OXFORD READINGS IN PHILOSOPHY

Series Editor G. J. Warnock

THE PHILOSOPHY OF EDUCATION

Oxford Readings in Philosophy

The Philosophy of Law, edited by Ronald M. Dworkin
Moral Concepts, edited by Joel Feinberg
Theories of Ethics, edited by Philippa Foot
The Philosophy of Mind, edited by Jonathan Glover
Knowledge and Belief, edited by A. Phillips Griffiths
Reference and Modality, edited by Leonard Linsky
The Philosophy of Religion, edited by Basil Mitchell
The Philosophy of Science, edited by P. H. Nidditch
Aesthetics, edited by Harold Osborne
The Theory of Meaning, edited by G. H. R. Parkinson
Political Philosophy, edited by Anthony Quinton
The Philosophy of Social Explanation, edited by Alan Ryan
The Philosophy of Language, edited by J. R. Searle
Semantic Syntax, edited by Pieter A. M. Seuren
Causation and Conditionals, edited by Ernest Sosa
Philosophical Logic, edited by P. F. Strawson
The Justification of Induction, edited by Richard Swinburne
Locke on Human Understanding, edited by I. C. Tipton
The Philosophy of Perception, edited by G. J. Warnock
The Philosophy of Action, edited by Alan R. White

THE PHILOSOPHY
OF EDUCATION

Edited by

R. S. PETERS

OXFORD UNIVERSITY PRESS

Oxford University Press, Walton Street, Oxford OX2 6DP

OXFORD LONDON GLASGOW
NEW YORK TORONTO MELBOURNE WELLINGTON
IBADAN NAIROBI DAR ES SALAAM LUSAKA CAPE TOWN
KUALA LUMPUR SINGAPORE JAKARTA HONG KONG TOKYO
DELHI BOMBAY CALCUTTA MADRAS KARACHI

ISBN 0 19 875023 4

© OXFORD UNIVERSITY PRESS 1973

First published 1913
Reprinted 1975, 1978

PRINTED IN GREAT BRITAIN
BY RICHARD CLAY (THE CHAUCER PRESS) LTD
BUNGAY, SUFFOLK

CONTENTS

INTRODUCTION   1

The Concept of Education

I. AIMS OF EDUCATION—A CONCEPTUAL INQUIRY   11
    by R. S. Peters, J. Woods, and W. H. Dray

II. WORK, LABOUR, AND UNIVERSITY EDUCATION   58
    by P. Herbst

III. REFLECTIONS ON EDUCATIONAL RELEVANCE   75
    by I. Scheffler

The Content of Education

IV. LIBERAL EDUCATION AND THE NATURE OF KNOWLEDGE   87
    by P. H. Hirst

V. TOWARDS A DEFINITION OF QUALITY IN EDUCATION   112
    by M. Warnock

VI. CURRICULUM INTEGRATION   123
    by R. Pring

VII. CURRICULUM PLANNING: TAKING A MEANS TO AN END   150
    by H. Sockett

Teaching and Learning

VIII. WHAT IS TEACHING?   163
    by P. H. Hirst

IX. HUMAN LEARNING   178
    by D. W. Hamlyn

X. THE LOGICAL AND PSYCHOLOGICAL ASPECTS OF LEARNING   195
    by D. W. Hamlyn

The Justification of Education

XI. EDUCATION, DEMOCRACY, AND THE PUBLIC INTEREST   217
    by P. A. White

XII. THE JUSTIFICATION OF EDUCATION   239
    by R. S. Peters

NOTES ON THE CONTRIBUTORS   269
BIBLIOGRAPHY   271
INDEX OF NAMES   275

INTRODUCTION

IN the past decade the philosophy of education has been steadily establishing itself in Britain as a branch of philosophy. It is beginning to appear as an option studied in philosophy departments as well as one of the main disciplines contributing to educational theory which is studied in education departments. Philosophers, of course, from the time of Plato onwards, have had thoughts about education and have dealt with it in the context of wider concerns about knowledge, reality, and the good life. But few philosophers, with the exception of John Dewey, have dealt with it in a systematic way. And neither Dewey's philosophy nor his approach to educational problems took root in Britain. In the main, philosophy of education in Britain has not been regarded as a branch of philosophy in any technical sense. It has taken the form of a discussion either of the thoughts of the great educators such as Comenius, Rousseau, and Froebel, or of general principles of education, as by Sir Percy Nunn in his *Education: Its Data and First Principles* or by A. N. Whitehead in his *The Aims of Education*. In works such as these, philosophical, moral, and psychological assumptions were combined in the advocacy of general policies and practices for education.

A landmark in the development of philosophy of education in Britain was C. D. Hardie's *Truth and Fallacy in Educational Theory*. This was first published in 1942 and took the form of a critique of 'Education According to Nature' and of the theories of Dewey and Herbart. This was followed by a general discussion of the nature of educational theory and of educational measurement. Hardie's approach relied greatly on the techniques of the Cambridge analytical school represented by G. E. Moore and C. D. Broad. It attracted little attention until after the war when it was discovered by other philosophers of the analytic school who were beginning to interest themselves in the application of their techniques to issues outside the central areas of epistemology and logic.

It would be out of place in this introduction to trace the development of philosophy of education subsequent to Hardie's book. The point of mentioning this work is that it represented a transition. Its jumping-off ground was the writings of great educators such as Froebel and Herbart, but it tackled them in a manner which was specifically philosophical. Philosophers of education nowadays attempt to do the same. Perhaps they lack the exuberance of the early days of 'the revolution in philosophy'; for what competent philosopher has ever eschewed analysis? They lack Hardie's conviction that disagreements between educators are 'factual or verbal or due to some emotional conflict'. They are hesitant about saying that conceptual issues can be clearly distinguished from empirical ones; they contemplate with equanimity the possibility that there may be moral facts; some of them even welcome the return of metaphysics. But in spite of their liberalism in comparison with the old guard of the 'analytic movement', they do appreciate that it is important to distinguish philosophical questions about education from the old mix of historical exposition and recommendations about policies and practices. They think that philosophy of education should be a branch of philosophy proper and should be in close touch with developments within it.

To claim, however, that philosophy of education is and should be a branch of philosophy is not to suggest that it is a distinct branch in the same sense that it could exist apart from established branches of philosophy such as epistemology, ethics, and philosophy of mind. Rather it draws on such established branches of philosophy and brings them together in ways which are relevant to educational issues. In this respect it is very much like political philosophy. Thus use can often be made of work that has already been done in philosophy. In tackling, for instance, issues such as the rights of parents and children, punishment in schools, the freedom of the child, and the authority of the teacher, it is possible to draw on and develop work done by philosophers on 'rights', 'punishment', 'freedom', and 'authority'. Questions are asked, as in any other sort of philosophy, about the concepts employed such as 'punishment', 'freedom', 'authority', and the grounds for making judgements are examined. What sort of right, for instance, is the right to education, and how is it to be justified?

Drawing on existing work in such cases is not at all a matter of mechanical application; for analysis and arguments often fail to fit easily into educational contexts. Most of the work on 'punishment', for instance, has been based on the paradigm of the operation of the legal system. When applied to problems of children in school there are important differences as well as similarities. Punishment presupposes responsibility for actions. But at what stage are children fully responsible for their actions? The school, too, is primarily concerned with education which suggests some kind of improvement in people as its rationale. Must this radically transform arguments which attempt to justify the punishment of children? Is more to be said for the reformative theory in the school than in the law-courts? Similar points can be made about the application of the concept of 'authority'; for teachers are meant to be authorities on what they teach. Must this affect the authority structure of the school and make some of the democratic arguments about the place and exercise of authority in it inapplicable?

But not all philosophy of education consists in attempting to apply existing work to a new context. There are many central issues, most of which fall within philosophy of mind, on which no work exists at all. What, for instance, is meant by 'education'? This is a question which has not been tackled in any precise way before. Perhaps it is not amenable to precise analysis. But this cannot be claimed in advance of making an attempt to give an analysis of it. Suppose it is claimed that 'education' involves at least the development of knowledge and understanding. There is then the queer anomaly, for which surely only some kind of historical explanation can be given, that there is a great concentration of work by philosophers on 'knowledge' but precious little on 'understanding'. 'Education' also implies some kind of learning. But there has been very little work done by philosophers on the concept of learning and still less on activities such as those of 'teaching', 'imparting', and 'indoctrinating' by means of which learning is promoted. Indeed it is approximately true to say that the philosopher of education has established work to consult if he is concerned with wider questions about the social aspects of education, about the nature of different 'subjects' in education such as history, science, mathematics, religion, art, and literature (there is a philosophy of all such subjects), and about wider psychological issues such as those of intelligence, concept-formation, language and thought, motivation, and emotion. But if he is concerned with central questions about education itself, about the curriculum, about learning and teaching, and about the justification of education, there is very little established work to consult. Most of it has in fact been done recently by philosophers of education. This fact of life in philosophy of education has determined the structure of this collection.

The editor is allergic to collections of articles that have no unifying theme. As this collection occurs in a series catering mainly for the needs of students of philosophy rather than for those of students of education, it was thought appropriate to concentrate on recent work which is specific to the philosophy of education, with which the student of philosophy may be quite unfamiliar. Articles have therefore been chosen that open up the most general and the most central issues about education in a clear and controversial way. This is the explanation of features of this collection that, at first sight, may seem rather anomalous. Three philosophers, for instance, contribute two articles each, while others who have contributed much to the subject do not feature in this collection. Three of the articles have been published in previous collections, yet there must surely be a few good articles around that have not yet appeared in any collection. And so on. These seeming anomalies are consequences of the decision that was taken about the structure of the collection. Priority has been given to articles which open up the most general issues which are specific to the philosophy of education.

Most of the articles in the collection present a point of view. They are not just a neutral map of the possible contours of concepts. This is as it should be; for what is the point of conceptual analysis unless it is connected with further questions that require answers? And can analysis be neutral? Is it separable from arguable assumptions and deep-seated presuppositions? Whatever is to be said about these fundamental questions concerning the nature of philosophy in general the purpose of this specific collection is plain. It is to present central issues in the philosophy of education with which the general philosophical public may be unfamiliar in the hope of stimulating further discussion of them which may, in time, contribute to the development of the subject. For philosophy of education is, at the moment, suffering from too little fundamental divergence in points of view.

1. *The Concept of Education*

The collection starts with a section on the nature of education itself. This is initiated by a symposium, which took place at the Ontario Institute of Educational Studies in 1965, in which the nature of education and its aims were discussed. Richard Peters gives a brief résumé of the analysis of 'education' which he had attempted previously and relates the formulation of 'aims' to this. John Woods and William Dray make criticisms of this to which Peters replies. This is followed by an extract from a later systematic attempt by Peters to reformulate his analysis in the light of objections. This introduces a strong note of controversy into the collection from the start, and should be useful to the student in highlighting most of the disputed issues.

In his analysis of 'education' Peters makes much of the distinction between 'education' and 'training' and of non-instrumental features of the development of knowledge and understanding. The second article, by Peter Herbst, is devoted to these issues. Drawing on the distinction made by Hannah Arendt between 'work' and 'labour' he outlines an account of 'education' which is allied to the values of production and to a non-instrumental attitude to life. He attacks the current emphasis on the values of consumption and the view of education that goes with it.

The final paper in this section on 'Reflections on Educational Relevance' is one read by Israel Scheffler at a symposium of the American Philosophical Association in 1969 on 'The Concept of Relevance in Education'. This conference took place at a time when student unrest was gathering momentum in the U.S.A. and is an attempt to make explicit what might be meant by the widespread demand for 'relevance' in education. Scheffler's purpose in writing this paper, however, was not just to make explicit different ways of interpreting this demand; it was also to question the educational relevance of educational relevance. It was a forthright contribution, at a philosophical level, to a continuing controversy.

2. *The Content of Education*

Central to the concept of education is the development of knowledge and understanding. In schools and universities explicit attempts are made to do this by means of an organized sequence of learning experiences which is called the curriculum. But what should be its priorities? Should depth of knowledge or breadth be the ideal? Are the divisions between the subjects on the curriculum arbitrary or do they reflect defensible epistemological distinctions? If there are defensible dimensions within knowledge what can be meant by 'curriculum integration'? And in what ways can learning experiences be regarded as means to achieving more specific objectives within the development of knowledge and understanding?

The first article is Paul Hirst's influential paper on 'Liberal Education and the Nature of Knowledge' which has been published in other collections. No excuse is needed for republishing it in this collection; for it raises most of the main issues with which this section is concerned. He argues for the importance of liberal education conceived of as initiation into several logically distinct forms of knowledge. In contrast to this Mary Warnock, in 'Towards a Definition of Quality in Education', emphasizes the importance of specialization in developing the imagination which, she argues, is a hall-mark of quality in education. Both these articles assume the differentiation of knowledge into distinct disciplines; but there is a widespread movement in educational circles for 'integrated' and 'interdisciplinary' studies. But what exactly are they? What is the case for introducing them? In the next article Richard Pring explores the various meanings which can be attached to 'Curriculum Integration' and investigates their presuppositions within the theory of knowledge. There is then the question of the objectives to be attained by such schemes of study, or by any curriculum, for that matter. What sense can be made of regarding the curriculum as a means to attaining specific educational objectives? Is the 'means–end' model really applicable in the sphere of learning and teaching? Hugh Sockett examines these issues in the final article in this section.

3. *Learning and Teaching*

Educated people are those whose states of mind and behaviour exhibit knowledge and understanding; but they are not born this way. Neither do they become this way just through a process of maturation; they achieve it through learning. Often this learning is stimulated by the teaching of others, but it need not be. It may be an empirical fact that some forms of learning are best brought about by teaching, but it is not part of our understanding of 'learning' that it must happen this way. 'Teaching', on the other hand, cannot be understood without some reference to 'learning'.

Learning is a subject about which psychologists have written much but philosophers little. It would be rash, however, for philosophers to discourse in too self-contained a way on such a subject; for obviously 'learning' is a process about which, to a certain extent, empirical general-izations can be and have been made by psychologists. And the gen-eralizations will depend very much on what it is that is learnt—skills, attitudes, concepts, etc. This collection is concerned with central ques-tions about the development of knowledge and understanding and there are theories of learning which are relevant to these features of human development. But one of the most puzzling questions about learning, especially in this area, is the extent to which questions about it are the province of the psychologist or of the philosopher. The two writers on learning who are now most discussed by philosophers of education, namely Chomsky and Piaget, raise these questions in acute form. Two articles by David Hamlyn have therefore been included which seem particularly pertinent to these problems. The first on 'Human Learning' is concerned mainly with Chomsky's theory in the general context of the development of knowledge. The second paper on 'The Logical and Psychological Aspects of Learning' gives an assessment of Piaget's theory and deals with the distinction between empirical and conceptual issues in human learning.

Far more work has been done by philosophers of education on the concept of 'teaching' than on that of 'learning'. Indeed there is already extant an American collection of articles on *Concepts of Teaching*, edited by C. B. J. MacMillan and T. W. Nelson, and articles on aspects of teaching are included in R. S. Peters (ed.), *The Concept of Education*. One of the clearest articles, called 'What is teaching?' by Paul Hirst, in which he maps the conceptual issues, has, however, only recently been published. This seemed, therefore, to be the obvious article of this type to include.

4. *The Justification of Education*

Teaching is usually an educative activity, but it need not be. We would not think of it as such if, for instance, somebody was taught every tenth name in a telephone directory or if he was taught to be superstitious. This is because we conceive of education as leading to desirable states of mind, which do not include heads stuffed with useless information or falsehoods. But, given the distinction between just teaching and teaching that is of educational value, a further question arises, which is that of the justification of education. Supposing that education is regarded as valuable mainly because of its connection with knowledge and understanding, questions must be asked about the grounds on which knowledge and understanding are so highly valued. Why should so much time and money be spent on their development in schools and universities?

The last two articles in this collection are concerned with this question. Pat White approaches it from the point of view of social philosophy. In a paper on 'Education, Democracy, and the Public Interest', she examines the claim that education is in the public interest. Richard Peters, in the final article on 'The Justification of Education' approaches the question more from the standpoint of ethics. In this revision of earlier work on 'Worth-while Activities' he examines instrumental arguments for education and those that attempt to establish the intrinsic value of education. Various considerations are discussed that support the claim that the possession and pursuit of knowledge make life less boring, and a rationale is finally attempted for Socrates' contention that the unexamined life is not worth living.

THE CONCEPT OF EDUCATION

I

AIMS OF EDUCATION—
A CONCEPTUAL INQUIRY

R. S. PETERS

I WAS recently commenting sourly to a colleague in psychology on the proclivity of educators to fasten on some small piece of research—for example, on 'discovery' or 'creativity'—and to puff it up into an educational panacea. He remarked wryly that teaching was such an uphill job that teachers had to have some sort of a booster every five or ten years to keep their spirits up. Bible texts are no longer any good; so snippets of research have to do instead! Traditionally, of course, such boosters have been called 'aims of education'. But why? Panaceas have abounded in politics; but we do not hear about aims of politics. Why should education in particular be associated with aims? Or has this a purely contingent explanation in that Dewey wrote about 'aims of education' and Whitehead later put together a collection of essays and addresses under the title of *The Aims of Education*, and so a fashioin was set? Or is there a more deep-seated explanation?

Had I the time—and also the necessary scholarship—I would like to follow up this question and discover the precise period at which educators became, as it were, so target-minded. But my task in this symposium, as I understand it, is to exhibit the approach of the analytical philosopher to questions about aims of education, not that of the historian of ideas. One has to ask, therefore, why the demand for educators to formulate aims seems so natural, whatever its historical origin, and what sort of function is performed by such formulations. In other words the concepts both of 'aim' and of 'education' have to be explored and some comments have to be made about the function performed in educational discourse by their juxtaposition.

I shall not have time to enter into questions to do with the *justification* of aims which are, both philosophically and practically speaking, the most interesting and important questions about them. Philosophy, as I

From *Philosophy and Education*, Proceedings of the International Seminar, Monograph Series No. 3, edited by B. Crittenden (Teachers College Press for The Ontario Institute for Studies in Education), pp. 1–32. Reprinted by permission of the authors and the editor.

understand it, is concerned mainly with the questions, 'What do you mean?' and 'How do you know?' I shall be concerned only with the first of these questions about the aims of education.

AIMS

Dewey has much that is illuminating to say about 'Aims in Education' in Chapter VIII of his *Democracy and Education*; yet one of the all-pervading weaknesses of his treatment of the concept of 'aim' is that he regards it as equivalent to that of 'purpose'.[1] Of course 'aim' belongs to the same family of concepts as does 'purpose'; so also do 'intention' and 'motive'. They are all conceptually connected with actions and activities; but there are subtle differences between them in the ways in which they are so connected.

Actions and activities are identified, in the main, by reference to how the agent conceives what he is doing. Of course, there are very often characteristic movements of the body; but these are never sufficient for identification. We might say, for instance, that a person was raising his hand. This would be a safe bet in normal circumstances because it is only on rare occasions that people have their hands raised. But such a specification of an action would be minimal; for it would be improbable that he was *just* raising his hand. Perhaps he was testing the direction of the wind, voting, or signalling to someone. We could thus identify the action as a case of any of these. But we would probably have to ask him which it was to be sure. We might say to him, 'Are you signalling to someone or testing the direction of the wind?' If, however, we were not very sure from the context what the alternative specifications might be, we might say, 'What is your purpose in raising your hand?' We would, in other words, identify it in a minimal sense as a hand-raising action and seek an explanation of it by asking for the agent's *purpose* in performing the action so specified. We might even, in certain specific contexts, when perhaps we were suspicious as well as puzzled, about his action, ask for his motive in raising his hand.[2] But we surely would not ask what he was *aiming* at in raising his hand, in order to remove our puzzlement. If we said this it would sound rather quaint—unless, that is, he looked as if he was going to throw something. What, then, is speci-

---

[1] John Dewey, *Democracy and Education* (New York: Macmillan Co., 1916), p. 120.
[2] For what is specific to the concept of 'motive', see R. S. Peters, *The Concept of Motivation* (London: Routledge & Kegan Paul, Ltd., 1960) and 'More About Motives' in *Mind*, Vol. 76 (Jan. 1967).

fic about the concept of 'aim' which gives rise to the quaintness of such a question?

The concept of 'aim' always carries with it some of the nuances associated with its natural home in contexts of shooting and throwing. It suggests, first of all, the concentration of attention, and the specification of some precise objective. The desires of the agent are directed, as it were, towards some distant target, and there must be concentration of effort and attention in order to hit it. The question 'What are you aiming at?' is therefore rather like the question 'What are you trying to do?' with the additional suggestion of concentration on some specifiable objective.

'Aiming' is also like 'trying' in that it suggests that there is some difficulty involved in the task and a very real possibility of falling short or of not bringing it off. Very often, indeed, when the question 'What are you aiming at?' is asked, there is a very definite implication of bungling and confusion, of effort not properly co-ordinated or directed. In this respect, however, talk about 'aims' is not as extreme, or as pessimistic in regard to practice, as talk about 'ideals'. 'Ideals' are connected with wishes; they pick out objectives which, by definition, cannot be realized in practice. If they become more practicable, if, as it were, the sights are lowered a bit, they become 'aims', which are objectives that can be attained, given concentration and co-ordination of effort. But there is still the very strong possibility of failure lurking in the background. Needless to say, the term 'purpose' carries no such suggestions, though the term 'intention' suggests the possibility of mistake rather than of failure. (Compare 'What did he intend to do?' and 'What was he aiming at?')

These features of the concept of 'aim' indicate the specific social function performed by raising questions about the aims of actions or activities. 'Aim' conveys, first of all, some suggestion of an objective that is not too near at hand or too easy to attain. It conveys, secondly, some suggestion that the action or activity in question is not obviously structured in relation to such an objective. We ask people what they are aiming at when they are working away at something but it is not quite clear at what. It is, in other words, an attempt to get them to specify an action or activity in relation to some objective that is not altogether obvious or near at hand. We are saying, as it were, 'What precisely are you trying to do?' To ask a person what he is aiming at is not primarily to demand an explanation for what he is doing. It functions more as a criticism or as an exhortation than as a request for an explanation. It is, as it were, putting the onus on him to specify his objective more precisely and to concentrate his efforts accordingly.

This explains why 'aims' are so typically associated with institutions such as clubs and political parties, in which people join together to work at achieving something of common concern. It is important for them to specify this fairly precisely in order to bring to the forefront what is distinctive of their efforts. The formulation of their aims has an important social function in focusing their efforts in a specific direction. Similarly, institutions like the police force and the army have aims definitive of them. In so far as an individual is a member of the police force his actions and activities must be conceived of under the aspect of preserving order in a community. He may have all sorts of idiosyncratic purposes; but in so far as he is a policeman he must conceive what he is doing as directed towards this over-all objective.

It would be fascinating to explore further the comparatively uncharted region of 'aims', 'ideals', 'intentions', and 'purposes'. But this paper is meant to be in the philosophy of education, and, though the cardinal philosophical sin is to fail to make important distinctions, it is almost equally sinful to make distinctions that are not used, that do not work in an argument. The points so far made on the concept of 'aim' should prove sufficient to clarify the question originally posed about the naturalness of talk about aims of *education*. The main points made are:

1. We tend to ask about aims in contexts where we think it important to get people to specify more precisely what they are trying to do.

2. Aims suggest the concentration on and the direction of effort towards an objective that is not too palpable or close to hand.

3. Aims suggest the possibility of failure or of falling short.

THE CONCEPT OF EDUCATION

Why should all this be so peculiarly apposite in the case of education? A quick answer might be that education is a highly diffuse and difficult activity in which many earnest people engage with great seriousness without being altogether clear what they are trying to do. The demand for the aims of education is therefore a salutary request for teachers to survey what they are doing, get their priorities straight, concentrate their attention on them, and discard irrelevancies. Also, as tangible results are very difficult to come by in education, the constant possibility of falling short, of never quite bringing it off, is always present to the educator. Hence the appropriateness of all the talk about 'aims'.

This answer is almost right. Or, to put it more concretely, the general contours of the answer are right; what are lacking are the specific features of the concept of 'education' which would make it interesting. The main respect in which it is not quite right is that education is not an activity. We do not say, 'Go along, go and get on with your educating' as we would say, 'Go along, go and get on with your teaching.' Educating is no more an activity than reforming or improving are. What is it, then?

'Education', like 'reform', is not a concept for picking out any specific activity, but for laying down criteria to which a family of activities must conform. We do not say, 'Have you been educating them *or* instructing them in algebra this morning?' though we might say, 'Have you been educating them *by* instructing them in algebra this morning?' There are innumerable activities which might count as educating people just as there are innumerable activities that might count as reforming them. To call such activities 'education' is to say that they conform to certain very general criteria.

The criteria involved can be divided into two main groups. There will be, firstly, those that characterize the successful outcome of education in the form of an educated man; there will be, secondly, those that characterize the processes by means of which people gradually become educated. The latter cannot, of course, be characterized without the former, but they cannot be characterized simply by saying that they are efficient means for producing a desirable end. They are, rather, a family of on-going tasks culminating in the manifold achievements involved in being educated.

It can immediately be seen why there is a tendency to talk both about the aims of education and about the aims of reform. For both these concepts have, as it were, a norm built into them, which functions as a very distant target for such activities, and which structures them in a certain direction. 'Education', like 'reform', picks out a family of processes culminating in a person being better; 'education' picks out a family of processes culminating in a person having an outlook and form of life that is in some way desirable. It could be just as much a logical contradiction to say 'My son has been educated, but nothing desirable has happened to him' as it would be to say 'My son has been reformed but has changed in no way for the better.' Both concepts, in other words, suggest a family of processes 'aiming at' a norm.

This connection with commendation does not, of course, prevent us from speaking of 'poor education' when a worth-while job has been botched, or 'bad education' when we think that much of what people are working at is not worth while, though it is a nice question to determine at what point we pass from saying that something is 'bad education' to saying that it is 'not education at all'. There is also the derivative derisive sense when we say that a person was 'educated' at a public school, just as we might say of somebody that he was a 'good' man. The word can also be used derivatively in a purely external, descriptive way when we speak of an 'educational system', just as we can use the term 'moral' of someone else's code without committing ourselves to the judgements of value of those whose code it is. Anthropologists can talk of the moral system of a tribe; so also can we talk as sociologists or economists of the educational system of a community. In employing the concept in this derivative sense, we need not think that what is going on is worth while, but members of the society, whose system it is, must think it is worth while.

This normative aspect of both 'educate' and 'reform' makes them both special cases of what Ryle calls 'achievement verbs'.[3] They are like 'win', 'find', 'remember', and 'learn' in that some sort of success is implied by them. They differ, however, in that there is no one activity such as running a race or searching that terminates in success, and in that the success in question, unlike that involved in winning or in finding something, *must* be of value. Any answer, therefore, to the question 'What are you aiming at?' given by educators or by reformers will consist in a more careful specification of the achievements constituting being educated or being reformed. As 'aim', however, suggests some distant objective, and as it is possible to teach things like science or mathematics, which are usually taught for educational reasons, with a view to increasing productivity or some other such extrinsic end, it is only too easy to slip into looking for some distant objective beyond education which educators might be trying to bring about qua educators. But this would be impossible if education means the initiation of people into a worth-while form of life; for how could there ever be any end of value beyond this which it would be possible to bring about? The mistake comes through raising questions about what *education itself* might lead on to which are pertinent enough when asked about activities of teachers that are usually, but not always, conducted for educational reasons. Engineering, for instance, can be taught in schools or colleges purely with a view to increasing productivity; but people cannot be

[3] See Gilbert Ryle, *The Concept of Mind* (London: Hutchinson, 1949), pp. 149–53.

educated by being taught engineering with a view to bringing about anything which would not itself fall under the concept of what an educated person is. And engineers can be highly educated people. Of course, economists or politicians can look at schools or educational systems, as it were, from the outside and can ascribe instrumental aims to them. But proposals of that sort are not, strictly speaking, proposals about the aims of *education*. Rather, they are suggestions that things should be taught, or schools used, for purposes that are not strictly educational.

It could rightly be remarked that this explication of a concept cannot settle the issue between the advocate of purely vocational training and the advocate of education. A defender of training might agree that education involves the initiation of people into a worth-while form of life but might maintain that the community had not the resources for such a luxury. To this, the advocate of education might reply that the economist's position is ultimately incoherent. For if education involves the transmission of what is intrinsically worth while, what is going to be done about its transmission if the schools are geared purely to the production of technicians to keep the wheels of industry turning? For either such productive work must itself become endowed with ultimate significance, or it must be regarded as instrumental to something else which is so endowed. In either case, some education will have to go on somewhere, as well as training. And so the argument might continue. The analysis of 'aims of education' would not, of course, settle the substantive issue; for moral decisions can never be extracted from conceptual analysis. But it does at least help to spotlight the points at which decisions have to be taken.

Education, then, like reform, has norms built into it, which generate the aims which educators strive to develop or attain. But the norms in question are highly indeterminate; for what constitutes a person becoming better or having a desirable outlook? Requests for aims of education or of reform are therefore requests to specify the norm more concretely. Is it a sense of responsibility that is important in the case of reform? Or is it concern for others? Is it the development of critical awareness in the case of education? Or is it sensitivity to others and to significant form? Probing into 'aims' is a way of elucidating the content that a person gives to the concept of 'being reformed' or 'being educated'. Countless 'aims of education' are, therefore, possible, depending upon what features of a worth-while form of life any educator thinks it most important to foster. In spite, however, of this inevitable multiplicity of 'aims', it is possible to sketch certain general criteria of 'being educated' which indicate the dimensions along which these 'targets' or priorities lie. This must now be briefly attempted.

GENERAL CRITERIA OF BEING EDUCATED

The first thing that must be said about an educated man is that he must be one who not only pursues some particular activity such as science or cooking, but who is also capable of pursuing it for what there is in it as distinct from what it may lead on to or bring about. Of course these activities can be and often are pursued for instrumental reasons; they contribute a great deal to keeping people fed and the wheels of industry turning. But we would not call a person educated unless he was capable, to a certain extent, of delighting in such things for their own sake. A hall-mark of a good school is the extent to which it kindles in its pupils a desire to go on with the things into which they have been initiated when the pressures are off and when there is no extrinsic reason for engaging in them.

This criterion of commitment to what is internal to worth-while activities, be it the pursuit of truth for its own sake or the determination to make something of a fitting form, is necessary but not sufficient for being educated. For a person could be a trained ballet-dancer or have mastered an eminently worth-while skill, such as pottery-making, without being educated. What might be lacking is something to do with knowledge and understanding; for being educated demands more than being highly skilled. An educated man must also possess some body of knowledge and some kind of conceptual scheme to raise this above the level of a collection of disjointed facts. This implies some understanding of principles for the organization of facts. We would not call a person who was merely well informed an educated man, as Whitehead so eloquently argued. An educated person must also have some understanding of the 'reason why' of things. The Spartans were morally and militarily trained. They knew how to fight and they knew what was right and wrong; they were also possessed of a certain stock of folklore, which enabled them to manage—provided they stayed in Sparta. But we would not say that they had received a moral or military education; for they had never been encouraged to get a grasp of the principles underlying their code.

Some development in depth of knowledge and awareness there must be for a man to be educated. But something still is lacking; for a man might be a very highly trained scientist, yet we might refuse to call him an educated man. This would not be because there is nothing worth while in science; for it is a supreme example of a worth-while activity. It could not be because such a man cares nothing about it and has no grasp of its principles; for the hypothesis is that he is dedicated to it and has a good grounding in its principles. What, then, is lacking which might make us withhold the description of 'educated' from such a person? It is surely the possibility that he might be narrowly specialized. He might work away at science and know almost nothing of anything else and not see its connection with much else in a coherent pattern of life.

When educationalists proclaim that 'education is of the whole man', they are enunciating a conceptual truth; for 'education' rules out narrow specialism just as it rules out a purely instrumental approach to activities. Think of the difference, for instance, between sex education and sex training. We use the phrases 'trained in' and 'trained for' when we wish to talk about vocational, utilitarian, or specialized pursuits. We do not speak of a person being educated *in*, or *for*, or *at* anything in particular. This does not mean, of course, that an educated man must not be trained in something. It only rules out the possibility of his being *just* trained. A trained artist, or scientist, or historian is not necessarily an educated man; for he may have a deep but circumscribed understanding in these spheres. To what extent a person has to develop in all the various forms of awareness (for example, scientific, historical, mathematical, moral, aesthetic, religious) in order to be educated would be difficult to determine. The main function of this criterion is to rule out narrow specialism rather than to suggest positive requirements.

There is one further positive requirement that must underpin all that has been said about the educated man in respect of knowledge and understanding. This is that it must permeate his way of looking at things rather than be 'hived off'. It is possible for a man to know a lot of history, for instance, in the sense that he can give correct answers to questions in examinations and classrooms; yet this might never affect the way in which he looked at the buildings and institutions around him. He might never connect what he had learnt about the Industrial Revolution with what he saw in the Welsh valleys or in Manchester. We might describe such a man as 'knowledgeable' but we would not describe him as educated; for 'education' implies that a man's outlook is transformed by what he knows.

This transforming quality of education is what makes the contrast often drawn between life and education ridiculous; for it is by education that mere living is transformed into a quality of life. For how a man lives depends upon what he sees and understands. In schools and colleges there is, of course, a concentration on activities like literature, science, and history, which have a high degree of cognitive content. But an educated person is not one who simply goes on engaging in such activities when he leaves such institutions; he is one whose whole range of actions, reactions, and activities is gradually transformed by the deepening and widening of his understanding and sensitivity. There is no end to this process; for as I have remarked elsewhere: 'To be educated is not to have arrived at a destination; it is to travel with a different view. What is required is not feverish preparation for something that lies ahead, but to work with precision, passion, and taste at worth-while things that lie to hand.'[4]

These, then, are the more specific features of being educated. But as multiple criteria are involved, it is obvious enough that emphasis will be given at different periods to different aspects of what it means to be educated. Such emphases emerge as 'aims of education'. For, as Dewey shrewdly remarks: 'For the *statement* of aim is a matter of emphasis at a given time. And we do not emphasize things which do not require emphasis—that is, such things as are taking care of themselves fairly well. We tend rather to frame our statement on the basis of the defects and needs of the contemporary situation; we take for granted, without explicit statement which would be of no use, whatever is right or approximately so.'[5] Some, for instance, in revolt against mere information and book learning, emphasize the importance of the inquiring and critical attitude or the necessity for understanding principles; others, perhaps appalled by the development of specialization, draw attention to the importance of 'wholeness'. The 'cult of the intellect' is attacked by those who stress 'the training of character'; others advance the claims of aesthetic sensitivity to counteract the blunting effect of the mass media. The very fact that education involves multiple criteria is perhaps one of the underlying reasons why statements of aim seem so necessary. If anyone is engaged in an activity like cooking or fishing that has a palpable and determinate point to it, talk of 'aims' seems rather otiose; but when there is a group of activities directed towards a cluster of ends that are highly indeterminate, the demand for 'aims' serves an obvious function. It focuses attention on some neglected priority.

[4] R. S. Peters, 'Education as Initiation', *Philosophical Analysis and Education*, ed. R. D. Archambault (New York: Humanities Press, 1965), p. 110.
[5] John Dewey, op. cit., p. 130.

It might be objected that some over-all aim might be ascribed to education as a group of activities, just as it might be ascribed to politics. Could it not be said, for instance, that just as *the* aim of reform is to make men better, so *the* aim of education is to initiate men into a reflective form of life. It could be said—but it would not be very informative; for it would be merely a way of drawing attention to what it means to educate or reform someone. There are times when it is necessary to say such things, just as there are times when it is necessary to say things like 'the function of government is to govern'. For instance, suppose a group of technically minded bureaucrats and businessmen were trying to transform an educational system into a system of vocational and technical training, it might then be appropriate to draw attention to the connection between education and some intrinsic values of a community by enunciating such an over-all aim. In other words, it would serve a useful function in a context where the educational function of schools or colleges, as distinct from their training, or selective function, was being neglected. But a remark like this would have little function in drawing the attention of educators to what was important *within* education—that is, assuming that they were all concerned with education and not with using schools and colleges for other purposes which are extrinsic to education. In a similar way, somebody speaking of what was done within a Borstal or Approved School, might say 'The aim of reform is to make men better, you know.' This would have point if the inmates of such reformative institutions were merely being used as cheap labour by the state, or if they were being brutally treated without any attempt to strengthen their desire to become respectable citizens. But the enunciation of such over-all aims would be pointless as aids to getting clear about priorities *within* reform or *within* education. And the function of talk about aims in education is usually to clarify the minds of educators about their priorities.

PRINCIPLES IMPLICIT IN EDUCATIONAL PROCEDURES

There is, however, another collection of what look like over-all aims for education which have a rather different function. I have in mind aims such as 'growth', and 'the self-realization of the individual'. These are often cited as omnibus aims of education; yet they do not seem to be tautologies masquerading as aims, in the way in which aims such as 'to initiate man into a worth-while form of life' seem to be. What is to be made of aims such as these?

Such aims go further than a general slogan such as 'the development of individual capacities', which functions as a demand that educators should take account of individual differences, that education should not be laid on in too uniform a way, but should be adapted carefully to differences in ability and aptitude. For such a demand could be made simply by those concerned about the efficient provision of functionaries for the state, though more often it is made by those who are claiming equality of consideration for the individual as a matter of individual right. But this general plea has to do with the distribution of education; it suggests no particular procedures of educating people. It could be made by those who are wedded to very formal and authoritarian methods. The plea, however, for self-realization, or that children should be allowed to grow, goes far beyond such a purely distributive demand.

Aims of this sort have their natural homes within an individualist system of thought and they draw attention to the claims of the individual to pursue his own bent. Perhaps there is a tendency for children to be treated in too uniform a way, or to be moulded too readily for some occupation demanded by the state. Such 'aims' proclaim that education must permit areas of discretion within the sphere of what is thought desirable, that autonomy and self-origination are important in education. The child must be allowed to discover things for himself and learn by making his own mistakes. Attention is thus focused on *procedures* of education which involve both psychological theories about learning and moral principles about how children should be treated—for example, with respect and with regard to their freedom.

The basic point, then, about aims of education which cluster around the cliché that the aim of education is 'the self-realization of the individual' is that they draw attention to a class of *procedures* of education rather than prescribe any specific direction or content for it. Indeed, child-centred theorists often went so far as to maintain, mistakenly in my view, that procedures involving what David Ausubel calls receptive learning,[6] are not education at all. Education, they argued, must involve some kind of 'leading out' procedure; as the usual sort of formal instruction involves no such 'leading out', it is not education at all. I have elsewhere attempted to uncover the minimal conceptual basis for this conversion of a moral policy into a definition,[7] so will not go over this again. Anyway, it has little bearing on the question of aims.

---

[6] David Ausubel, *The Psychology of Meaningful Verbal Learning* (New York: Grune & Stratton, 1963), *passim*.

[7] See Peters, 'Education as Initiation', sec. 2, and *Ethics and Education* (London: George Allen & Unwin, 1966), chap. i, sec. 4.

Those who draw attention to the importance of individual avenues of exploration in education by enunciating aims to do with 'growth' or self-development often give the impression that this can replace reference to old-fashioned matters to do with content. It is not so much the acquisition of knowledge that matters, they argue, as the inquiring attitude. It does not now matter that the child should master some science or become skilled in art; what matters is that his capacity for choice should be nurtured by being presented with alternatives. But reflection, I think, will reveal that what Dewey said about 'aims' in general applies pre-eminently to aims such as the self-realization of the individual, which emphasize the importance of learning by individual experience and discovery and the importance of a principle of options in a curriculum. For this stress on individual self-realization has point when an educational system is either geared to the demands of the state, such as for more scientists or technicians, or when individuals are being moulded relentlessly in accordance with some dull or doctrinaire pattern. There is point, under such conditions, in stressing the difference between people and the ethical principle of respect for each individual's right to develop in his own way. But although aims such as these can be enunciated under such circumstances, the standard *content* of education is more or less taken for granted, though not explicitly stated. For no educator. when confronted with abilities and inclinations such as those of a lotus-eater or of a Marquis de Sade, would say that these ought to be developed to the full. No educator would advocate bingo and billiards on the curriculum if a child 'chose' them. The plea for self-realization is a plea for types of procedure which takes for granted matters of content, in the old-fashioned sense; it is a plea for principle of options within a range of activities and modes of conduct that are thought to be desirable. For not all desirable things are within the scope of every individual; not all of them fan in some minds even the faintest spark of inclination. The plea is both for cutting the coat of what is desirable according to the cloth of individual aptitude and for the procedural principle that individuals should be allowed some say in discovering what this is.

The self-realization of the individual, then, is limited to the development of self in modes of thought and conduct that are regarded as desirable, or at least as not undesirable. The traditional content of the curriculum and of the community's form of life is taken for granted; but within this the demand is that the individual should be allowed to grow at his own pace and follow his own bent. Furthermore all such avenues of self-development are inescapably social in character. They are engaged with others; there is usually a body of knowledge or at least some kind of 'lore' attached to them even if they take the form of games or pastimes; there are good and bad ways of proceeding, which the individual has to pick up from others more experienced in them. The 'potentialities' of the individual can be developed only within the framework of some socially structured pursuit into which he has to be initiated.

So much, then, for general aims to do with 'growth', 'the self-realization of the individual', and so on. The burden of my argument has been to show:

1. These 'aims' draw attention to the importance of a group of principles involved in certain types of educational *procedures*, connected with autonomy, self-origination, individual choice, and individual differences.

2. Stress on such principles more or less takes for granted aspects of education which were dealt with above under the concept of being educated. The values of a community provide the background of content in relation to which a plea can be made for individual differences and a principle of options.

THE FUSION OF CONTENT AND PROCEDURE

It seems, then, that aims of education can draw attention to principles immanent in types of educational procedure as well as to aspects of what it means to be educated. But why, it might be asked, should *anything* to do with procedures of education have bearing on its aims? If the cash value of all the talk about the self-realization of the individual is to emphasize certain procedures for developing educated people, why should anyone erect the principles immanent in such procedures into over-all aims? 'Aim' suggests the structuring of an activity in a certain direction. Procedures are, as it were, processes with rules built into them. How can principles immanent in them be regarded as aspects of aims which give direction and concentration to the activities of educators? The answer, surely, is connected with the impossibility of conceiving of educational processes in accordance with a means–end model and of making any absolute separation between content and procedure, matter and manner, in the case of education. This point I must now try to explain.

In dealing with the concept of education I distinguished first of all various criteria of being educated and tried to relate aims of education to emphases on some one criterion rather than another within this general area. I then dealt briefly with other sorts of aims which draw attention to principles immanent in the procedures—for example, instruction, learning by experience, and discovery—by means of which educated people are developed. But the point must now be made that what I have called principles of procedure can also be regarded very much as a matter of content. This, indeed, is one of the features of 'education' which makes any attempt to conceive it as taking a means to an end, or as developing a product by means of processes, quite inappropriate.

Consider, first of all, the general rules which must be imposed as conditions necessary for classroom teaching. The discipline imposed by the teacher, the equality of consideration with which he treats individuals, the respect and degree of liberty which he accords to them, are, on the one hand, rules which are necessary for the distribution and organization of education. But, on the other hand, an essential part of the moral education of children is that they should make these principles, which form the framework of their explorations, their own. They will develop as moral beings if they treat the principles immanent in such procedures as content which is subtly imparted to them. The same sort of point applies negatively. If a child is always provided with some extrinsic incentive for learning—for example, marks or prizes—he may learn quite a bit of what he is expected to learn. But he may also pick up the principle that effort is only worth while if something has some palpable use or reward attached to it. And this is a negation of one of the basic criteria of being educated.

Secondly, there are those principles of procedure which are presuppositions of worth-while activities such as science or history. There must be respect for evidence and a ban on 'cooking' or distorting it; there must be a willingness to admit that one is mistaken; there must be non-interference with people who wish to put forward objections; there must be a respect for people as a source of argument and an absence of personal invective and contempt for what they say because of who they are. To learn science is not just to learn facts and to understand theories; it is also to learn to participate in a public form of life governed by such principles of procedure. In so far, therefore, as a person is educated scientifically, he will have to absorb these principles of procedure by means of which the content of scientific thought has been accumulated and is criticized and developed. He must take this sort of social situation into his own mind. Indeed, the mind of the individual is largely structured by the principles of such public situations in which he participates.

Educational theory has too long been haunted by misleading models of what an educational situation is. On the one hand, there are those who regard it as one in which some high-minded operator 'shapes' children

according to some specification, or 'tops them up' with knowledge; on the other hand, there are those who mingle the assumptions of a consumer-oriented society with biological metaphors, and think that the teacher's function is to encourage the child to 'grow' or to 'follow his own interests', as if he were an organism unfolding some private form of life. Both accounts have their own specific defects; but they both share the common defect of ignoring the central fact that education consists essentially in the initiation of others into a public world picked out by the language and concepts of a people and structured by rules governing their purposes and interactions with each other. In relation to this the teacher is not, as it were, an external operator who is trying to impose something of his from the outside on children, or trying to develop something within them which is their own peculiar possession. His function is rather to act as a guide in helping them to explore and *share* a public world whose contours have been marked out by generations which have preceded both of them. There is always what D. H. Lawrence called 'the holy ground' that stands between teacher and taught to which *both* owe an allegiance. The problem is to get others to enter it and to enjoy the public heritage.[8]

As the forms of knowledge and understanding defining the outlook of an educated man are inseparable from the principles of procedure which characterize the public situations in which they are acquired, developed, and transmitted to others, there is no inappropriateness in emphasizing as 'aims' of education the procedural aspects of this situation. For principles immanent in them, such as freedom, or respect for evidence, can be treated as priorities and can structure the activities of education as well as more usual aims. For instance, emphasis can be given to the independent, inquiring attitude rather than to the actual acquisition of knowledge. It is, of course, a further question, how coherent such an aim is which neglects the more traditional ones. For what sense is there in making children critical without giving them anything to be critical about, or in stressing inquiry without worrying about whether knowledge is acquired as well?

THE FUNCTION OF PHILOSOPHICAL ANALYSIS

In the old days, when the philosopher was thought of as 'the spectator of all time and all existence', too much was claimed for the philosopher of education. It was thought that he could issue high-level directives for education as well as pronounce on God, freedom, immortality, and

[8] For further development of this, see Peters, *Ethics and Education*, chap. ii.

the meaning of life. In more recent times, after the 'revolution in philosophy,' there is a danger of too little being claimed. He still has a spectatorial role all right; for his concern with the second-order questions 'What do you mean?' and 'How do you know?' assures him of that. But it is thought that the inappropriateness of the philosopher pronouncing qua philosopher on matters of substance must make his contribution to educational theory of greatly diminished importance. Rather than make any general comments about this topic, I propose instead to conclude this paper by indicating the general implications for educational theory of the analysis that I have given of 'aims of education'.

GENERAL IMPLICATIONS FOR EDUCATIONAL THEORY

1. The analysis both of 'aim' and of 'education' should reveal the inappropriateness of conceiving of an aim of education as some end *extrinsic* to education which education might lead up to or bring about. On this general point I am very much in agreement with Dewey.

2. The analysis reveals the absurdity of the expectation that there could ever be one agreed aim of education. If such an over-all aim were ever produced it would be tantamount to a tautology, to saying that there ought to be concentration on education. The ineluctable multiplicity of aims is due to two main features of the concept of 'education':

(a) The fact that the concept of 'an educated man', which represents the achievement aspect of education, encapsulates distinct criteria, attention to which may pull the educator in different directions. For instance, emphasis on the criterion of 'wholeness' may militate against the emphasis on understanding of principles—that is, breadth and depth are difficult aims to combine.

(b) Aims can also relate to principles immanent in procedures of education, such as the importance of freedom and individual self-origination. It was argued, however, that if these are to be aims of *education*, they can be understood only against a background in which the general criteria involved in being educated are taken for granted. This is an important point to make against some child-centred educators who emphasize principles of procedure with a seemingly cavalier disregard for matters of direction and content.

3. Sometimes, when people fasten on to the idea that philosophy involves the analysis of concepts, they embark on this without asking

themselves what is illuminated by such analysis or what further philosophical questions are thereby opened up. My claim is that the above analysis of 'aims of education' does provide some sort of illumination of the issues by sketching the contours both of 'aim' and of 'education' and by showing what makes their juxtaposition a natural one. But it also opens up vast vistas for further philosophical work.

(a) It was claimed that most 'aims of education' are attempts to emphasize aspects of what it means to be educated. But no substantive pronouncements were made about the content to be given to the concept of 'being educated'. It was, however, suggested that this involves certain formal criteria—commitment to modes of thought and conduct that are regarded as worth while in themselves, which involve some depth of understanding, and which are not pursued with cavalier disregard for other ways of looking at the world. A curriculum is largely composed of such activities and forms of awareness. The question inevitably arises, why these should be thought worth while rather than things like bingo and billiards. This raises, of course, in an acute form, the old Utilitarian question about the grounds of the preferability of poetry over push-pin. An answer to this can be developed only by delving deep into ethics. But I would claim that making explicit these criteria involved in 'being educated' helps to map the paths along which such a justification must proceed. I cannot substantiate this without deploying the arguments. I can say only that I found these criteria of great help in making the attempt elsewhere.[9]

(b) It was also claimed that 'aims of education' can relate to principles such as freedom and respect for persons, which are built-in to procedures of education. Now questions can be raised about the efficiency of such procedures; but there are also crucial questions, seldom asked by educators, about the justification of the principles which are immanent in them. It might be found, for instance, that 'learning by discovery' was rather an inefficient method of learning; but, in so far as such a procedure involves an emphasis on freedom, it might be preferred, in spite of its inefficiency. But this would necessitate arguments to show why freedom is desirable. This analysis, therefore, draws attention to the need for more fundamental work in ethical theory to justify the fundamental principles underpinning the whole 'progressive' approach to education.

[9] *In Ethics & Education* ch. v. and in No. XII of this collection on 'The Justification of Education'.

4. I think that it is possible to produce arguments to show both why some sorts of pursuits are more worth while than others and why some principles rather than others are justifiable in dealing with children. In other words, I think it possible for a philosopher of education to produce some kind of ethical foundations for education, the guiding lines for which are provided by the above analysis of 'aims of education'. But what I think a philosopher cannot do, qua philosopher, is to pronounce on the relative weight to be attached to such principles, to proclaim that, for example, literature is more important than science, or that a principle of options in a curriculum should be stressed rather than 'wholeness', which might involve a greater element of compulsion. The justification of principles is one thing; their application in concrete circumstances is another. It is one thing to give arguments for general aims; it is quite another to say which particular one should be emphasized in contingent circumstances. Philosophy has an important contribution to make to practical wisdom; but it is no substitute for it.

COMMENTARY

JOHN WOODS

Although I agree with much of the substance of Professor Peters's paper, I confess to having some misgivings about its philosophical underpinnings. Professor Peters has undertaken to provide, for the concepts of 'aim' and 'education', a linguistic analysis which will reveal the appositeness of our speaking of education (as opposed, say, to nose-pulling or squash) as *having* aims. We need to ask, therefore, (1) whether the analysis of *aim* and *education* are tenable, and (2) whether their analyses do indeed underscore the naturalness of regarding education as being possessed of aims. Because I will answer the first question negatively, I do not see how I can properly address myself to the second. Neither will I speak to the more general question, whether analytic philosophy is capable of any real contribution to theories of education.

But first a preliminary, of almost appalling brevity, on what a linguistic analysis of a concept is supposed to be. It is true, is it not, that if someone is a bachelor then that person satisfies a certain condition, the condition, namely, of being unmarried. Suppose, however, that if someone is a bachelor, then, thanks to special legislation, he satisfies another condition: he pays a bachelor tax. Both are conditions pertaining to bachelors, but they pertain differently. The difference is this: If I say of someone both that he is a bachelor and that he fails the conditions of being unmarried, I contradict myself; but if I say he fails the condition of paying a special tax, what I say is self-consistent, although it may be false. It is fashionable to say that the first condition is part of the concept 'bachelor', whereas the second condition is only a *de facto* regularity pertaining to people who happen to be bachelors. Let us say more generally, that a condition C is part of the analysis of a concept K only if to say that something exemplifies the concept but fails to satisfy the condition is to say something inconsistent, para-doxical, or conceptually odd;[10] and that where C is thus part of K, then were C violated and we continue to *use* K as if nothing had gone wrong, we should have a *different concept of K.*

It is of the utmost importance, for evaluating the success of any putative piece of linguistic analysis, to determine whether the words analysed occur with their standard meanings, whether they occur as customarily used and understood by fluent speakers of the language. In particular, one has to guard against the possibility that what is offered as the analysis of a concept K, *as ordinarily used by fluent speakers of the language,* is in fact a *disguised recommendation* to the effect that the concept be assigned a meaning different from the one it has. Linguistic analysis is designed to reveal what a word does mean and not what the word should be made to mean; and if a so-called analysis accomplishes the latter and not the former, it fails. It fails because linguistic analysis is not a normative enterprise, even though it may inquire into all manner of normative concepts and set the stage for any number of normative decisions.

AIM

Turning now to professor Peters's analysis of 'aim', we see that he has given us three conditions:

---

[10] Professor Peters, I'm sure, would find this too narrow. Perhaps a better, though murkier, formulation would be that C is part of the analysis of K if, and only if, it would be in some sense inconsistent to say that exemplifica-tions of K frequently or always fail C. Thus, a single or even a few failures might be tolerated, but not all that many. The main point still remains: the relation between K and C might not be logically necessary, but it cannot be merely contingent. This broader formulation is the one against which the adequacy of Professor Peters's analysis is to be tested.

1. We tend to ask about aims in contexts where we think it is important to get people to specify more precisely what they are trying to do.

2. Aims suggest the concentration of attention on and the direction of effort towards an objective that is not too palpable or close to hand.

3. Aims suggest the possibility of failure or of falling short.

Now, let me make it plain that I take these statements to be unarguably true; but what I cannot accept is that they stand to the concept 'aim' in any such relation as the condition of being unmarried stands to the concept 'bachelor'. That is, I cannot believe that these constitute even part of the analysis of the concept 'aim'; nor that if we found out that people used 'aim' in violation of just these conditions we should think that their concept of 'aim' was different from ours.

Consider condition (1). It is, of course, false that always, in asking about aims, we are asking for a more precise specification of what people are up to. How often, indeed, are the aims of education inquired into mainly as a prelude to a discussion of their merits and not as an invitation to describe more determinately what people are doing? The question is, then: Is it *inconsistent*, even if false, to say that people rarely, if ever, ask about aims in order to get more precise descriptions? I submit not; but those who feel themselves demurring might consider the possibility that what generates the oddness of speaking this way is not the concept 'aim', but rather the concept of 'asking a question'; if we never questioned people in order to get more precise information, then perhaps we would not have the concept of 'questioning' which we do have; but we needn't thereby have lost our concept of 'aim'.

What, then, of condition (2)? Is it in some sense inconsistent or linguistically deviant to say, 'At long last people have had the good sense to aim only at those things which are fairly near to hand and fairly easily achieved'? What if virtually everyone undertook to aim for just those things we could comfortably achieve? Would we be obliged to say that the concept 'aim' had changed? Or would we say that *people* had changed? The latter, surely. (Suppose you ask an ancient and gouty, blue-nosed Tory what are the aims of his party; could he not reply, perfectly coherently, that they are to leave everything as it is? According to Professor Peters our politician would be abusing, not the national interest, but rather, the concept 'aim'!) In making aims 'kissing cousins' of ideals (which are defined as being unrealizable in practice), Professor Peters is stipulating a meaning for 'aim' for which condition (2) holds only vacuously. In effect, Professor Peters has changed the subject. He purports to be speaking of the concept of 'aim' when in fact he seems to be talking about something importantly different, namely the concept of a 'distant aim'.

Of course, one can easily sense the temptations of condition (2). *As a matter of fact*, many of our aims are rather distant; were it otherwise we could hardly be ambitious. But more important, there are certain aims, intelligibly described as limiting cases of aims, that are very close to hand, namely those that once achieved can never be achieved again. If, for example, I now aim at being elected president for 1967–8 of the local chapter of the Sigismondo Society, and if later I succeed, then, to be sure, I can no longer aim at *that*. So we have two facts; (1) there there is now some distance between me and the presidency; and if I win, there will be no distance whatever; and (2) if I win, I can't have *that* aim any longer; for me, winning can't be an aim. In examining these facts one might be inclined to think that *because*, after my election, there is no distance between me and my aim, it is not any longer properly called an aim. But, in reply to this, I suggest that it is not because what I aim at has become maximally close to hand, but rather because its description incorporates reference to a date such that the achievement of the aim, of *that very aim*, is logically unrepeatable. Indeed, if all aims were thus logically insusceptible of continuous or repeated realization, then we should have at least one model for 'aim' which sustains one possible interpretation of the claim that aims not only are not, but cannot be, too palpable or near to hand. But unhappily, it is far from true that all, or even most, aims satisfy this model.

A similar protest can be made about condition (3). Must we agree that if most of the things we aimed at were practically certain of realization, we should then have a different concept of 'aim'? Can I not say, without inconsistency, that all I aim for in life is a roof over my head, twenty dollars a week, and the freedom to stroll the parks of Toronto, and that, happily, I regularly get what I aim for? And if I do say this have I in any way bruised our notion of 'aim'?

Suppose, finally, that we had all the know-how to achieve easily and with virtually practical certainty the aims of education (whatever these might be). Then, in the light of Professor Peters's analysis of 'aim', it would be inconsistent or conceptually misguided to say that education had any aims; but what is this but to say that education would thereby be made aimless?—All of which, surely, is hopelessly paradoxical.

EDUCATION

If I understand him, the following is a list of conditions each of which Professor Peters takes to be part of the concept 'education'. A person is educated only if (1) he takes delight in what he does for its own sake; (2) he understands the principles which underlie such worth-while activities; (3) he engages in many such pursuits: he is not narrowly specialized; (4) his outlook is influenced and his sensitivity deepened by what he knows.

Of course, I accept these as being, in the main, *de facto* regularities pertaining to many educated persons. But permit me three cavils. First, we speak of a person as having had a *specialized* education; we speak of him as being educated, but because of laziness, impecuniosity, ambitiousness, or other considerations, as not having followed through, as having narrowly focused his concerns, or as no longer taking delight in the matters he had proper time for in his youth. These ways of speaking, which are not surely to be thought of as conceptually odd, actually imply that the person in question *is* educated. (Of couse he may not be ideally or perfectly educated, but Professor Peters is not speaking of these; he is speaking, rather, about what the unadjectived word 'education' means. Indeed, it is here that I am bound to charge him with offering us an analysis but giving us a proposal—to change the meaning of 'education'—in the guise of an account of what we do in fact mean by it. What supports me in this, I think, is that according to Professor Peters's criteria we should be required to withdraw the word 'educated' from virtually all the people we presently believe to *be* educated. Which is just to say that Professor Peters would have us drop the word as ordinarily *used* by fluent speakers of our language.) Second, we regularly (and rightly) withhold the appellation 'educated' from persons who *satisfy* each of the above conditions: the craftsman who pursues many trades, who engages in a sparkling variety of hobbies and pastimes, who knows the ins and outs of navigation, book-keeping, swordfishing, karate, cabinetmaking, weaponry, combustion mechanics, birdwatching, boxing, plastering, flower-arranging, roofing, and Montana Red Dog, but who has no academic competence, is not educated, even though he might fulfil our conditions.

Professor Peters would certainly reply to this that these formal conditions are relevant only when they pertain to the right *sorts* of activities. Indeed, he alleges that what counts as the right sort of activity is somehow socially determined. Hence my third point: a primitive society, wholly barren of academic riches, might well specify a wide range of activities as worth while (hunting, archery, mating, dancing, feats of strength and endurance, magic, medicine); and if any member of that society pursued the whole range of such activities in satisfaction of the four conditions, Professor Peters's position would oblige him to say that the man was educated. And this, I believe, Peters would not want to say.

COMMENTARY

WILLIAM H. DRAY

Professor Peters has discussed the question whether education has aims, with a view to displaying the sort of contribution analytical philosophers can make to educational theory. Let me confess that I should be delighted to find him showing that our expertise is badly needed in this inviting field. Like Professor Woods, however, I have to report some misgivings. Mine are not so much about particular analytical conclusions Professor Peters draws, as about the whole conception of the analytical philosopher of education's task which, in spite of the many wise things he says about education along the way, may seem to emerge from his analysis. Let me draw your attention first to a respect in which I think he may have misrepresented the philosopher's task, and then to one in which I think he has left that task obscure.

Whether or not Professor Peters's analysis of 'aim' and 'education' are satisfactory in detail, I take it that it is a major claim of his argument that there is something logically odd about speaking of education having aims at all. No problem is raised by saying something like 'The aim of vocational training is increased productivity', for this would be either an empirical report of what people hope to achieve by means of such training, or a perfectly intelligible prescription of what they should aim at. But such statements as 'The aim of education is initiation into a worth-while form of life,' or 'The aim of education is cultivation of the intellect', according to Professor Peters, only 'masquerade' as pronouncements of a similar sort. In reality they are empty tautologies. They are tautologies, however, into which it is quite 'natural' for educators to slip, since the various subject-matters used in educating *can* all themselves be studied for extrinsic purposes or aims. Such tautologies, furthermore, often have a 'social function'. The first sort reminds us, in circumstances where this may have been forgotten, what education really is; the second claims, in a confused but nevertheless effective way, educational priority for a certain subject-matter, skill, or procedure at a certain place and time.

Now, what is disturbing to me about this as a specimen of analytical philosophy of education is what may appear to be the philosopher's *acceptance* of what his analysis, especially in the second sort of case, represents as a defective way of talking. It is true that Professor Peters explains how 'natural' this way of talking is; but the reason it needs explanation is that, on his own showing, it is an error. It is true that he justifies the error; but he does so only in the sense of showing its tactical advantage as a persuasive device in the warfare of educational policy-makers. I do not want to suggest that the offering of such explanations and the detection of such linguistic tactics fall completely outside the analytical philosopher's proper function. But I regard it as even more central to his function, given his interest in conceptual logic, that he should *expose* and *deplore* the errors in so far as he believes them to enter into educational theory. What Professor Peters's conceptual analysis challenges us to recognize, it seems to me, is that typical uses of statements of the form 'The aim of education is ...' are not only false, but depend for their utility on their falsehood. Whether Dewey, whom Professor Peters quotes in this connection, would be prepared to put it this way is perhaps debatable; but I think Professor Peters should be.

Even this, however, does not really bring out the extent of the conceptual irregularity which I take Professor Peters's analysis to represent as typical of educational theory. According to him, when we say the aim of education is initiation into a worth-while form of life, or the cultivation of the intellect, what we call its aim is in fact its *nature*, or a part or aspect of it. That is the case for interpreting 'aim' statements as unwitting tautologies. But such statements, I would want to claim, are, on Professor Peters's own analysis, not even well-formed tautologies—as, for example, 'Education *is* initiation' or 'Education *is* cultivation of the intellect' would be. The incoherence of taking a part or aspect of something as its own aim may perhaps appear more clearly if we look at a more homely example. Compare the following two statements about baseball:

'Baseball is (among other things) aiming to hit pitched balls.'
'The aim of baseball is (among other things) to hit pitched balls.'

The first of these may indeed be a tautology, baseball being, in conception, a game requiring the constituent aim of hitting pitched balls. But given the conceptual truth of the first, the second statement is a logical monster. So are the alleged tautologies about the aims of education. In tolerating them, what Professor Peters fails to denounce, I fear, is not just the venial sin of taking conceptual truths for substantive empirical or prescriptive utterances; it is the mortal one of mistaking nonsense for sense. It would be a pity if his interest in what might be called the 'pragmatics' of educational discourse gave educational theorists the impression that analytical philosophers would not generally make a fuss about this sort of thing.

The second general question about the job of the analytical philosopher which Professor Peters's paper leads me to raise is an old favourite among critics of philosophy as analysis; yet it seems to be one which it is especially important to have articulated in philosophy of education. This is the question, *whose* concepts the philosopher conceives himself as analysing in order to make his distinctive contribution to educational theory. Professor Peters's discussion proceeds as if he will have little difficulty finding a relatively clear and generally shared, if rather complex and often theoretically misunderstood, concept of education to work upon. Many of the specific conceptual conclusions he draws, however, make me wonder about this assumption. Let me indicate a few examples.

Professor Peters defines education as initiation into a worth-while form of life, and he emphasizes at various points and in various ways the *evaluative* aspect of the concept. At one point he endeavours to display this aspect by claiming that it would be logically self-contradictory for a father to say 'My son has been educated but nothing desirable has happened to him.' I find this difficult to accept. For the father might surely be taken to be asserting quite coherently that the state of his son *after* being educated was, on the whole, less valuable than his state at the beginning—a judgement he might be driven to, for example, if his son, in the process, had become self-satisfied or a snob. Nor does it seem to violate the logic of the concept to imagine the same judgement being expressed by an anti-intellectual religious fundamentalist, who has no difficulty recognizing the marks of the educated man in his university-trained son, but thinks them *in themselves* all to the bad. The latter's concept, especially, seems to me much more likely to reflect what Professor Peters says about initiation into a *public* form of life than about initiation into a *valuable* one. In this respect, it conforms also to the concept I find myself employing and I doubt that this is just a case of what Professor Peters calls 'derivative' use.

Even if we accept the formula 'initiation into a worth-while form of life', an associated difficulty arises for me out of what is to be understood by 'initiating'. By this, Professor Peters sometimes appears to mean no more than 'introducing', although in a way which facilitates understanding rather than mere knowledge. Much of the time, however, he clearly means a good deal more. Thus, although at one point he makes it a criterion of being educated only that a person should be *capable* of pursuing a worth-while activity 'for what there is in it', he goes on almost immediately to tell us that what is required is *commitment* 'to what is internal in worth-while activities'. This seems to me to interpret the concept in far too behavioural a way. One paradoxical consequence would be the impropriety of calling a man educated who revolts against his own culture. It would require Jews, for example, to say that St. Paul suddenly lost his education on the road to Damascus, whereas they are much more likely to regard him as an educated renegade. And it would make questions about a man's character logically redundant, once we have assurance that his moral education is empeccable, whereas I should want to leave logical room for saying that it was, in part, the excellence of a man's moral education that enabled him to be so wicked: he fully grasped the moral enormity of what he nevertheless chose to do.

I have reservations also about Professor Peters's central claim that there is a conceptual error in asserting that someone seeks to become educated for some extrinsic purpose or aim. It seems to me perfectly coherent, for example, to say of a person who believes that God Himself is a snob, that he is preparing himself for the life everlasting by becoming educated. I can understand Professor Peters ruling this out, having read what he regards as certain desirable motivations into the concept of an educated man; but his reading them in strikes me as highly prescriptive. I find it even more difficult to follow him when (unless I have misunderstood his point) he makes it a conceptual requirement that the man's *teachers* also be properly motivated. 'People cannot be educated', he insists, 'by being taught engineering *with a view* to bringing about anything which would not itself fall under the concept of what an educated person is.' [My italics.] But it would surely be strange to withdraw our judgement that a man is educated on discovering that his teachers had only pretended to value education for its own sake. Thus, when Professor Peters declares that economists and politicians, who ascribe instrumental aims to the schools, do not 'strictly' make proposals about the aims of education, I can agree only that education *shouldn't*, not that it *couldn't* have such aims. And this is not a conceptual thesis.

Finally, I begin to wonder whether I in fact share Professor Peters's concept of education when he incorporates certain *procedures* into the concept. 'Education', he tells us, is a concept 'for laying down criteria to which a family of activities must conform'. These criteria characterize both the successful outcome, the 'educated man', and the 'processes by means of which people gradually become educated'. By including the latter in his explication of the concept, Professor Peters presumably makes it a *logical* impossibility to educate anyone other than by the proper procedures (some of which he goes on to discuss). These would certainly appear to exclude, say, plugging a man into an 'instant education' machine. It seems not implausible to me, however, to hold that the impossibility of 'instant' education, if any, is a causal rather than a logical matter; it is not obvious that 'educated', like 'evolved', entails certain things about the history of its referent. Yet if Professor Peters were to carry a majority against me on this point, I should not mind too much. For what I want to emphasize is simply the difficulty for philosophical analysis that may arise out of genuine differences of concept among individuals and groups, and perhaps also sometimes (for example, in the present case) out of indeterminacy of concept as well. This difficulty needs to be distinguished from the sort Professor Woods raises when he claims that Professor Peters did not in fact get the logical analysis of 'education' right. For the question is, what it would be to get it 'right'.

Not that the problem of identifying exactly what the analytical philosopher is supposed to analyse is unique to the philosophy of education. But there is a tremendous difference between the problem of analysing the concept of education and the problem, say, of analysing the concept of knowledge in general epistemology, or (to suggest what may seem a more relevant comparison) the concepts of fact or interpretation in philosophy of history. The epistemologist can claim with considerable plausibility that, on the whole, he finds people agreeing about what they can say they know and on what would count as supporting or undermining claims to knowledge. The philosopher of history can limit himself usefully to analysing the fairly stable conceptual networks of those who are generally recognized to be historians; and even if he is forced to admit that he takes account only of what 'reputable' or 'good' historians do, he may still feel that his feet are on reasonably firm ground. Such ground is not so obviously available to the analytical philosopher of education. He could always, of course, mark out useful work for himself by attempting analyses only of specific educational theorists or schools, with little further ambition than to help us (and them) understand what they are saying, and perhaps to police it for internal consistency. But Professor Peters's paper suggests that he, at any rate, would accept no such limitation. It would thus be interesting to know more precisely what he takes to be the objects of the analytical philosopher of education's analysis. Would he, for example, resist the suggestion that what the philosopher really does is *fabricate* a concept of education out of his vision of what people ought to become, and then hope its circulation may have a beneficial effect upon the schools? If educators are asked to consider the contribution that analytical philosophers can make to educational theory, they deserve the clearest possible answer to this question.

REPLY[11]

RICHARD S. PETERS

The conditions under which my paper was read and discussed were scarcely ideal from the point of view of the philosopher. To start with, it was the opening paper of the International Seminar, which had to be addressed to the general public and not simply to members of the Seminar. It had, therefore, to be a talk fit for philosopher kings and yet one that preserved the common touch. This, by the way, is the usual predicament of anyone working in the philosophy of education. If he gets too technical, he loses touch with most teachers, whose activities he is trying to clarify, criticize, or justify. If, on the other hand, he succeeds in communicating with teachers, he is in danger of being criticized by philosophers for being too crude or superficial, even though they may pay him a back-handed compliment by remarking that what he says is wise!

Secondly, I had no preview of the comments on my paper made by Professor Dray and Professor Woods, which followed each other in rapid succession. I was therefore able only, in the time allotted, to pick a few of the many acute points made and to plunge around trying to

[11] [This reply was written after the termination of the Seminar; selections from the discussion between Professors Peters, Dray, and Woods are included as footnotes at appropriate points.]

answer them 'off the cuff'. It therefore seems appropriate to attempt to do both the commentators and myself justice by adding a few further remarks, either dealing with points that I missed altogether in my immediate reply, or expanding some of the replies that I then gave, now that I have had some time to study more carefully what they said.

PROFESSOR DRAY'S COMMENTS

Logical Impropriety of Talk about 'The Aim of Education'

I entirely accept Professor Dray's first point about the logical impropriety of talk about 'the aim of education'. His account of what I was trying to say is both accurate and probably more clearly put than my own version. He is, perhaps, a bit sharp with me when he scolds me for not being rather more critical of this way of talking. I have, in the past, been very critical of it in various talks and writings, and thought that my whole analysis was an implicit criticism.

I must confess, however, that when I was asked to utter yet again on this subject for the International Seminar, I said to myself: 'What new is there for me to say about it?' I decided to pursue my long-standing puzzlement a bit further about the concept of 'aim' (on which, like the concept of 'education', no previous work has been done) and to try to work out what could have led people to talk in this way about education. Hence my mention of 'naturalness' which Professor Dray finds so distressing. Such 'naturalness' is not a purely psychological matter; it is connected in my analysis with the social function of talk about 'aims'. Professor Dray seems to think that once the philosopher has shown that talk about *the* aim of education is often an unfortunate way of proclaiming a tautology or uttering an analytic truth, he should stop people talking like this and then shut up shop. But surely, just as it is philosophically interesting to explore the analytic *use* of statements and the functions served by uttering tautologies, so it is interesting to see why this may get mixed up with talk about 'aims' in educational discourse. My analysis shows, too, that there are many quite appropriate ways of using 'aim' in educational discourse—for example, 'My aim as a teacher is . . .' In other words, it does not rule out the propriety of *all* talk of aims in educational situations.

The Case of the 'Educated' Snob

A father who comments that his son has turned out to be a snob *because* of, rather than in spite of, his education is, I think, using 'education' in an external, descriptive sort of way, like a person who says of a criminal, 'He is reformed all right; but as a result he just takes it out on his wife.' Would this show that 'reform' is not connected with making people better? This external, descriptive use certainly covers the case of the anti-intellectual fundamentalist who regards university education as all to the bad. In his own Bible classes he might equally well remark that what people got in universities was not education at all. It is like saying, 'He is a moral man all right; but he fiddles his income-tax', where 'moral' is used in what Hare calls the 'inverted commas' sense![12]

I do not think, by the way, that Professor Dray's suggestion that I should change my first criterion from 'initiation into a valuable form of life', to 'initiation into a public form of life', will do. For swearing, going to watch horse-racing and greyhound racing are very much part of a public form of life. But we would hesitate to associate them with education.

Commitment to What Is Worth While

Professor Dray's ingenious objections to my suggestion that an educated person is one who is 'committed' to what is internal to worthwhile activities involve a too substantive rendering of what I had in mind. I meant that such a person must care, to a certain extent, about the point of the activity and be not unmoved by the various standards of excellence within it. I am not sure to what extent he would have to accept any particular *content*, for example, the law of supply and demand if he had been initiated into economics. But in the case of science, for instance, a man must think that, to a certain extent, truth matters and that relevant evidence must be produced for assumptions; in the case of morals, the suffering of others, or fairness, must not be matters of indifference to him. What sort of philosophical education would a person have had if he did not bother much about consistency or cogency in argument? This does not imply that such a man will not be capable of 'cooking' the evidence, of being ruthless or unjust, and of being inconsistent at times. But it does imply that he will feel bad if he does behave in such ways. What the Jews would have said about Saul on the Damascus road, I am not sure. It would depend on the extent to which they believed in indoctrination, with the rigid insistence on an unshakeable *content* of belief that goes with it. But certainly they would

[12] See R. M. Hare, *The Language of Morals* (Oxford at the Clarendon Press, 1952), pp. 121–6.

have said that he was not educated if he had been quite insensitive to all aspects of religious experience.

The Motivation of Teachers

The reply I made during the Seminar to Professor Dray on the question of the motivation of teachers needs to be a bit expanded.[13] In my paper I was mainly concerned with the achievement aspects of education. I did, however, say, 'Engineering, for instance, can be taught in schools or colleges purely with a view to increasing productivity; but people cannot be educated by being taught engineering with a view to bringing about anything which would not itself fall under the concept of what an educated person is.' Professor Dray understandably took 'people cannot be educated' to relate to the achievement aspect, and raised his eyebrows at the suggestion that a certain kind of motivation of teachers is necessary if people are to emerge as educated men. But in my clumsy sentence, 'people cannot be educated' was meant to refer to the *task* aspect. I meant that in so far as teachers work away at educating people and regard the teaching of engineering as part of this, then they must emphasize those aspects of engineering which are consonant with their concept of an educated person. I went on to point out that engineers can be highly educated people. But it would obviously be only empirical speculation to suggest that they will emerge as such if, and only if, their teachers emphasize the educational aspects of engineering rather than just train them for a job.

A Moral, Not a Conceptual, Thesis?

Professor Dray thinks that it is a moral, not a conceptual, thesis that education cannot be related purely to vocations and skills. I argue that it is a conceptual thesis; for we do not speak of people being educated *as* cooks, *in* engineering, or *for* anything specific such as farming. In

[13] [The following is the relevent passage from the discussion at the Seminar.]
Peters: About the question of the teacher's motive. I think one has to distinguish, in talking about the concept of 'education', between two points of view: that of *task* and that of *achievement*. Now, in my paper, what I was mainly concerned with was the achievement aspect. Whatever the motives of the teacher—he might be interested in pay, or prestige in the community —he might, nevertheless, be an inspired teacher, and some of the pupils might end up by being educated. I wasn't concerned with the motives of the educator, only with people being educated. I was only dealing with what the state of mind is of the person who emerges from this sort of process, with the achievement aspect.

such contexts we speak of training. That is perhaps why people say vacuous things like 'Education is for life'; for they want to say that it is for something extrinsic; yet the logic of the concept forbids them to specify anything in particular which education is for. I think I am right about this. It may be the case—indeed it is almost a platitude nowadays—that people are of much more use in industry if they are educated rather than just trained in some skill that quickly becomes outdated. So education is a good investment from the point of view of the economy. But that does not make industrial productivity the aim of education. What I did argue in my paper, however, is that this conceptual point about education does not straight away settle the dispute about policy between those who advocate education and those who advocate technical training.

A Fabricated Concept?

Of course it was not my intention, as Professor Dray darkly hints at the end of his comments, to *fabricate* a concept of education out of my vision of what people ought to become. Actually, my analysis is rather content-free, which Professor Woods, for different reasons, found unsatisfactory in his fascination with carpenters and games-players. I take the concept of 'education' to be *almost* as unspecific in terms of content as something like 'good' or 'worth while', with the notion of 'transmission of' or of 'initiation into' prefixed to it. It is slightly more specific than 'good' because of the cognitive criteria to do with depth and breadth of understanding and awareness that I suggested also went with it. But I am more prepared to entertain the suggestion that I may have tightened up the concept a bit in my analysis when it emanates from Professor Dray than when it emanates from Professor Woods; for I do feel that Professor Dray is more sympathetic to the *sort* of conceptual analysis that I was attempting both of 'education' and of 'aim'.

PROFESSOR WOODS'S COMMENTS

Tight or Loose Conceptual Connections

Professor Woods obviously has little sympathy for the type of conceptual analysis that stems from the later Wittgenstein, in spite of his softening down of his approach in his footnote;[14] for no one who had much sympathy for such an approach would take the hoary example of the relationship between 'being a bachelor' and 'being unmarried' as

[14] See above, p. 30 n. 10.

a particualry helpful one if he was interested in getting clearer about concepts as general and as elusive as those of 'aim' and 'education'. Much more appropriate parallels would be concepts such as 'motive' and 'reform', as I suggested. Nevertheless, as I made clear in the discussion, I accept his general point that the connection between the concepts and what is suggested as part of their analysis must be conceptual rather than *de facto*.[15] But I obviously have a much looser notion of what counts as a conceptual connection, or of what it would be 'logically odd' to say, than he has. But more of this later.

Hobbies and All-round Understanding

Perhaps there was a slight misunderstanding on Professor Woods's part of my third criterion of 'wholeness' or 'not narrowly specialized'. He interprets this as implying that an educated person must engage

[15] [The following are the relevant passages from the discussion at the Seminar.]

Peters: I don't take it to be the philosophical analyst's job, with a concept like 'education', to formulate hard and fast, necessary and sufficient conditions which must always be satisfied if the word is to be used correctly. The point of approaching the concept as I did can be expressed as follows: We have developed certain ways of talking in which we use the word 'education' rather than 'training'. There are clear examples of when we would use one rather than the other: the stock example which I gave is the difference between sex education and sex training. Now, given that a way of talking has emerged to mark such a difference, the point of doing what I did is to get clear about the distinctions which lie behind the use of our words. Really, the main point is to become clearer and clearer about the contours of the concepts which have emerged; we cannot pin them down with a definition.

Phenix: I heard Professor Woods say, in effect, that the kind of analysis that has been undertaken, namely showing the kinds of situations in which one *uses* the term 'aims', is not what he calls philosophical analysis.

Woods: I'm not sure that I would be right in saying that it is not relevant to philosophical analysis, but I think I am right in saying that the inquiry into use, à la Peters, is certainly not the specification of conditions pertaining to the use of the given word associated with the given concept, which conditions stand to that word in other than a merely contingent or *de facto* relation. English-speaking analytic philosophers have introduced a number of terms to describe the kind of relation which must obtain between such conditions and what they are conditions of. They all have at least this one thing in common, namely the denial of the relation of merely *de facto* regularity. It is something stronger than that, although it need not be strict logical necessity.

I would think that what Professor Peters has to say, on the strength of his understanding of the analysis of a concept in terms of the job it does in a given linguistic context, could all be true and illuminating. But what would be true would, in my opinion, be *de facto* true. It would be a plain matter

in a wide variety of pursuits as hobbies, and this leads him to have problems about carpenters and games-players.[16] I meant only that we would say that a person is not educated if his *understanding* is very narrowly specialized. It would be a further question, how a man spends his time. A carpenter, in this view, could be an educated man, even though he spends most of his day on carpentry. He would have to have some depth of understanding in carpentry, not just a know-how, and his understanding and sensitivities would have to be not limited to carpentry. His 'education', in this sense, could be revealed in, for example, his personal relationships, his conversation with his friends, his grasp of politics and world affairs. He would not necessarily have to spend a great deal of his time listening to music, reading history, and doing scientific experiments at home. This criticism only *rules out* narrow specialization of thought. I made clear in my paper that it lays

---

of fact that when we inquire into somebody's aims, very frequently we want a more determinate specification of what they are up to. It would equally be a plain fact that on other occasions when people ask other people about their aims they do so to introduce a discussion about the merits of those aims. They are not interested in a more precise specification of what people are up to.

Peters: If Professor Woods can show that the relation is purely contingent, then I agree that it is bad analysis. What one tries to establish is some kind of a conceptual connection. Consider a well-known example. People thought at one time that 'good' meant 'what people desire'. Now this obviously doesn't fit all those cases where people say that something is good but that they don't desire it. I would want to hold that there is, nevertheless, some kind of conceptual connection between the notion of 'good' and people's desires. In other words, this isn't purely a *de facto* relation. However, it is very intricate to work out what these sorts of connections are, and one needs a much more sophisticated notion of 'meaning'. Often what is taken as the word's meaning is just what falls under the concept in some purely denotative way, as it were. One could never give the meaning of something like 'aim' or 'education' in that way. But there are all sorts of possible connections that might be explored between concepts other than just the purely *de facto* connections.

[16] [The following is the relevant passage from the discussion at the Seminar.]

Woods: Suppose there is a man who is a carpenter, who delights in carpentry for its own sake, who appreciates and understands the underlying principles of his trade. He extends his interest to a whole range of worthwhile pursuits, both hobbies and pastimes, crafts, other trade pursuits. He delights in them for their own sake, understands their underlying principles, is so affected by his understanding of those principles, that his life takes on a new quality. These are surely worth-while pursuits engaged in for their own sake.

down no *positive* requirements; I also made it clear that this is a *cognitive* requirement. People often suppose that educated people are those who continue doing, when they leave schools and colleges, all those things that they did there as distinct activities. This is obviously absurd. What is not absurd, however, is that their awareness should be sensitized in various dimensions—for example, moral, aesthetic, scientific, historical—and that they should continue to learn and explore in them without making all of them their hobbies. I do not see why a man who takes up carpentry, or who is a devotee of some game, should not develop in this way.

I think that my own answer, together with Professor Dray's intervention in the discussion, dealt adequately with the point about a primitive society, in which Professor Woods also failed to grasp what I was trying to say about cognitive requirements.[17]

Specialized Education

Professor Woods's point about 'specialized education' is not difficult to deal with either; for often we add an adjective to cancel out a criterion built into a concept that has multiple criteria. The example of 'knowledge' is a good parallel, which should be more acceptable to one with Professor Woods's purist proclivities. When a woman says that she knows that a man is a scoundrel, she suggests (*a*) that she thinks he is a scoundrel, (*b*) that she has good grounds for her view, and (*c*)

---

[17] [The following are the relevant passages from the discussion at the Seminar.]

Peters: On Professor Woods's point about the primitive society. I don't think people in a primitive society would have developed a concept of 'education' as distinct from something like 'training' or 'brought up in the ways of society'. I would suspect that it is only at a late stage of social sophistication that one begins to distinguish being trained from being educated.

Woods: The point of choosing the example of the primitive society in part hangs upon what you have just said. It seems to me that a member of that society would not be required to admit that he was educated. He, in fact, may not have the concept. But it occurred to me that you would have to say that he was educated simply because he engaged in a wide variety of activities said to be worth while by that society in ways that fulfilled your four conditions of what constitutes being educated.

Dray: I wonder if Professor Woods has really done justice to your criterion about understanding and knowledge. In fact, you do say that an educated man 'must also possess some body of knowledge, and some kind of conceptual scheme'. And this would pretty well rule out primitive man for you.

that it is true that he is a scoundrel. But we could say of her that she has 'intuitive knowledge' of this. 'Intuitive' here has the main function of cancelling the criterion (*b*), that she has good grounds for her view. I do not see why 'specialized education' should not be a similar sort of case.

Educated but Lazy

To Professor Woods's point about the person who, through laziness, and so on, does not go on with the worth-while pursuits of his youth, I would reiterate what I have just said about hobbies. If his outlook on his specialized occupation and on life generally was very little influenced by 'the matters he had proper time for in his youth', I would say that he was uneducated. If, however, the precipitates of them were not altogether 'inert', why, in my view, should he not be called educated? The question of degree comes in, of course; but I do not propose to go over all that again.

Aiming at What Is Close at Hand and Easy to Hit

To turn to the concept of 'aim' which I too have always found rather elusive: The preliminary point needs to be made that I would count as a conceptual connection one that appertains to the general use of a concept in a public language. It is quite possible, however, that once a concept has been learnt and begins, as it were, to acquire a life of its own, usages develop that seem inconsistent with the general use. But they are parasitic on the general use and would not be intelligible apart from the general use. To take a well-known example: G. E. M. Anscombe has argued[18] that no one could intelligibly be said just to want a saucer of mud. For whatever could one *do* with it if one had it? ('Wanting', it is argued, implies some criterion such as this.) But could it not be argued in reply that the concept of 'wanting' is learnt in standard situations when this criterion is satisfied, and that its general use is connected with such situations; but that, once it has been learnt, it can be applied perfectly intelligibly by the odd individual to situations where this condition is not fulfilled? There is, then, a conceptual connection between 'wanting' and 'being able to do something with what is wanted'; but this does not mean that there cannot be idiosyncratic usages where this connection does not hold. But these later usages could not be the general practice. I would call this sort of connection a conceptual one and not just a *de facto* one.

[18] G. E. M. Anscombe, *Intention* (Oxford: Blackwell, 1957), p. 70.

This general thesis about conceptual connections enables me to deal with most of Professor Woods's objections to my thesis about the general use of 'aim'. He suggests, in his second objection, that there is nothing inconsistent or linguistically deviant in saying that we are aiming at something that is fairly near at hand and fairly easy to obtain. (Note the use of 'fairly'! When does 'fairly near' turn into 'fairly far'?) But his example does not show this; for he has to add a *special background* to make such talk sound convincing. He has to put in: '*At long last* people have the *good sense* to aim only at those things which are fairly near at hand and fairly easily achieved.' He then asks whether we would say that our concept of 'aim' had changed or that people have changed, if virtually everyone undertook to aim at those things that he could comfortably achieve. But does he then think that the general use of the concept of 'aim' is independent of general facts about human nature? I would think that, because people in the main are as they are—that is, somewhat prone to set themselves difficult and distant targets—that the concept of 'aim' has developed a general use outside its natural home of shooting and throwing. If people had been different they probably would not have developed this concept. To take a parallel: The concept of 'ought' has a very important function only because men can reason and have inclinations which suggest alternative courses of action to them. Once, however, men have developed such concepts, they can use them in derivative and idiosyncratic ways.

As a matter of fact, Professor Woods's third objection seems to me to depend not just on a derivative but on a quaint way of speaking. I would never normally say that all I *aim* for in life is a roof over my head, twenty dollars a week, and so on. If I did say such a thing I would use the word 'aim' to produce a certain kind of deflationary effect, because *usually* talk about people's aims in life is linked with the specification of more distant and exalted types of objectives. Professor Woods's claim that there would be no inconsistency in this shows his determination to fit the analysis into a logically tight straitjacket. My case is that it would be quaint because of the primary use of the concept of 'aim'. Conceptual analysis should take account of quaintness as well as of inconsistency. It should also be sensitive to the manifold purposes served by ways of speaking.

The Assessment of Aims

Professor Woods's first objection is surely pretty naïve. He thinks that the fact that we can discuss people's aims from the point of view of their merits is a counter-example to my thesis that the general function of talk about aims is to get people to specify their objectives more precisely. Surely all one has to reply is that the assessment of aims is second-order type of talk. The concept of 'aim' gets off the ground in contexts such as those that I have suggested. But once this way of talking gets established, we can classify aims and pronounce on their merits. To take a parallel case: The fact that we can compare the types of commands given by schoolmasters and drill sergeants and assess them in various ways affects in no way the analysis we give of the distinct function performed by the language of commands as distinct, say, from that of advice.

Conclusion

I agree, then, with Professor Woods that the connection between the concepts that I have dealt with and the type of analysis that I have suggested is not as tight as that between the concept of 'bachelor' and that of 'being unmarried'. It would take me too long to explain why, in the case of the concept of 'aim' especially, it would be absurdly simple-minded to look for a connection as tight as this. But I hope I have done something to make implausible Professor Woods's suggestion that the connections I have suggested are purely *de facto* connections. I have a suspicion, however, that he thinks that, if the connections are not as tight as that of his favoured example, they are too elusive to be philosophically important. Such a purist view, I suggest, would stop most works in ethics, philosophy of mind, epistemology, political philosophy, aesthetics, and the philosophy of religion—as well as in the philosophy of education. And that would be a pity.

FURTHER THOUGHTS ON THE CONCEPT OF EDUCATION

R. S. PETERS

The matter, however, is not quite as straightforward as this; for 'education' is not quite so straightforward a concept as 'cure' or 'reform'. In particular it is doubtful whether 'education' is always used

From *The Logic of Education* by P. H. Hirst and R. S. Peters (London: Routledge & Kegan Paul; New York: Humanities Press, 1970), pp. 20–8. Reprinted by permission of the authors and publishers.

to designate processes that lead up to a general end in the way in which 'cure' and 'reform' always seem to be used. Doubts can be thrown on this parallel by probing to see whether any conditions that even begin to look like logically necessary conditions have been provided for the use of the term 'education'. To test this counter-examples have to be produced.

(a) *Objections to the desirability condition*. Roughly speaking, two types of conditions have been suggested for the use of the term 'education', namely desirability conditions and knowledge conditions Let us consider first counter-examples to the desirability condition. They are as follows:

(i) We often talk of the educational system of a country without commending what others seem concerned to pass on. This objection can be met by citing the parallel of talking about the moral code of another community or of a sub-culture within our own. Once we understand from our own case how terms such as 'educate' and 'moral' function, we can use them in an external descriptive sort of way as do anthropologists, economists, and the like. As observers we appreciate that, in the moral case, their way of life is valuable to them, and, in the case of an educational system, we appreciate that those, whose system it is, consider that they are passing on what they think valuable. But *we*, as observers, do not necessarily commend it when we use the word 'moral' or 'educational' to refer to it.

(ii) We can talk of poor education or bad education. This can be met by saying that we are suggesting that the job is being botched or that the values with which it is concerned are not up to much.

(iii) A much more serious objection, however, is that many regard being educated as a bad state to be in. Their objection is not to a particular system of education, but to *any* sort of education. They appreciate that 'education' has something to do with the transmission of knowledge and understanding. Indeed they probably associate it with books and theories. And this is why they are against it; for they think of it either as useless or as corrupting. Of course they bring up their own children, perhaps in traditional skills and folk-lore. But they do not see any connection between what they think valuable and 'education', and have no specific word to differentiate the handing on of what they think valuable from handing on a lot of other things.

This last point suggests one way in which the objection could be met.

It could be argued, with some cogency, that people who think that being educated is a bad state to be in lack our concept of being educated. Their understanding has not become differentiated to the extent of needing a special word for referring to the passing on of what they do think is valuable. They have *a* concept of education; for they use the term to refer to what goes on in schools and universities. But they have not *our* concept. The only trouble about this way of dealing with the objection is that people who lack our concept of education are, at the moment, rather numerous. 'We', in this context, are in the main educated people and those who are professionally concerned with education; and 'we' are not in the majority of people who use the word 'education'. So it is doubtful whether the desirability condition of 'education' is a logically necessary condition of the term that is in current use. It stands in this relation to a more specific, differentiated concept that has emerged. This possibility will be considered in more detail later (see pp. 54–5).

Another way, not of really meeting the objection but of accounting for the discrepancies with regard to the desirability condition, is to suggest that the knowledge conditions are the only proper logical conditions, and that the desirability condition is dependent on them. On this view the fundamental notion involved in being educated would be that of having knowledge and understanding. Because knowledge and understanding are valued in our culture, both for their own sake and for what they contribute to technology and to our quality of life generally, being educated has come to be thought of as a highly desirable state to be in—but not by everybody. Whether or not the desirability condition is fulfilled would depend, therefore, upon contingent facts about the attitude of people talking about education to the passing on of knowledge and understanding. The desirability condition, therefore, would not be, properly speaking, a logically necessary condition of the use of the term 'education'. It would rather be a contingent consequence of certain people's valuations.

This way of simplifying the analysis has much to commend it:

(i) It certainly takes care of those who regard education as a bad thing. As, on this view, the connection between education and something that is valued depends only on the contingent fact that people value knowledge and understanding, it is not surprising that simple people or hard-headed practical men are against it. For it seems to serve no useful function in their lives; indeed it may be seen as an influence that is likely to undermine their way of life. If they see that it may help them to run a farm or to cure a disease they may accord a limited value to it, but only of an instrumental type.

(ii) There would be no need to make any elaborate philosophical moves to deal with cases where we speak of education and educational systems without approving or disapproving of what goes on. Education would be, as indeed it is sometimes called, the 'knowledge industry'. We could talk of it in the same way as we talk of any other set of practices that we might or might not think important.

(iii) 'Poor' or 'bad' education would simply mark the efficiency with which knowledge was handed on or the worth of the type of knowledge that was handed on.

This, then, is a most attractive simplification of the analysis. Its main feature, however, is that it puts all the weight of the analysis on the knowledge conditions, and it is questionable whether they are strong enough to support it. They must therefore be tested by counter-examples in the same way as was the desirability condition.

(b) *Objections to knowledge conditions.* The knowledge conditions, it will be remembered, include both depth and breadth of understanding.

(i) An obvious counter-example would be, therefore, that we often talk of specialized education. This objection could be met by saying that often, when we have multiple conditions, we can withdraw one of them by using a countermanding word. For instance, people talk of knowing things 'intuitively', where 'intuitively' countermands one of the usual conditions of 'knowledge', namely that we have grounds for what we believe. Similarly 'specialized' could be regarded as withdrawing the breadth condition of 'education'.

(ii) We might talk of Spartan education, or of education in some even more primitive tribe, when we know that they had nothing to pass on except simple skills and folk-lore. This objection could, perhaps, be met by saying either that the term was being extended analogically, as when dogs are spoken of as being 'neurotic', or that the people using the term had not yet developed a differentiated concept of 'education' which takes us back to the case already mentioned of people who think that education is a bad thing. As there are a lot of people who talk in a quite unabashed way about Spartan education, it is difficult to maintain that the knowledge conditions are logically necessary conditions of the term in general use. This point is strengthened by the third objection.

(iii) The case of 'Spartan education' is just one of a wider class of cases. A little etymological research reveals the fact that 'education' is, or has been, used without this conceptual connection which is suggested with knowledge. The Latin word 'educere' was usually, though not always, used of *physical* development. In Silver Latin 'educare' was used of the rearing of plants and animals as well as children. In English the word 'education' was originally used just to talk in a very general way about the bringing up of children and animals. In the seventeenth century, for instance, harts were said to delight in woods and places of their first education. The word was often used of animals and birds that were trained by human beings such as hounds and falcons. In the nineteenth century it was even used of silkworms! (See *O.E.D.*) Nowadays we sometimes use it in this general way as when, for instance, we talk about Spartan education or when we use it of our own forms of training that do not have any close connection with knowledge and understanding. In other words the older usage still survives.

Arguments from etymology, of course, establish very little. At best they provide clues which it may be worth while to follow up. In this case, for instance, it seems that the word originally had a very generalized meaning. With the coming of industrialism, however, and the increasing demand for knowledge and skill consequent on it, 'education' became increasingly associated with 'schooling' and with the sort of training and instruction that went on in special institutions. This large-scale change, culminating in the development of compulsory schooling for all, may well have brought about such a radical conceptual tightening up that we now only tend to use the word in connection with the development of knowledge of understanding. We distinguish now between 'training' and 'education', whereas previously people did not. We would not now naturally speak of educating animals and we would never speak in this way of plants. But we do speak of training animals and of training roses and other sorts of plants.

These counter-examples to both the desirability condition and the knowledge conditions of 'education' make it very difficult to maintain that an adequate analysis has been given of the concept. It is possible, however, that there is some explanation of these counter-examples. It could be the case, in other words, that the cases that fail to fit the analysis could themselves be linked in some way. If we could get clearer about the principle underlying the counter-examples further light would be shed on the concept of 'education' generally.

(c) *Education and the educated man.* As a matter of fact there is another etymological point that may put us on the track of the explanation of cases that do not fit the original analysis. A little research in the *O.E.D.* reveals that the notion of 'educated' as characterizing the allround development of a person morally, intellectually, and spiritually only emerged in the nineteenth century. It was also in this century that the distinction between education and training came to be made explicitly. This use was very much connected with instruction by means of which desirable mental qualities were thought to be produced, as well as with the drawing out and development of qualities thought to be potential in a person. The term, however, continued to be used, as it had previously been used, to refer to the rearing and bringing up of children and animals, as well as to the sort of instruction that went on in schools. In other words, though previously to the nineteenth century there had been the ideal of the cultivated person who was the product of elaborate training and instruction, the term 'an educated man' was not the usual one for drawing attention to this ideal. They had the concept but they did not use the word 'educated' quite with these overtones. Education, therefore, was not thought of explicitly as a family of processes which have as their outcome the development of an educated man in the way in which it is now.

Nowadays, especially in educational circles, the concept of an educated man as an ideal has very much taken root. It is natural, therefore, for those working in educational institutions to conceive of what they are doing as being connected with the development of such a person. They have become very sensitive to the difference between working with this ideal in mind and having more limited and specific goals, for which they use the word 'training'. Witness, for instance, the change in nomenclature, following the Robbins Report, from Training Colleges to Colleges of Education. Witness, too, the change from Physical Training to Physical Education. In brief, because of the development of the concept of an 'educated man', the concept of 'education' has become tightened up because of its natural association with the development of such a person. We distinguish between educating people and training them because for us education is no longer compatible with any narrowly conceived enterprise.

Now in the analysis previously given of 'education' as being comparable to 'reform' and 'cure' a connection was assumed between education and the development of an educated man. It was admitted that other people may not have developed this more differentiated type of conceptual structure, but it was maintained that it is important to make these distinctions even if people do not use terms in a specific enough way to mark them out. But it could well be that the older use of 'education' is widespread in which there is no such tight connection between various processes of bringing up and rearing and the development of an educated man. It may well be that many people still use the word 'education' to cover not only any process of instruction, training, etc., that goes on in schools but also less formalized child-rearing practices such as toilet training, getting children to be clean and tidy, and to speak with a nice accent. They may think these achievements desirable, though they have little connection with knowledge and understanding. I do not think, however, that the word is now used, except semi-humorously, to talk about the training of animals, and I have never heard it used to honour the labours of gardeners with their plants. At least the concept has shifted more or less universally in these respects from that of the seventeenth century.

It looks, therefore, as if the concept of 'education' is a very fluid one. At one end of a continuum is the older and undifferentiated concept which refers just to any process of bringing up or rearing in which the connection either with what is desirable or with knowledge is purely contingent. There may be uses which link it just with the development of desirable states without any emphasis on knowledge; there may be uses which pick out the development of knowledge without implying its desirability. The more recent and more specific concept links such processes with the development of states of a person that involve knowledge and understanding in depth and breadth, and also suggests that they are desirable. The analysis of 'education' which compares it to 'reform' is of this more differentiated specific concept.

Aims of education

How, then, would reasons deriving from the later, more specific concept of 'education' provide guidance for a teacher concerned about educating his pupils? The general injunction to promote desirable states of a person, that involve depth and breadth of understanding, would indicate only a general direction; it would offer no specific guidance.

More specific guidance would have to be obtained by the teacher getting clearer about his aims in educating people. For the function of the formulation of aims is to specify more precisely what one is trying to achieve, one's target in a metaphorical sense. This attempt to specify precise targets also takes over a further suggestion from the context of shooting and throwing, where the concept of 'aim' has its natural home, namely that the end in view is not altogether easy to achieve.

Distance and difficulty seem to be endemic to ends that we would characterize as 'aims'. Aims, however, cannot specify states of affairs that it would be manifestly impracticable to bring about. In this respect they differ from 'ideals'. A person can expatiate on his ideals as a teacher without having to raise awkward questions about practicalities. If, on the other hand, he attempts to formulate his aims, he has to have regard to practicalities. He also has to be more specific than he is licensed to be if he is asked about his ideals. An educational ideal, for instance, might be that every child should learn out of the joy of discovery. A teacher's aim, in the same context, might be a more specific and attainable objective such as that every child in his class should be brought to see some point in learning what had to be learnt.

Formulating aims in education must be distinguished from attempting to answer the general question 'What is *the* aim of education?' This is an unhelpful sort of question to ask in this context because the answer must either be a conceptual truth or a persuasive definition. It would be a conceptual truth if it specified an adequate analysis of the general end brought about by processes of education. In other words, if the foregoing analysis of the specific concept of 'education', as the family of processes leading up to desirable states of mind in people involving depth and breadth of understanding, is more or less adequate, then it would be a conceptual truth that the production of this general end is the aim of education. It would be like saying that the aim of reform is to make men better. And to reiterate this would not provide much guidance for the teacher. Suppose, however, that something more concrete were produced as a specification of this general end. Suppose it were said that *the* aim of education is to produce specialized knowledge. Then a stipulative definition would be produced which would have the function of recommending a specific policy. Instead of coming out into the open and saying '*My* aim in educating people is to develop specialists' covert support would be obtained for this policy by trading on the suggestion that pursuing this, and only this end, is consistent with educating people. This, it is true, would help the teacher in giving more specific guidance. But the help would be at the expense of conceptual clarity.

Suppose, then, the teacher attempts to specify *his* aim in educating people or the aims of a particular educational institution. What sort of answer could be given? Roughly speaking any answer which could be a more precise specification of what an educated man is considered to be. Features would be emphasized—e.g. critical thinking, specialized knowledge, autonomy, aesthetic sensitivity—which would be part of the teacher's understanding of what it means to be 'educated'. Content would be given to the general form of 'an educated man' provided by the analysis in terms of desirability and knowledge conditions. Arguments, of course, would have to be produced for emphasizing some desirable qualities rather than others. Indeed this is one important respect in which educating people differs from curing them, to revert to the comparison with medicine. For in education there is as much debate about the ends of education as there is about the methods to be adopted to promote these ends. The same is not true of medicine. There is much more consensus about what constitutes being 'cured' than there is about what constitutes being 'educated'.

It is important to distinguish 'aims of education' in these cases from aims of education when the more general undifferentiated concept of 'education' is being used—e.g. by politicians talking about the educational system. A politician or administrator, in an economic frame of mind, might think of education as the means by which a supply of trained manpower is assured. He might think of education purely in this way and have no regard for the endeavours of educators who might in their turn be impervious to the economist's frame of reference. They might be concerned purely with the development of educated men and women. Of course looking at what goes on in schools and universities from this economic point of view is not *necessarily* antagonistic to being concerned with education in the more specific sense. Indeed a teacher might regard the development of responsible citizens, who have the competence to fulfil some occupational role, as his unifying aim as an educator. For him this civic consciousness might be the hall-mark of an educated person. He might, in his approach, concentrate on getting his pupils technically equipped to do certain jobs, and attempt to make technical skill and knowledge the linch-pin of a person's depth and breadth of understanding as a citizen.

Similarly a teacher might teach a subject such as science with purely vocational or economic ends in view. He might regard himself just as equipping people for vocations or as serving a national need for trained manpower, without much thought about the development of the individuals concerned, as individuals. He might conceive of what he was doing just as contributing to economic growth. But teaching science with these limited ends in view should be distinguished from educating people. Teaching, as has already been pointed out, is not necessarily educative. On the other hand, though not unmindful of the nation's needs, a teacher might also teach science because he regarded this form of understanding as central to his concept of an educated person.

II

WORK, LABOUR, AND UNIVERSITY EDUCATION

P. HERBST

THE central idea of this paper is to apply a distinction of Hannah Arendt's[1] to the educational scene; the distinction is between work and labour. The thesis is briefly that education is work rather than labour, and that to educate well is to work, as well as to teach people to work. Some critical conclusions will then be drawn about contemporary education and some unflattering remarks made about contemporary universities.

The work–labour distinction may be interpreted as an application of certain theories in the philosophy of action. The relevant investigations have mainly occupied continental philosophers, existentialists, and phenomenologists for instance. The Marxists and neo-Wittgensteinians have also contributed. The theme of these philosophers is that human actions are subject to certain characteristic defects which make them less characteristically actions and which make the agents less characteristically human. Such defects are variously called alienation, bad faith, viscosity, anomie, and so on. People who elect life-styles which involve them in habitually defective action are sometimes said to lack authenticity, or to be dehumanized.

Roughly speaking, work is conceived to be a species of unalienated action, labour is activity tending to alienation. (It must be conceded from the outset that the distinction between work and labour cannot be made very sharp. More than one criterion for distinguishing them will need to be introduced, and there will be cases which will answer to one criterion, but not to another.)

Work and labour have this in common, that they consume the time and energies of people, and that, being directed to a purpose, they may be done more or less quickly, or more or less competently, or more

---

A revised version of a paper, first written in 1967 as a contribution to a symposium on education in the Australian National University.

[1] Hannah Arendt, *The Human Condition* (Chicago: University of Chicago Press, 1958), chs. 3 and 4.

or less conscientiously, and so on. Also, and for these reasons, both work and labour tend to exclude other human pursuits. They call for a certain discipline or self-direction, and so, whether you work, or whether you labour at a task, you cannot at the same time make love or engage in sport.

Both work and labour are commonly directed to production, though not everything which is produced is a commodity, or a negotiable possession. For present purposes we must subsume the provision of services, and the tasks of planning, administration, and exchange under the heading of production, even though, in an obvious sense, much labour is quite unproductive. An instance is the labour which is expended in the service of the war-industry.

The products of work are works. I am sorry that the only available English word is so weak and colourless. I shall use the Latin word 'opus' instead. The opus, as I conceive it, is the point of the workman's work; if the opus is well done, he has not worked in vain. I shall argue that in order to work well, a workman needs to love or value that at which he works and if so, he aims at good workmanship. The excellence of an opus will be sharply distinguished from its instrumental goodness, and in particular, from its propensity to procure satisfaction for consumers. At the same time it is not denied that in objects which belong to a telic species, what counts as their excellence may depend on their telos. For instance, because a chair may be defined as something for sitting on, being comfortable is a virtue in chairs.

The satisfaction of consumers is not a measure of the excellence of a product. This seems pretty evident, particularly if the consumers themselves have been exposed to sales talk. Thus efficient advertising induces consumers positively to prefer shoddy to good workmanship, and sometimes, to regard all goods as being made purely for consumption, so that, unlovely and unmemorable, they will have served their turn, if, by being consumed, they perish.

Palmström, a creation of the German poet Morgenstern, did not share this attitude. He had a handkerchief of such exquisite beauty and workmanship, that, meaning to blow his nose in it, he was overawed by its grandeur. The handkerchief was re-folded; the nose betrayed. I mention him because he illustrates the mistaken idea that if the telos of an opus is not utilitarian satisfaction, the object must become a mere museum-piece.

Labour is toil, labour is hardship. It is the price which we pay for whatever advantages the rewards of labour will buy. A typist who neither understands nor cares for the material which she is typing, is hired to work in an office. She accepts the inconvenience of having to perform an uncongenial task for the sake of keeping body and soul together and for the sake of the activities and amusements which her wages and her social contacts at work bring within her reach. If she could obtain these advantages without having to type, that would be better, but typing is better than forgoing the advantages. It is a ledger-calculation.

Labour may in some circumstances cause us to have pleasurable experiences, and very commonly, it puts us into a position to buy pleasures. But, if it is not justified puritanically, as the *aspera* which are involved in the pursuit of *astra*, it must be justified by the pleasures or satisfactions to which it is a means. Work need not similarly cause or give us pleasures; congenial work on the contrary *is* a pleasure. The pleasure consists in doing the work, not in some consequence, or state of mind, produced by the work. The pleasure of labour on the other hand (if any) is always extrinsic to it.

The view of happiness on which the argument relies is Aristotelian. Happiness *consists in* activities: it is not compounded of pleasures which are *produced by* activities. Activities conceived as pleasure-producers are labour. Activities conceived as happiness-constituents are work.

Labour is contingently related to its product. Artifacts of the same kind may be produced by radically different productive processes. Human labour may be made more productive, more efficient, by being aided or even supplanted by machines. The process of production and the product are conceptually distinct. Many process-workers do not even know to what product their labour contributes: the finished artifact is no concern of theirs.

Work is non-contingently related to its product. The description of the process and the description of the product are part of a single conceptual scheme. The excellences of the product may be described in terms of workmanship, the productive work as aiming at these excellences.[2] Education is a case in hand. To be educated, is to bear the marks of having been through the educational process. Thus finished product and productive processes are correlatively understood.

The adequacy of work and the excellence of its product are *judged*

---

[2] The view that work does not play a part in the *causation* of opera (assuming its intelligibility) is not expressed here, and must not be ascribed to the author.

together. If the unified conceptual scheme is abandoned, this advantage is lost and the point of the work is no longer clear. It is then, poor thing, fed into the machine of means and ends and justified by the calculus of satisfactions. The ironic outcome is that the workman comes to hate his work, or in bad faith, to invent a myth in order to persuade himself that he likes it, and thus its fruits are mortgaged, even before they have been gathered. The workman then becomes a labourer.

A simple, but perhaps not over-simple account of unalienated action is that the aims and purposes of the agent, as a person, accord with the general telos of his enterprise. Unalienated work is a case in hand; there has to be some enterprise in which an opus of a certain kind is produced, subject to standards of excellence for *that kind* of work, and such that the workman desires to produce that kind of work under a description such that these standards of excellence are appropriate, which he endorses in any case.

The view that work, unlike labour, must have a point which the workman can endorse, and a purpose with which he can associate himself, has been apparently bypassed by some doctrines, recently orthodox, in the philosophy of action. The position which I have in mind is that any performance or activity may be described in indefinitely many ways of which none is more basic or more revealing than another, and it is held that the frustration of not being free to do as one purposes is avoided, provided that one endorses what one does under some description which one's exertions will bear. Thus, for instance, since much labour is correctly described as making money and most labourers are keen on making money, it seems that, except through their failure to make money, they cannot be frustrated.

The theory of multiple descriptions is also used to deflect the point of the remark that the frustration of labour arises as much from the absence of standards of excellence to which the labourer can aspire, as from the lack of a real object in labouring. In certain situations, especially under conditions of modern advertising, there may be a performance which is a bad way of earning money but a good way of building a house, or a good way of achieving promotion in a university but a bad way of teaching pupils. Here again it will be argued that if the labourer really wants money and promotion, then he can take a pride of workmanship in his endeavours, provided that they are adequately described as successful money-getting or promotion-earning. Thus, according to this relativist thesis, conceptions of skill and excellence of workmanship vary with different descriptions of the same activity, and the labourer will not go without reward if he conceptualizes his activities under some description under which they come out well.

These arguments seem to be nothing better than sophistries. It is clearly wrong to say that people *care* about making money or achieving status; they *desire* these things. The concept of care connects with the idea that there are some things which we cherish, and to which we devote ourselves. We care for things lovingly, or tenderly, or devotedly, but except in bad faith we pursue our interests quite unsentimentally.

The workman then *cares* for his opus, and he will have a reason for proceeding thus rather than thus, in terms of the qualities and excellences at which he aims in the finished product. Thus his performance bears a description under which it is a condition of quality in his product, there being a description of his product under which he wants to make it, and to make it well.

Now it is not evident that these conditions can be met by activities of which the point is money-making, or some such other extrinsic end. The money which a man earns is not his product, but rather what he gets in exchange for his product. Money is not an opus. One lot of money differs from another lot of money only by way of more or less; money does not bear the marks of craftsmanship. Similarly, the activities which are addressed to the task of money-making have the qualities and excellences of which they are capable only relative to some opus which is saleable, or some purpose from the pursuit of which an income happily results.

Let us meet the critics of our viewpoint who proceed from the theory of multiple descriptions by experimenting with an example. Consider a man who, being a devoted builder, has conceptions of excellence in houses, and under these conceptions cares about what and how he builds. Incidentally, he wants to earn a living out of building. Now let us attempt to invert the example. Thus we get a man who, being a devoted money-getter, has conceptions of excellence in money-getting, and under these conceptions cares for the sums of money which he makes, and for what he does by way of getting them. Incidentally, what he does by way of money-getting is house-building.

Now it makes sense to suppose that a man builds houses, no matter whether well or badly, in order to obtain money, but it does not make the same sense to suppose that a man makes money, no matter whether well or badly, in order to obtain a house. The only interpretation which we can place on that suggestion is that he makes money in order to be in a position to *buy* a house, and if so, he had better do well at money-making, because the house of his choice may turn out expensive.

There seems to be a confusion between constitution and instrumentality in the arguments of the cynics. Good workmanship is constitutive of a good work, but (with good luck) only a means of obtaining rewards. Good workmanship on the other hand is as little constitutive of rewards as it is instrumental to a well-made opus. By these tests not all descriptions under which a man may be said to be acting when he makes something come out equal. For instance 'earning a living', 'making a reputation for himself', 'earning promotion', 'serving his company', 'doing his duty', cannot be descriptions of work, while 'building a house', 'composing a quartet', 'working at a philosophical problem', and 'educating a student' may serve as work descriptions proper. A workman is one who avowably acts under such a description.

Universities, despite the composition of their councils, are, by and large, self-governing institutions still, but more than the armed forces, or the institutionalized professions, the pressures of society affect them everywhere. Governments hold the purse-strings; they do not find it difficult to persuade universities to volunteer research in areas deemed useful, nor do they hesitate to encourage subject-areas and educational techniques to produce students who will accept the roles envisaged by the official planners. The media and the politicians, not to mention the representatives of business interests and the trade unions, are for ever admonishing universities not to abuse their positions of privilege, but to shoulder their social responsibilities, and to assist in the accomplishment of some task which, at the time, is conceived to be essential to progress, or to the country's well-being (or to that of the nation, mankind, society, or some other likely recipient of people's fundamental loyalties). The funds and the support which universities receive from the public purse are insufficient for their needs, however, and thus they must seek the assistance of industry, and trade, and the professions to enable them to branch out into areas of research on which their prestige depends. It seems likely that funds would no longer be readily available if the interests of learning and the interests of the donors came to be in serious conflict. Situations in which the consciences of individual university teachers conflict with the interests of a donor are now increasingly common, specially in the ecological field. The results will need to be studied.

Some university people feel slightly guilty about the pursuit of learning: the image of the ivory tower puts them on the defensive. In such a mood they are anxious to stress the continuity of their outlook with that of society at large, and they become active in organizations to which the idea of thought, directed to the telos of truth, is alien, but in which they can prove themselves good fellows.

The attachment of some university teachers to their institutions, and to the traditions and ideals of universities, is often only partial. Take a department in a vocational branch of university teaching: law, for instance. Some of its most distinguished members are fully functioning members of their profession, perhaps on temporary loan to a university. The department as a whole has its moorings at least as much in chambers and in the law-courts as in the cloisters, it invites distinguished counsel, judges, and attorneys general for talks and dinners: in return its members sit on committees which make them influential in the profession, and are allowed to appear in an advisory capacity on various bodies designed to solve the legal problems of governments, banks, trade unions, and public corporations. The interests of the legal profession, however, are no more guaranteed to coincide with the interests of the students in acquiring an education than the interests of General Motors are guaranteed to accord with those of the American nation. Thus, for a teacher who has the education of his students at heart (as distinct from their careers) there may be a tension, a case of divided loyalties. The students themselves undoubtedly often feel this tension, and the disinterested desire to emerge as educated men and women struggles with the desire for a meal ticket. What it is to receive an education remains to be discussed below.

The professions and the institutions to whose service students are destined have influence, not only through their members or nominees on university councils, grants commissions, research foundations and such bodies which control universities and their work, but also because they have it in their power to employ or to reject graduates. This power is great, and to many, fearful.

Thus, for many reasons, and not least, because it is a universal tendency for people to rationalize the pressures upon them and to contrive an ideology designed to make these pressures bearable, universities reflect the ethos of the societies in which they operate, even where this ethos is incompatible with the enterprise of teaching and research. That seems to be the present situation in the technologically advanced affluent societies of the western world. Some remarks about this ethos are called for.

To begin with a cliché: we live in a society of consumers. It is true, the pundits and the politicians are for ever exhorting us to production, and seem to regard the indefinite expansion of production as the greatest good, but production is conceived of as a mere correlative of consumption. We produce either what we anticipate that we will consume, or we produce the means of accelerated production, machines, that is to say. Sometimes we even produce the means of accelerated consumption, as in the advertising industry. Society as a whole is here conceived to be acting on the supposition that consumption is the only worth-while human function, and that the indefinite expansion of the production–consumption cycle, together with the unhampered freedom to produce and consume, are the only worth-while ends of action.

The greater part of our political energy is devoted to economic matters, to welfare, the enhancement of the standard of living, the expansion of output, the procurement of 'jobs', and the provision of common services which otherwise would have to be purchased by the individual. To this we must add our preoccupation with stability and security, the protection of our vast and infinitely complex system of production, administration, commerce, and organized consumption against organic imbalances, and against internal and external foes. The question whether the ideological emphasis in our society is on production or consumption is bound up with whether we are concerned with the health and stability of the system, growth-rates for instance, employment opportunities and the avoidance of slumps, or whether, concerned to advertise the benefits of the system, we point to the bonanza of an indefinitely rising 'standard of living'. It seems clear that, despite the emphasis on growth-rates, few believe in production for its own sake. Our consciences are ruffled when the alleged needs of the stability of the system cause us to dump foodstuffs in the sea, even without the thought of the starving millions of Bangla Desh.

To consume a commodity is so to put it to use that in the process it disappears or perishes. Thus a commodity is given in exchange for a service or a satisfaction. Not all consumer commodities are as ephemeral as food: some, the so-called durable consumer goods, are consumed slowly. There are also consumer services (banking, for instance); and there are those objects which are not, in any obvious way, consumed at all, but which are produced, bought, sold, and disposed of as if they were consumer goods. I mean 'desirable residences', gardens, jewels, and the palpable artifacts of learning and art (books, paintings, stereo, etc.).

It has been remarked that the central ethos of capitalist production is puritanism, that is, justification by achievement wrought from self-sacrifice, self-discipline, frugality, and labour. Paradoxically enough, the central ethos of capitalist consumption is utilitarianism,[3] that is the doctrine that the discipline and toil of the productive process can only by justified by the personal satisfactions of the consumers. Since the most successful producers acquire wealth, they also become major consumers, and thus we have that grotesque historical joke, the tycoon who practises frugality in luxury, and who pursues his pleasures in the same spirit of grim determination in which he approaches his managerial role. The puritan ethos is irreducibly individualistic, no man can hope to win merit for another, none can assuage his conscience through the sacrifices or exertions of another man. The utilitarian ethos on the other hands is social and impersonal. Any man may glean satisfactions from consuming a commodity, no matter who produced it, and society as a whole is conceived to be in a state of well-being if the majority is happy, that is, according to that ideology, if the level of consumption is high.

The early philosophers and economists who set the intellectual tone of our system of production saw one thing very clearly: the destiny of a consumer-good is to be consumed, and there is no point in consuming it unless one derives some pleasure or satisfaction from doing so. Thus we produce in order that we may consume, and we consume for the sake of the satisfactions to be derived from doing so; thus our satisfactions alone are an end, and everything else, the goods themselves the productive process of which they are the fruit, and the labour which is expended in the process are but means. Viewed from this standpoint nothing has intrinsic value but human satisfactions, and the best life is that in which the capacity for consumption is maximized, and the opportunities do not lag behind.

From our point of view the crucial thing about the consumer ideology is its indifference to the opus, the work which a workman makes. Since the opus is conceived to be a mere means, a cog in a process of which the end-product is pleasure or satisfaction, there are no conceptions of excellence for it as such; its goodness becames a

---

[3] The popular, not the 'philosophical' variant is intended.

relational property; to be good it must be such that out of its consumption the consumers derive satisfactions. Thus art is debased to amusement, literature to journalism, the serious and rational debate of public issues to image-building and gimmickry, and that part of learning which is not a mere service industry for trade, industry, government, or the professions is made to provide a cultural varnish for the young barbarians whom the system needs and nourishes.

The labourer is a social being.[4] He subserves the 'needs of society', and, if properly socialized, conceives of himself as subserving these needs. If society cannot consume his products, he has laboured in vain. If his products are not good to consume, or if they are inefficiently produced, or produced at too great a cost to society, he has laboured badly. Labourers, as I here conceive them, include some of the most highly paid men in the kingdom, and most of our society consists of labourers.

The things which we value or love engage our interest: we care about them and they concern us. We cannot *care* about what touches us only through its effects or its potential uses. A key for instance, common and undistinguished, is unlikely to be something about which we care, even if it puts a fortune within our reach. The attitudes of interest, concern, or care depend on the intrinsic properties of an object. If an object touches us only because we can use it, or because we want what it will bring about, then we do not care about it as such. Our attitude to it will then be commercial. That which is treated exclusively as a means, commercially that is to say, is thereby degraded if it is degradable. The time-honoured example is a prostitute. Even if no money changes hands, the girl's dignity is undermined if, viewing her only as an instrument of sexual gratification, we do not care whether she be happy or unhappy, religious or atheistical, interested in mountaineering or politics, and so on. In the commercial state of mind we do not even care whether she likes or abominates her partner, nor will we be concerned about her subsequent fate.

The consumer's society degrades whatever it touches, work, nature, art, its own history and traditions, and the creations of men of genius. Work (being confused with labour) is but toil, the process of production is distinct from and merely instrumental to the product; it is the product and, beyond it, a satisfaction which are desired, not the process. Since the process of producing is troublesome, we abandon it with

[4] A thesis of Mrs. Arendt's.

relief and turn to its natural counter-pole, which is play (or fun as the newspapers now call it). This increasingly becomes the really serious business of our lives; besides, it has the advantage of opening up quite unlimited new opportunities for consumption.

The ideological producer for consumption, despite his rockets to the moon, is the world's most unambitious creature and also the most destructive. All, or nearly all, the immense array of ingenious and amazing objects to the manufacture of which his intelligence is harnessed are made for consumption. At the same time, as the opportunities for consumption magnify, so does the consumer's appetite, until, as things stand now, the earth itself stands in danger of being devoured. He destroys the beauty of nature, the animal kingdom is expended for his satisfaction, he destroys whole cultures and traditions to stimulate trade, and finally he destroys men themselves. I do not mean in warfare only, which is nothing peculiar to our times, but by a process of depersonalization which results from being made a means to an end.

It is time we returned to the universities. Universities do not fit in well in a consumer's society. I do not mean that the structure and fabric of a university cannot survive in such a society; that would clearly be wrong. Universities are growing still. They receive unprecedented attention from the mighty, and a degree has become a passport to worldly success as never before.

Nevertheless universities do not flourish in a consumer's society without suffering a sea change. The ethos of a university has in the past been principally an ethos of work, and the objects to the achievement of which universities used to be committed were conceived as of intrinsic worth. These objects were twofold, namely the pursuit of learning (or inquiry as I propose to call it) and the education of the young. They seem to me to be the proper aims of universities still. Unfortunately they are in danger of being lost. If they are lost, it will not be as a result of an open change, but imperceptibly, ostensibly under the old ethos still. They will be lost, like liberty in a society grown totalitarian in the defence of liberty. Even in 1984, the academic credo affirming the pursuit of learning and the education of the young will be intoned. But it seems that the pursuit of learning will be transmuted into the pursuit of skills and know-how, and that education will become training or instruction. It seems probable that the matter of education will increasingly be parcelled out into one or other of two broad categories, on the one hand essential knowledge, that is, knowledge which is good for some socially acceptable purpose, and luxury knowledge, a sort of prestigious top-dressing on the other. It is possible even that the pursuit of luxury knowledge will altogether disappear from the syllabus, and that activities which fall within its sphere will become extra-curricular. There will be concerts, exhibitions, poetry-readings, and meditation-sessions, and these will be calculated to perform a function in that parcel of life which is now called leisure.

We are sufficiently imbued with the ethos of our era for the thought that universities are primarily for the service of society to be natural to us. Thus we conceive of our role in terms of the satisfaction of social needs. We provide society with trained men for the professions, with experts to advise government and industry, and we produce persons with cultural graces to dignify our voracity. When we think of university expansion, we naturally look at the market to see what graduates it will absorb, and we plan research training as immediately addressed to social needs.

Thus we become a factory for making a certain kind of equipment which society needs, people as well as computers. But perhaps this account of the matter may strike you as too pessimistic. There is a current development which seems to belie it; I mean the expansion of research in universities, and the prestige which it enjoys.

Research is surely work. Many of us, perhaps a majority, regard it as the real business of universities, and think of the advancement of knowledge as the ultimate aim. Teaching is viewed as a slightly inferior activity, necessary, alas, both because society demands it and for the perpetuation of academic institutions, but an imposition on a true man of learning. Adapting Plato's famous simile, academic people have to earn a place in the sun of pure research by a temporary sojourn in the cave of education. They do their duty, earn their release, and go off on sabbatical leave.

There are few images as appealing as the image of ourselves adding to the sum of human knowledge. Knowledge seems to us like a vast impersonal edifice, to which, by the sheer exercise of our industry and wit, we can add a brick. What could be a more enduring monument than this? Our knowledge is not and cannot be consumed, neither could it conceivably have accrued from some activity generically different from inquiry. It is therefore non-contingently related to the activity from which it results. Our claims to knowledge are tested by the tools of logic and the resources of experiment and these alone provide the tests of workmanship.

This image is pretty, but it does more than justice to most contemporary academic research. There is a sense of course in which all knowledge is enduring. Copies of our monographs and journals will continue to accumulate in our libraries at an ever-expanding rate, but much of this work is undertaken as labour rather than work.

The idea that work may be undertaken in the spirit of labour presents no difficulty. Analogously a puritan may debauch himself in the spirit of duty, and an intending lover may trade his affections in the spirit of a ledger-clerk. In each case the conception which the agent has of his act ill accords with its point, and this argues confusion or self-deception on his part. The agent does not know what he is about: he acts katatelically.

Research-labourers do research katatelically, though not necessarily without results, if 'results' are a kind of pay-off to society or to some interest represented in it. (Discoveries of genuine interest to intellectuals are not excluded.) A research-labourer works in the spirit of labour. He puts his highly trained labour-force at the disposal of society or its agencies. He works in its interests, and conceives that to be its point. The beneficiaries generally reward him, but not from love of the intellectual enterprise. The beneficiaries use him, even as he will presently use his students, or prepare them for social use after they have obtained their 'qualification'. The beneficiaries accept useful results, whether or not they have accrued from intellectually reputable work. They know what they want: unfortunately he generally does not.

Inquiry absorbs a man. It is an extension of his personality. Roughly, if a man is content to engage in a piece of research from nine to five as a job, he will not engage in it as inquiry. The workman is involved in his work. The sort of involvement which I have in mind is not unlike what is called commitment. One cannot change one's work as one can change one's job. The workman who is deprived of his work is deprived *tout court*.

Research, it seems, has become a sort of independent empire. There is indeed a myth that people who have gone through the research-mill make good university teachers, and if the function of a good university teacher is simply to train people in the techniques of research, it may not be a myth entirely. The belief that research produces good teachers adds to our notion of its utility.

Research begets research. Much of it is addressed to the expansion of the research-culture, which nobody, not even the research workers, regards as intrinsically valuable. We tend the dog, clip its fur, polish its teeth, publish its pedigree, and enter it for every available dog-show, but we are not really fond of animals.

Now we come to teaching. This presents us with our thorniest problem. It is in our attitudes to students that we most clearly show whether we accept or reject the ethos of consumption. Our traditions demand that we should educate our students. Education is one of the excellences of which human beings are capable, and just as the excellence of a painting cannot be defined in terms of its monetary value or in terms of its social usefulness, so also the state of being educated cannot be defined in careerist or social-utility terms.

An educated student is one in whom certain potentialities are developed, including the potentiality for work in a certain field. Students are intelligent or stupid before they enrol, but good teachers develop their intelligence and teach them to use it, to apply it, to delight in its exercise. An educated man is sensitive, perceptive, daring in imagination, subtle in distinction, lucid and powerful in reasoning, and articulate. An educated student understands the enterprise of inquiry. This may take the form of reflection, discussion, or internal dialectic, it need not consist in writing articles. For instance, the preparation of a creative lecture is also part of the enterprise. Often the kind of inquiry which most obviously lends itself to publication is from the point of education, infertile. For this reason, among others, the greater part of our journal literature is almost at birth embedded in the sedimentary deposits of the academy, and will never be looked at again.

The education of a student is an end in itself, and the making of him is our noblest work. This work requires no further justification, and by attempting to justify it further, in terms of the values of the consumer society, we only succeed in undermining it.

We educate students by working with them in a field or discipline. One cannot do everything at once, and a certain concentration in a field ensures that work is done in depth and discourages superficiality. But the field is never more than the locus in which the work of education is accomplished. Competence in a field is not the aim of education, but only one of its expedients. The emphasis on a field as against the potentialities which work in a field makes actual is inimical to the enterprise of education.

The consumer mentality makes education wellnigh impossible. First a relatively mild and engaging variant, the idea that it is our task to equip students to earn a livelihood, or to make a position for themselves in society. If a teacher is fond of his students, he will not wish them to come to grief in life, and thus he may skimp their education in order to increase their value in the market.

The more insidious forms of consumer education mould the student, not in his own material interests but in the alleged interests of society. The student and his skills are debased into a means for the achievement of social ends. The student becames a capital investment. He is there for the performance of certain kinds of labour which will procure satisfactions for his fellow citizens, and the teachers are there in order to train him in the skills which will make him a useful instrument in procuring these satisfactions. *He* ceases to matter, provided only that he performs the part which the diviners of social needs have cast for him. The diviners of social needs are roughly men in authority, with their academic advisers.

The replacement of education by instruction is a serious matter. It naturally goes hand in hand with the abandonment of any real interest in students or their maturation, which in turn is the inevitable result of the mass-production techniques which are now being forced on us. Instruction is a practical enterprise in which a set skill, or a standard quota of information is imparted for a purpose. The point of instruction is to suit the subject to a task. Thus soldiers are instructed in the use of weapons, and trainee-policemen are instructed in their duties. Instruction is standardized, uncritical, undialectical, and it discourages speculation about ends and means alike. Some university courses seem to be almost pure instruction. All available teaching time is parcelled out into segments each of which is devoted to imparting some particular item of information, or to allow time for the practice of some particular skill. Directives to tutors are printed in detailed cyclostyled sheets; these ensure that all tutorials will operate in parallel. The student is there to absorb this material. He contributes nothing and his intellect remains unengaged. The teachings of some psychologists have aggravated this state of affairs.

Education is a dialectical enterprise, critical, discursive, and largely idiosyncratic on the teacher's and the student's side alike. It is true that education presupposes the mastery of some skills and the possession of some information. These are ancillary to education. In the consumer's society, however, they tend to replace it. One cannot educate a student well at a distance. Education is a meeting of two intellects, and therefore of two persons, and this requires a common life. But in the contemporary academy the teacher is becoming ever more inaccessible. Many students do not even know their lecturers by name.

The students who are subjected to this sort of pseudo-education are not fully conscious of what is happening, but they are dimly aware that they are being used for purposes not of their own choosing. Many feel cheated. They came to the university for an education, and find themselves being moulded for the purposes of a society of which the official representatives often strike them as unadmirable. 'Society' speaks to them through members of the establishment.

The view that their teachers lack capacity, or knowledge, or skill is not essential to this state of mind, and it is not the principal cause of discontent. On the contrary, student disaffection is often associated with a sense of inferiority. Students feel that their teacher's interest in them is inauthentic. The jargon-word 'alienation' is not easily banished from one's lips.

To sum up, the danger in modern universities is that students will be regarded as capital equipment and that by being 'instructed' they will be conditioned to take their place in the technical, commercial, or administrative machinery of a society which recognizes no values but consumption. They will therefore be made ready for being used. When that happens, the university will have played a part in the production of highly skilled and (unless there is an oversupply) extremely precious labourers, but it will not have taught them to work, albeit both their well-being and that of society depends on their capacity for action, which, in the productive field, is work. Neither is the producing of such young men and women anything but labour, and thus some of the most imaginative and ingenious men and women in the land are reduced to the status of labourers. Thus, given the tedious absurdities of the research-empire, specially in subjects which are insecure in their standing and seek to prove that they too are hard-headed and 'scientific', the university and its *raison d'être* pass each other by.

The idea that universities should subserve social needs, as these are understood in the dominant ideology, has been disparaged in this essay, and the traditional values of men of learning have been defended in opposition to ideological, economic, and political demands. Society, in so far as it can be said to have judgement and articulation, is a poor judge of its own needs, and universities sacrifice a good to promote an evil if they think themselves committed to the utilitarian objectives (or the ideologically inspired projects) which worldly spokesmen advocate. The consumer's ethos does not serve its exponents well. By undermining the human personality, it deprives people of the power of happiness. True, it provides us with the technical means of abolishing the miseries of disease and want, but it also destroys that capacity for love and care, and that freedom of the spirit, which vouchsafe fulfilment, and which are a condition of the enjoyment of worldly things. We do no service to society by making ourselves into its servants.

A society is no better than the persons who compose it. If by education we produce men and women of excellence, we have no need of a higher aim.

III

REFLECTIONS ON EDUCATIONAL RELEVANCE

I. SCHEFFLER

J. L. Austin used to query the importance of importance. I want here to question the educational relevance of educational relevance.

To do so may seem paradoxical, even absurd. For if relevance is not relevant, what is? And who, in his right mind, would wish learning to be irrelevant? The air of obviousness about these questions misleads, however. It derives, not from some mythical relevance axiom of the theory of education, but from the characteristic value-laden import of the word in its categorical use. To stand against irrelevance is like opposing sin and to favour relevance is akin to applauding virtue. The theoretical problem, with relevance as with virtue, is to say in what it consists and why, thus specified, it ought to be pursued. Relevance is, in particular, not an absolute property; nothing is either relevant or irrelevant in and of itself. Relevant to what, how, and why?—that is the question. That is, at any rate, the question if the current demand for relevance is to be taken not merely as a fashionable slogan but as a serious educational doctrine.

There being no single official elaboration of such a doctrine, I shall sketch three philosophical interpretations that might plausibly be offered in defence of current emphases on relevance, and I shall organize my comments around each of these interpretations. The first is primarily epistemological, concerning the nature and warrant of knowledge. The second is primarily psychological, having to do with the character of thought. The third is mainly moral, treating of the purposes of schooling.

I. EPISTEMOLOGICAL INTERPRETATION

According to a venerable tradition, knowing is a state of union of the knower and the known. In apprehension, the knower is at one with the object, contemplation a form of love in which rational man finds his

From the *Journal of Philosophy*, Vol. 66, No. 21 (Nov. 1969), pp. 764–73. Reprinted by permission of the author and editor. The paper is included in *Reason and Teaching* (London: Routledge & Kegan Paul; Indianapolis: Bobbs–Merrill Co.).

highest consummation. The state of union is of course not physical; to know a thing is not to be in physical proximity to it. Rather, it is to understand it, that is, to apprehend through the mind its essential structure or abstract form. Knowledge is union, then, not with the ordinary things of the world, but with their ideal essences. Such union affords, however, an indirect grasp of ordinary things and processes, inasmuch as the latter are crude approximations or rough embodiments of the pure forms seen by the eye of intellect alone.

For the Platonic tradition just sketched, knowing thus involves a withdrawal from the immediate world as well as an identification of the mind with the abstract forms which alone render this world intelligible. Education is not an immersion in the ordinary world but an approach to a superior abstract reality remote from it. Ideally, education is mathematical and dialectical, and the mind illuminated by abstract forms is best able to deal with the ordinary processes of the physical and human environment when it is once again directed towards them.

The classical conception we have been discussing has been largely abandoned. The doctrine of abstract forms, in particular, has been severely criticized. Not only are there fundamental difficulties in conceiving the nature and interrelations of these forms, as well as their relations to the ordinary world. The rise of scientific modes of thought has made it increasingly implausible to suppose that knowledge consists in contemplation of a world of essences, of superior reality, lying behind the changing phenomena of the common-sense environment. The world of changes is the one real world. Through addressing itself actively to this world, science seeks the provisional experimental truths that dwell amid change.

From this point of view, an education that draws the student away from the phenomena of his environment diverts him from the task of achieving truth. If the notion of a static world of essences is rejected as myth, an education that encourages the mind to dwell in such a world must frustrate the pursuit of truth. Detached and abstract, it is irrelevant to the only reliable processes available to man for establishing true beliefs by which he can guide his conduct. Such epistemological irrelevance is to be shunned if rational conduct is our ideal. Instead of withdrawal, education must encourage immersion in the changing phenomena constituting the live environment of the student. The radical rejection of classical doctrines of knowledge thus leads us to reject equally a detached and remote education.

Now the trouble with this line of thought, as I see it, is not that it rejects classical epistemology, but that it does not sufficiently reject it. Denying the Platonistic assumption of a superior world of essences, it retains the ancient and even more primitive assumption that knowledge consists in a state of union between knower and known. To know is to draw near to, and be one with, the object of knowledge, to eliminate the distance between. Instead of the object of knowledge being thought to consist in an essential and superior reality, it is now conceived simply as the ordinary world of material and historical processes. To know this object is, however, again to be understood as consisting in a state of union with it. This ordinary world must be directly confronted, without conventional or ideological intermediaries. Education is to abolish distance and detachment, bringing the learner into intimate engagement with the environment to be known.

The underlying assumption of knowledge as union is, however, radically false. Glued to the phenomena, the mind can no more attain perspective than can the viewer with eyeballs glued to the painting. Cognition is inextricably dependent upon categorization, analysis, selection, abstraction, and expectation. It is the very antithesis of dumb contact. If the scientist does not seek to contemplate a static world of essences, neither does he immerse himself in the phenomenal changes of his immediate environment in an effort to confront the facts. Facts, in any case, presuppose conceptualization and derive significance through their bearings on theory. The scientist, far from rejecting the mediation of concepts and theoretical construction, seeks ever newer and more comprehensive intellectual schemes for understanding. These schemes bring with them fresh modes of analysis and order; they create novel definitions of fact and bring forth new dimensions of relevance. What the scientist rejects is the rule of the familiar. His job is precisely not to take for granted the customary conceptual apparatus of his environment but, through criticism and invention, to develop more adequate intellectual equipment which will encompass this very environment along with other actual and possible ones.

Such a mission requires that he should step back from the material and conceptual surrounding in which he finds himself. He seeks the distance that lends perspective and the critical detachment that facilitates alternative testable visions. There is a world of difference between such withdrawal and the retreat into never-never lands of myth or pendantry. The alternative to such retreat is not a warm bath in immediate phenomena but a search for theoretical comprehension that transcends the merely local and the merely customary. Epistemological relevance, in short, requires us to reject both myth and mystic union. It requires not contact but criticism, not immersion in the phenomenal and conceptual given, but the flexibility of mind capable of transcending, reordering, and expanding the given. An education that fosters criticism and conceptual flexibility will transcend its environment not by erecting a mythical substitute for this world but rather by striving for a systematic and penetrating comprehension of it.

II. PSYCHOLOGICAL INTERPRETATION

Thought, according to a widely prevalent doctrine, is problem-oriented. It originates in doubt, conflict, and difficulty. Its function is to overcome obstacles to the smooth flow of human activities. When action is coherent and well adapted to its circumstances, human energy is released in overt channels set by habit and custom. The blocking of conduct, either through internal conflict or environmental hindrance, turns its energy inwards, transforming it into thought. Playing out multiple possibilities for future action, thought proceeds until an envisaged feature of some such possibility sparks overt conduct once more, conduct which, by its impact on surrounding conditions, may succeed in overcoming the initial hindrance to the regular outward flow of action. In the evolutionary perspective, thought is an adaptive instrument for overcoming environmental difficulties. Scientific inquiry, the most highly developed form of thought, is the most effective reaction to such difficulties, and the most explicitly problem-directed.

In general, we may say that when thought is genuine and effective it is a response to an objective breakdown in the organization of habit and belief, an answer to the torment of doubt. Controlled by its initiating perplexity, its effectiveness may be gauged by the extent to which it achieves resolution of the difficulty that gave it birth. Thought which is not thus relevant to a problem does not constitute genuine inquiry or deliberation. An education geared to the encouragement of the latter must, then, take its starting point in the doubts and difficulties of the student, originating in his life conflicts and the social issues of his environment. Its relevance to live problems must be evident in its ultimate motivation, which is to solve these problems, and in its evaluation as facilitating or retarding such solutions.

Now it is easy to read this pragmatic doctrine of thought as a merely descriptive account, but such a reading would be mistaken. The doctrine is not designed to embrace all activity that might readily be described as thinking in everyday parlance. In musing, recollecting, or imagining, one is thinking though not necessarily solving problems. The work of painter, writer, or composer, thoughtful and focused as it is, cannot readily be taken as a species of problem solving: Of what problem is *Macbeth* the solution? The artist's activity does not always originate in the breakdown of habit, nor is it plausibly split into internal deliberation and overt unthinking action, rather than taken as a continuous flow in which making and thinking are smoothly meshed. In attending to my words now, you are thinking, but you have not, I hope, experienced an objective breakdown at the outset of my paper.

The fundamental import of the pragmatic doctrine is, I suggest, rather normative than descriptive. It purports to tell us what *genuine* thinking consists in. Taking its cue from evolutionary categories, it stresses the adaptive function of thinking in the organism's struggle to survive in a hostile or indifferent environment. Interpreting science as the most refined and effective development of such adaptive thinking, it urges the ostensible problem-solving pattern of scientific reasearch as the chief paradigm of intellectual activity, to be favoured in all phases of education and culture.

To say that the problem theory of thinking is normative in its import does not, however, imply that it rests on no factual assumptions whatever. As we have just noted, it draws particularly upon a special reading of science as the prime example of responsible and effective thinking, growing out of practical problems and issuing in reconstructed modes of conduct. And this reading cannot, I believe, be sustained. It holds at best for simple types of practical thinking and for technological applications, but it does no justice to science as an autonomous theoretical endeavour. Scientific theories do not, generally, grow out of practical conflicts, nor do they, in themselves, serve to guide practical activities; they are embedded in complex intellectual structures linked only indirectly, and as wholes, to contexts of evidence and experiment. Their assessment is intimately dependent upon these intellectual structures, and involves, aside from practical efficacy, theoretical considerations bearing on their relative simplicity, naturalness, comprehensiveness, elegance, and connectibility with associated structures.

The scientist's work may perhaps be plausibly described as problem-oriented, in that much of it is directed towards the answering of certain questions. But these questions cannot be identified with practical breakdowns in the personal life or social environment of the scientist. They typically cannot even be understood outside the historical context of prior theorizing and experimentation, which determines independent canons of intellectual relevance. The scientist's questioning is, moreover, often hypothetical and speculative. Born of a sophisticated curiosity, it may come to torment his waking hours; it does not itself need to originate in personal or social torment. Even Charles Sanders Peirce, the father of pragmatism, who began by insisting on real and active doubt as the first phase of thought, had increasingly to emphasize the significance of feigned doubt in order to account for the autonomous context of scientific problem solving. An educational conception of thinking as directly addressed to the alleviation of conflicts and breakdowns of behaviour would, in sum, constitute not the foundation of a scientific attitude of mind but the death-knell of scientific thought. By confining thought to the immediacies of practice, it would eliminate its leverage on practice, reducing its characteristic effectiveness in transforming the environment.

Nor does the problem theory of inquiry, even broadly interpreted in terms of questions, tell the whole story. Thought does not subside when doubts are, for the moment, stilled. A scientist without questions is not a happy thoughtless theorist. Problem finding is at least as important to him as problem solving. He does not, in any event, wait upon difficulties that happen to occur to him but strenuously seeks new difficulties of the widest critical significance. An education modelled on scientific thinking could not possibly remain content with the student's initial problems; it would seek to introduce him to new ones and train him to explore further for himself. More generally, it would strive to create wider perception as well as to improve problem-solving capacity, to develop an alertness to unsettled and conflicting elements in experience as well as a drive to organize, unify, and resolve. It would, in short, aim not only to assess ideas by their relevance to given questions but also to discover new questions by expanding the sense of relevance.

III. MORAL INTERPRETATION

If a defence of educational relevance is to be found neither in the notion of knowledge as union nor in the conception of thought as a response to practical difficulty, can we not hope to find such a defence by considering the purposes of schooling? Granted that knowledge presupposes critical perspective and that the life of thought has its own integrity, is there no practical value to be gained by the development of theoretical understanding? Do we not need to make special provision for bringing such understanding to earth, for applying it towards the resolution of the practical problems of men? Indeed, considering the institution of schools, is it not clear that their primary purpose is to foster the employment of knowledge for desirable social ends?

Reflections such as these, by offering a more restricted interpretation of relevance than the preceding two we have considered, seem to gain in persuasiveness. Social relevance is not to be construed as a necessary feature of all knowledge or thought. Rather, it is a consequence of the primary institutional function of the school. The school's job is, after all, not confined to the advancement of knowledge and the fostering of scientific habits of mind. For knowledge and critical thought are themselves valued for their potential contribution to the achievement of social goals. Such contribution requires not merely the advancement but also the employment of knowledge; it depends upon developing not only habits of inquiry but also arts of application. Indeed, application is the ultimate end to which inquiry is a means, and, from the standpoint of society, the school must thus be viewed as an instrument for the realization of its goals. The relation between knowledge and application is, furthermore, not an internal or necessary one; without special care, knowledge may very well be pursued without thought of its practical use. All the more reason, then, to build the context of social application into the life of the school as an encompassing emphasis in relation to which training in inquiry may be seen in its proper instrumental light.

Seen in long-term perspective, then, the school is a means for the improvement of society. The ultimate fruit of the knowledge it seeks is its use in life. Schooling must thus be so organized as to bring knowledge to bear on life's problems and, in so doing, to train students in the proper application of what they may know or come to know. Practical problems of the larger community should serve to provide the major framework within which all the school's activities are set. Separate as abstract intellectual specialties, the school's subjects are to be brought together in their common application to shared social problems. Curricular integration is to be accomplished not by some internal structural scheme but by a pervasive view of the content of schooling as an instrument in the service of the larger society. Education is thus to be made relevant by making its instrumental values dominant. A remote education, bringing nothing to the resolution of the problems of society, is a luxury society neither can nor should allow.

There is much in the foregoing interpretation that seems to me compelling. To argue, as I did earlier, that thought is not generally to be conceived as a response to practical difficulty and that theoretical inquiry involves critical distance and autonomous development does not, after all, imply that practical application is to be shunned. There is no warrant for the stark doctrine that schooling is practical only if thought itself is a practical tool, that, conversely, if thought is independent of practice then schooling must itself be divorced from the life of the surrounding community. The root assumption that the scope of schooling is fixed by the limits of thought must itself be rejected as the source of much mischief.

Theoretical inquiry, independently pursued, has the most powerful potential for the analysis and transformation of practice. The bearing of inquiry upon practice is, moreover, of the greatest educational interest. Such interest is not, contrary to recent emphases, exhausted in a concern for inquiry within the structures of the several disciplines. Students should be encouraged to employ the information and techniques of the disciplines in analysis, criticism, and alteration of their practical outlooks. Habits of practical diagnosis, critique, and execution based upon responsible inquiry need to supplement theoretical attitudes and disciplinary proficiencies in the training of the young. In so far as the doctrine of educational relevance is to be taken as emphasizing this point, I find myself in complete agreement with it. The example of professional education here points the way. Medical education, for example, must embrace not only disciplinary inquiries but also the arts of judgement and application to cases. And what holds for the specialized concerns of the professions seems to me to hold for schooling generally as an institution of society.

Yet reference to professional education suggests also certain respects in which the interpretation we have been considering is overdrawn. To insist that application is essential to professional training does not imply that it must dominate; to acknowledge the contribution of theoretical inquiry in transforming practice is not to argue that theory is to be treated as solely instrumental. Theory is effective in so far as it provides insight into fundamental processes, and the quest for such insight cannot be systematically bent to any external requirement without hampering its development and its consequent effectiveness. Professional education needs to bring the concerns of independent inquiry and the challenge of a specific range of practical problems into communication; it needs to foster mutual respect and understanding between researchers and practitioners. It cannot require research to be pursued in a practical frame of mind nor impose a uniform instrumental framework upon its constituent activities without reducing its own efficacy.

The conclusion is even stronger when we consider not professional education, oriented as it is towards special social functions, but schooling generally. For the potential ramifications of knowledge cannot be determined in advance; to encase all schooling within the framework of specified applications to practice is to hinder severely its unknown developments in other directions as well as its capacity to generate alternative conceptions of application.

Indeed, the notion that education is an instrument for the realization of social goals, no matter how worthy they are thought to be, harbours the greatest conceivable danger to the ideal of a free and rational society. For if these goals are presumed to be fixed in advance, the instrumental doctrine of schooling exempts them from the critical scrutiny that schooling itself may foster. On the other hand, if these goals are themselves to be subject to public criticism and review, schools may be conceived as social instruments only in the broad sense in which they also facilitate independent evaluation of social practice, only if they are, in effect, conceived as instruments of insight and criticism, standing apart from current social conceptions and serving autonomous ideals of inquiry and truth. A society that supports this conception of schooling is one which, rather than setting external limits to its work, is prepared to incorporate the school's loyalties to independent inquiry and free criticism into its own basic structure and ideals. In effect, such a society must view itself as instrumental to the values of schooling quite as much as it takes schools to serve its own goals.

A conception such as this is indeed what one would expect from an instrumentalism inspired by Dewey's notion of the continuity between means and ends, and it is ironic that the main stress in certain passages of his work is on the school as means. When one considers, however, that Dewey takes the end to be not society as it happens to be, but a reformed society, illuminated by an ideal imagination and a critical intelligence that it is the school's office to foster, it becomes clear that any simple-minded doctrine of the school as social instrument is inadequate, both as an expression of Dewey's views and as an independently persuasive educational philosophy. For the fact is that the larger society that the school is said to serve at any given time cannot be taken for granted as providing an ultimate end. It must itself be judged worth while by reference to the rational standards and the heritage of critical values to which the school bears witness. If the fruit of knowledge is its use in life, it must be a life itself infused with a respect for knowledge and criticism. It is, in short, one thing to say that the content of schooling should be brought to bear upon practice, that free inquiry and practical concerns are to be put into communication. It is quite another to say that schooling is to be conceived as an instrument for the implementation of designated social values, taken as ultimate.

This point of difference is decisive. To make education relevant by making it instrumental in the latter sense is to destroy its autonomy and to deliver it to the rule of uncriticized social values. To recognize, on the other hand, that the responsibility of education is not only to serve but also to criticize, enlighten, and create—that its job is not only to provide persons with techniques but, more importantly, to provide techniques with critical, informed, and humane persons—is to realize that it has its own dignity and its own direction to follow. Its primary task is not to be relevant but to help form a society in which its ideals of free inquiry and rationality shall themselves have become chief touchstones of relevance.

THE CONTENT OF EDUCATION

IV

LIBERAL EDUCATION AND THE NATURE OF KNOWLEDGE

PAUL H. HIRST

THE phrase 'liberal education' has today become something of a slogan which takes on different meanings according to its immediate context. It usually labels a form of education of which the author approves, but beyond that its meaning is often entirely negatively derived. Whatever else a liberal education is, it is *not* a vocational education, *not* an exclusively scientific education, or *not* a specialist education in any sense. The frequency with which the term is employed in this way certainly highlights the inadequacies of these other concepts and the need for a wider and, in the long run, more worth-while form of education. But as long as the concept is merely negative in what it intimates, it has little more than debating value. Only when it is given explicit positive content can it be of use in the serious business of educational planning. It is my contention in this paper that whatever vagaries there have been in the use of the term, it is the appropriate label for a positive concept, that of an education based fairly and squarely on the nature of knowledge itself, a concept central to the discussion of education at any level.

THE GREEK NOTION OF LIBERAL EDUCATION

The fully developed Greek notion of liberal education was rooted in a number of related philosophical doctrines; first about the significance of knowledge for the mind, and secondly about the relationship between knowledge and reality. In the first category there was the doctrine that it is the peculiar and distinctive activity of the mind, because of its very nature, to pursue knowledge. The achievement of knowledge satisfies and fulfils the mind which thereby attains its own appropriate end. The pursuit of knowledge is thus the pursuit of the good of the mind and, therefore, an essential element in the good life. In addition,

From *Philosophical Analysis and Education*, ed. R. D. Archambault (London: Routledge & Kegan Paul; New York: Humanities Press, 1965), pp. 113–38. Reprinted by permission of the author and publishers.

it was held that the achievement of knowledge is not only the attainment of the good of the mind itself, but also the chief means whereby the good life as a whole is to be found. Man is more than pure mind, yet mind is his essential distinguishing characteristic, and it is in terms of knowledge that his whole life is rightly directed.

That knowledge is equal to its task was guaranteed by the second group of doctrines. These asserted that the mind, in the right use of reason, comes to know the essential nature of things and can apprehend what is ultimately real and immutable. Consequently, man no longer needs to live in terms of deceptive appearances and doubtful opinions and beliefs. All his experiences, life, and thought can be given shape and perspective by what is finally true, by knowledge that corresponds to what is ultimately real. Further, the particular way in which reason is here represented as attaining knowledge results in a view of the whole of man's understanding as hierarchically structured in various levels. From the knowledge of mere particulars to that of pure being, all knowledge has its place in a comprehensive and harmonious scheme, the pattern of which is formed as knowledge is developed in apprehending reality in its many different manifestations.

From these doctrines there emerged the idea of liberal education as a process concerned simply and directly with the pursuit of knowledge. But the doctrines give to this general idea particular meaning and significance; for they lead to a clear definition of its scope and content, and to a clear justification for education in these terms. The definition is clear, because education is determined objectively in range, in structure, and in content by the forms of knowledge itself and their harmonious, hierarchical interrelations. There is here no thought of defining education in terms of knowledge and skills that may be useful, or in terms of moral virtues and qualities of mind that may be considered desirable. The definition is stated strictly in terms of man's knowledge of what is the case. The development of the mind to which it leads, be it in skills, virtues, or other characteristics, is thought to be necessarily its greatest good.

The justification that the doctrines lend to this concept of education is threefold. First, such an education is based on what is true and not on uncertain opinions and beliefs or temporary values. It therefore has a finality which no other form of education has. Secondly, knowledge itself being a distinctive human virtue, liberal education has a value for the person as the fulfilment of the mind, a value which has nothing to do with utilitarian or vocational considerations. Thirdly, because of the significance of knowledge in the determination of the good life as a whole, liberal education is essential to man's understanding of how he ought to live, both individually and socially.

Here, then, the Greeks attained the concept of an education that was 'liberal' not simply because it was the education of free men rather than slaves but also because they saw it as freeing the mind to function according to its true nature, freeing reason from error and illusion and freeing man's conduct from wrong. And ever since Greek times this idea of education has had its place. Sometimes it has been modified or extended in detail to accommodate within its scheme new forms of knowledge: for instance Christian doctrines and the various branches of modern science. Sometimes the concept has been misinterpreted: as in Renaissance humanism when classical learning was equated with liberal education. Sometimes it has been strongly opposed on philosophical grounds: as by Dewey and the pragmatists. Yet at crucial points in the history of education the concept has constantly reappeared. It is not hard to understand why this should be so.

Education, being a deliberate, purposeful activity directed to the development of individuals, necessarily involves considerations of value. Where are these values to be found? What is to be their content? How are they to be justified? They can be, and often are, values that reflect the interests of a minority group in the society. They may be religious, political, or utilitarian in character. They are always open to debate and detailed criticism, and are always in need of particular justification. Is there not perhaps a more ultimate basis for the values that should determine education, some more objective ground? That final ground has, ever since the Greeks, been repeatedly located in man's conception of the diverse forms of knowledge he has achieved. And there has thus arisen the demand for an education whose definition and justification are based on the nature and significance of knowledge itself, and not on the predilections of pupils, the demands of society, or the whims of politicians. Precisely this demand was behind the development by the Greeks of an education in the seven liberal arts, an introduction to and a pursuit of the forms of knowledge as they were conceived. It was precisely this demand that prompted Newman and Arnold in the nineteenth century to call for an education that aimed at the cultivation and development of the mind in the full range of man's understanding. It is the same demand that today motivates such classical realists as Maritain and R. M. Hutchins.

A TYPICAL MODERN STATEMENT: THE HARVARD REPORT

It may well be asked, however, whether those who do not hold the doctrines of metaphysical and epistemological realism can legitimately subscribe to a concept of education of this kind. Historically it seems to have had positive force only when presented in this particular philosophical framework. But historical association must be distinguished from logical connection and it is not by any means obvious that all the characteristic features of the concept are dependent on such philosophical realism. If the doctrines about mind, knowledge, and reality mentioned at the beginning of this paper are regarded as at best too speculative a basis for educational planning, as well they may be, the possibility of an education defined and justified entirely in terms of the scope and character of knowledge needs re-examination. The significance of the concept originally came directly from the place the basic doctrines give to knowledge in a unified picture of the mind and its relation to reality. Knowledge is achieved when the mind attains its own satisfaction or good by corresponding to objective reality. A liberal education in the pursuit of knowledge is, therefore, seeking the development of the mind according to what is quite external to it, the structure and pattern of reality. But if once there is any serious questioning of this relationship between mind, knowledge, and reality, the whole harmonious structure is liable to disintegrate. First there arise inevitably problems of definition. A liberal education defined in terms of knowledge alone is acceptable as long as knowledge is thought to be necessarily developing the mind in desirable ways, and hence promoting the good life. But if doubt is cast on these functions of knowledge, must not liberal education be redefined stating explicitly the qualities of mind and the moral virtues to which it is directed? And if knowledge is no longer seen as the understanding of reality but merely as the understanding of experience, what is to replace the harmonious, hierarchical scheme of knowledge that gave pattern and order to the education? Secondly there are equally serious problems of justification. For if knowledge is no longer thought to be rooted in some reality, or if its significance for the mind and the good life is questioned, what can be the justification for an education defined in terms of knowledge alone?

Difficulties of both kinds, but particularly those of definition, can be seen in the well-known Harvard Committee Report: *General Education in a Free Society*.[1] (In the Committee's terminology the aims of

---

[1] *General Education in a Free Society*, Report of the Harvard Committee (London: Oxford University Press, 1946).

a 'liberal' and a 'general' education are identical.) Though certain of the doctrines that originally supported the concept of a liberal education are implicit in this work, the classical view of the significance of knowledge for the mind is considerably weakened, and the belief that in metaphysics man has knowledge of ultimate reality is ignored, if not rejected. The result is an ambiguous and unsatisfactory treatment of the problem of definition and a limited and debatable treatment of the question of justification. Some examination of the Report on both these scores, particularly the former, will serve to show that adequate definition and justification are not only not dependent on the classical doctrines but can in fact be based directly on an explication of the concepts of 'mind' and 'knowledge' and their relationship.

The Report attempts the definition of a liberal education in two distinct ways: in terms of the qualities of mind it ought to produce and the forms of knowledge with which it ought to be concerned. What the precise relationship is between these two is not clear. It is asserted that they are 'images of each other', yet that there is no escape from 'describing general education at one time looking to the good man in society and at another time as dictated by the nature of knowledge itself'.[2] Which of the forms of description is to be given pride of place soon emerges, however. First, three areas of knowledge are distinguished, primarily by their distinctive methods: the natural sciences, the humanities, and social studies. But it is made plain that 'the cultivation of certain aptitudes and attitudes of mind' is being aimed at, the elements of knowledge being the means for developing these. Liberal education is therefore best understood in terms of the characteristics of mind to which it leads. 'By characteristics we mean aims so important as to prescribe how general education should be carried out and which abilities ought to be sought above all others in every part of it. These abilities in our opinion are: to think effectively, to communicate thought, to make relevant judgements, to discriminate among values.'[3] The meaning of each of these four is elaborated at some length. Among the many things detailed of 'effective thinking' it is first said to be logical thinking of a kind that is applicable to such practical matters as deciding who to vote for and what wife to choose; it is the ability to extract universal truths from particular cases and to infer particulars from general laws; it is the ability to analyse a problem and to recombine the elements by the use of imagination. This thinking goes

<hr>

[2] Ibid., p. 58.   [3] Ibid., pp. 64–5.

further than mere logic, however. It includes the relational thinking of everyday life, the ability to think at a level appropriate to a problem whatever its character. It includes too the imaginative thinking of the poet, the inventor, and the revolutionary. 'Communication', though 'obviously inseparable from effective thinking', is said to involve another group of skills, those of speaking and listening, writing and reading. It includes certain moral qualities such as candour, it covers certain vital aspects of social and political life and even the high art of conversation. 'The making of relevant value judgements' involves 'the ability of the student to bring to bear the whole range of ideas upon the area of experience', it is the art of effectively relating theory to practice, of abstractions to facts, of thought to action. Finally there is 'discrimination among values'. This includes the distinction of various kinds of value and their relative importance, an awareness of the values of character like fair play and self-control, intellectual values like the love of truth and aesthetic values like good taste, and, in addition, a commitment to such values in the conduct of life.[4]

As to how exactly these abilities come to be those developed by the three types of knowledge, little is said. It is noted that 'the three phases of effective thinking, logical, relational, and imaginative, correspond roughly to the three divisions of learning, the natural sciences, the social studies, and the humanities, respectively'.[5] The difficult connection between education in the making of value judgements and the formation of moral character is noted. Otherwise the remarks are of a general nature, emphasizing that these abilities must be consciously developed in all studies and generalized as far as possible.

This double, if one-sided, characterization of liberal education seems to me unsatisfactory and seriously misleading if what is said of the four abilities is examined more closely. In the first place, the notion that a liberal education can be directly characterized in terms of mental abilities and independently of fully specifying the forms of knowledge involved is, I think, false. It is the result of a misunderstanding of the way in which mental abilities are in fact distinguishable. From what is said of 'effective thinking', it is perfectly plain that the phrase is being used as a label for mental activity which results in an achievement of some sort, an achievement that is, at least in principle, both publicly describable and publicly testable—the solving of a mathematical problem, responsibly deciding who to vote for, satisfactorily

[4] Ibid., pp. 65–73.　　[5] Ibid., p. 67.

analysing a work of art. Indeed there can be effective thinking only when the outcome of mental activity can be recognized and judged by those who have the appropriate skills and knowledge, for otherwise the phrase has no significant application. Thus although the phrase labels a form of mental activity, and such mental processes may well be directly accessible only to the person whose processes they are, its description and evaluation must be in public terms occurring in public language. Terms which, like 'effective thinking', describe activities involving achievements of some sort, must have public criteria to mark them. But in that case, none of the four abilities can in fact be delineated except by means of their detailed public features. Such characterization is in fact forced on the Committee when they come to amplify what they mean. But their approach is simply illustrative, as if the abilities are directly intelligible in themselves, and the items and features of knowledge they give merely examples of areas where the abilities can be seen. If the public terms and criteria are logically necessary to specifying what the abilities are, however, then no adequate account of liberal education in terms of these can be given without a full account in terms of the public features of the forms of knowledge with which it is concerned. Indeed the latter is logically prior and the former secondary and derivative.

In the second place, the use of broad, general terms for these abilities serves in fact to unify misleadingly quite disparate achievements. For the public criteria whereby the exercise of any one of these abilities is to be judged are not all of a piece. Those that under the banner of 'effective thinking' are appropriate in, say, aesthetic appreciation are, apart from certain very general considerations, inappropriate in, say, mathematical thinking. In each case the criteria are peculiar to the particular area of knowledge concerned. Similarly, for instance, 'communication' in the sciences has only certain very basic features in common with 'communication' in poetic terms. It is only when the abilities are fully divided out, as it were, into the various domains and we see what they refer to in public terms that it is at all clear what is involved in developing them. To talk of developing 'effective thinking' is like talking of developing 'successful games playing'. Plainly that unifying label is thoroughly misleading when what constitutes playing cricket has practically nothing in common with what constitutes playing tiddly-winks. The implications of the term are not at all appreciated until what is wanted is given detailed specification. It is vitally important to realize the very real objective differences that there are in forms of knowledge, and therefore in our understanding of mental processes that are related to these. Maybe this unfortunate desire to use unifying concepts is a relic of the time when all forms of knowledge were thought to be similar, if not identical, in logical structure and it was thought that the 'laws of logic' reflected the precise psychological operations involved in valid thinking. Be that as it may, the general terms used in the Report are liable both to blur essential distinctions and to direct the attention of educational planners into unprofitable descriptions of what they are after.

Thirdly, in spite of any protestations to the contrary, the impression is created by this terminology that it is possible to develop general unitary abilities of the stated kind. The extent to which this is true is a matter for empirical investigation into the transfer of training. Nevertheless such abilities must necessarily be characterized in terms of the public features of knowledge, and whatever general abilities there may be, the particular criteria for their application in diverse fields are vital to their significance for liberal education. But to think in these terms is to be in danger of looking for transfer of skills where none is discernible. We must not assume that skill at tiddly-winks will get us very far at cricket, or that if the skills have much in common, as in say squash and tennis, then the rules for one activity will do as the rules for the other.

Failure to appreciate these points leads all too readily to programmes of education for which quite unwarranted claims are made. It is sometimes said, for instance, that the study of one major science can in itself provide the elements of a liberal education—that it can lead to the development of such abilities as effective thinking, communication, the making of relevant judgements, and even to some extent, discrimination among values. But this facile view is seen to be quite untenable if it is once understood how these abilities are defined, and how any one form of knowledge is related to them. Much more plausible and much more common is the attempt to relate directly the study of particular subjects to the development of particular unitary abilities. The Harvard Committee do this with subdivisions of 'effective thinking' when they suggest that, roughly speaking, logical thinking is developed by the sciences, relational thinking by social studies, and imaginative thinking by the humanities. This, of course, could be said to be true by definition if logical thinking were taken to be just that kind of thinking that is developed by the study of the sciences. But such a straight and limited connection is not at all what is indicated in the Report. The forms of thinking there are much more generalized. It follows then that logical, relational, and imaginative thinking must be independently defined. Because of the vagueness of the terms it might appear that this would be simple enough. But in fact this very vagueness makes the task almost impossible, for any one of the three terms might, with considerable justice, be applied to almost any example of thinking. (And the appropriateness of using such a term as 'imaginative' to describe a distinct type of thinking rather than its manner or style is very debatable.) Even if these forms of thinking can be satisfactorily defined, it remains to be shown that each of them demands the exercise of one distinct but general ability and that this ability can be developed in one particular area of human learning. Generally speaking there is little such evidence. What there is on transfer of training suggests that it occurs only where there is marked logical similarity in the elements studied.[6]

Finally the characterization of a liberal education in these terms is misleading owing to the tendency for the concept to be broadened so that it is concerned not only with the development of the mind that results from the pursuit of knowledge, but also with other aspects of personal development, particularly emotional and moral, that may or may not be judged desirable. This tendency can be clearly seen in the Report's comments on the abilities of communication, making relevant judgements, and discriminating among values. Stretching the edges of the concept in these ways leads to a much wider, more generalized notion of education. It then ceases to be one defined directly in terms of the pursuit of knowledge as liberal education originally was, and thus cannot be justified by justifying that pursuit. But this is surely to give up the concept in favour of another one that needs independent justification. The analysis of such a concept is beyond our present concern.

A REASSERTION AND A REINTERPRETATION

On logical grounds, then, it would seem that a consistent concept of liberal education must be worked out fully in terms of the forms of knowledge. By these is meant, of course, not collections of information,

---

[6] Precisely the same criticisms might be made of some remarks by Professor P. H. Nowell-Smith in his inaugural lecture, *Education in a University* (Leicester University Press, 1958), pp. 6–11. In these he suggests that the prime purpose of the study of literature, history, and philosophy is that each develops one of the central powers of the mind—creative imagination, practical wisdom, and logical thought. Once more we are up against the question of the definition of these 'powers' and if that problem can be solved, the question of sheer evidence for them and the way they can be developed.

but the complex ways of understanding experience which man has achieved, which are publicly specifiable and which are gained through learning. An education in these terms does indeed develop its related abilities and qualities of mind, for the mind will be characterized to a greater or less degree by the features of the understanding it seeks. Each form of knowledge, if it is to be acquired beyond a general and superficial level, involves the development of creative imagination, judgement, thinking, communicative skills, etc., in ways that are peculiar to itself as a way of understanding experience. To list these elements, picking them out, as it were, across the forms of knowledge of which they are part and in each of which they have a different stamp, draws attention to many features that a liberal education must of course include. But it draws attention to them at the expense of the differences among them as they occur in the different areas. And of itself such listing contributes nothing to the basic determination of what a liberal education is. To be told that it is the development of effective thinking is of no value until this is explicated in terms of the forms of knowledge which give it meaning: for example in terms of the solving of problems in Euclidean geometry or coming to understand the poems of John Donne. To be told instead that it is concerned with certain specified forms of knowledge, the essential characteristics of which are then detailed explicitly as far as possible, is to be given a clear understanding of the concept and one which is unambiguous as to the forms of thinking, judgement, imagination, and communication it involves.

In his Gulbenkian Foundation Report: *Arts and Science Sides in the Sixth Form*, Mr. A. D. C. Peterson comes considerably nearer than the Harvard Committee to the definition of a liberal education (once more termed here a 'general education') by proceeding in just this fashion. Being concerned that this should not be worked out in terms of information, he shies away from any direct use of the term 'knowledge' and defines the concept modestly as one that 'develops the intellect in as many as possible of the main modes of thinking'.[7] These are then listed as the logical, the empirical, the moral, and the aesthetic. The phrase 'modes of thinking', it is true, refers directly to forms of mental activity, and Mr. Peterson's alternatives for it, 'modes of human experience', 'categories of mental experience', and (elsewhere) 'types of judgement', all look in the same direction. Yet the 'modes' are not different aspects of mind that cut across the forms that human knowledge takes,

[7] *Arts and Science Sides in the Sixth Form*, Gulbenkian Foundation Report (Oxford University Department of Education, 1960), p. 15.

as the Harvard Report's 'abilities' are. They are, rather, four parallel forms of mental development. To complete this treatment so that there is no ambiguity, however, it must be made clear in a way that Mr. Peterson does not make it clear, that the four forms can only be distinguished, in the last analysis, in terms of the public features that demarcate the areas of knowledge on which they stand. Logical, empirical, moral, and aesthetic forms of understanding are distinguishable from each other only by their distinctive concepts and expressions and their criteria for distinguishing the true from the false, the good from the bad. If Mr. Peterson's 'modes' are strictly explicated on the basis of these features of knowledge, then his concept of education becomes one concerned with the development of the mind as that is determined by certain forms of knowledge. This is to be in sight of a modern equivalent of the traditional conception of liberal education.

But the reassertion of this concept implies that there is once more the acceptance of some kind of 'harmony' between knowledge and the mind. This is, however, not now being maintained on metaphysical grounds. What is being suggested, rather, is that the 'harmony' is a matter of the logical relationship between the concept of 'mind' and the concept of 'knowledge', from which it follows that the achievement of knowledge is necessarily the development of mind—that is, the self-conscious rational mind of man—in its most fundamental aspect.

Whatever else is implied in the phrase, to have 'a rational mind' certainly implies experience structured under some form of conceptual scheme. The various manifestations of consciousness, in, for instance, different sense-perceptions, different emotions, or different elements of intellectual understanding, are intelligible only by virtue of the conceptual apparatus by which they are articulated. Further, whatever private forms of awareness there may be, it is by means of symbols, particularly in language, that conceptual articulation becomes objectified, for the symbols give public embodiment to the concepts. The result of this is that men are able to come to understand both the external world and their own private states of mind in common ways, sharing the same conceptual schema by learning to use symbols in the same manner. The objectification of understanding is possible because commonly accepted criteria for using the terms are recognized even if these are never explicitly expressed. But further, as the symbols derived from experience can be used to examine subsequent experience, assertions are possible which are testable as true or false, valid or invalid. There are thus also public criteria whereby certain forms of expression are assessable against experience. Whether the 'objects' concerned are themselves private to the individual like mental processes, or publicly accessible like temperature readings, there are here tests for the assertions which are themselves publicly agreed and accepted.

It is by the use of such tests that we have come to have the whole domain of knowledge. The formulating and testing of symbolic expressions has enabled man to probe his experience for ever more complex relations and for finer and finer distinctions, these being fixed and held for public sharing in the symbolic systems that have been evolved. But it is important to realize that this progressive attainment of a cognitive framework with public criteria has significance not merely for knowledge itself, for it is by its terms that the life of man in every particular is patterned and ordered. Without its structure all other forms of consciousness, including, for example, emotional experiences, or mental attitudes and beliefs, would seem to be unintelligible. For the analysis of them reveals that they lack independent intelligible structure of themselves. Essentially private though they may be in many or all of their aspects, their characteristic forms are explicable only by means of the publicly rooted conceptual organizations we have achieved. They can be understood only by means of the objective features with which they are associated, round which they come to be organized and built. The forms of knowledge are thus the basic articulations whereby the whole of experience has become intelligible to man, they are the fundamental achievement of mind.

Knowledge, however, must never be thought of merely as vast bodies of tested symbolic expressions. These are only the public aspects of the ways in which human experience has come to have shape. They are significant because they are themselves the objective elements round which the development of mind has taken place. To acquire knowledge is to become aware of experience as structured, organized, and made meaningful in some quite specific way, and the varieties of human knowledge constitute the highly developed forms in which man has found this possible. To acquire knowledge is to learn to see, to experience the world in a way otherwise unknown, and thereby come to have a mind in a fuller sense. It is not that the mind is some kind of organ or muscle with its own inbuilt forms of operation, which if somehow developed, naturally lead to different kinds of knowledge. It is not that the mind has predetermined patterns of functioning. Nor is it that the mind is an entity which suitably directed by knowledge comes to take on the pattern of, is conformed to, some external reality. It is rather that to have a mind basically involves coming to have experience articulated by means of various conceptual schemata. It is only because man has over millennia objectified and progressively developed these that he has achieved the forms of human knowledge, and the possibility of the development of mind as we know it is open to us today.

A liberal education is, then, one that, determined in scope and content by knowledge itself, is thereby concerned with the development of mind. The concept is thus once more clearly and objectively defined in precisely the same way as the original concept. It is, however, no longer supported by epistemological and metaphysical doctrines that result in a hierarchical organization of the various forms of knowledge. The detailed working out of the education will therefore be markedly different in certain respects. The distinctions between the various forms of knowledge which will principally govern the scheme of education will now be based entirely on analyses of their particular conceptual, logical, and methodological features. The comprehensive character of the education will of course remain, since this is essentially part of the definition of the concept, but any question of the harmonious organization of its various elements will depend on the relationships between them that are revealed by these analyses.

But if the concept is reasserted in these terms, what now of the question of its justification? The justification of a liberal education as supported by the doctrines of classical realism was based on the ultimacy of knowledge as ordered and determined by reality, and the significance of knowledge for the mind and the good life. Having weakened these doctrines, the Harvard Committee's justification of their concept ignores the question of the relationship between knowledge and reality, and there is a specific rejection of the view that knowledge is in itself the good of the mind. They assert, however, the supreme significance of knowledge in the determination of all human activity, and supplement this, as is certainly necessary because of the extended nature of their concept, by general considerations of the desirability of their suggestions. When once more the concept is strictly confined so as to be determined by the forms of knowledge, the return to a justification of it without reference to what is generally thought desirable on social or similar grounds becomes possible. And such justification for the concept is essential if the education it delineates is to have the ultimate significance that, as was earlier suggested, is part of its *raison d'être*. This justification must now, however, stem from what has already been said of the nature of knowledge, as no metaphysical doctrine of the connection between knowledge and reality is any longer being invoked.

If the achievement of knowledge is necessarily the development of mind in its most basic sense, then it can be readily seen that to ask for a justification for the pursuit of knowledge is not at all the same thing as to ask for the justification for, say, teaching all children a foreign language or making them orderly and punctual in their behaviour. It is in fact a peculiar question asking for justification for any development of the rational mind at all. To ask for the justification of any form of activity is significant only if one is in fact committed already to seeking rational knowledge. To ask for a justification of the pursuit of rational knowledge itself therefore presupposes some form of commitment to what one is seeking to justify. Justification is possible only if what is being justified is both intelligible under publicly rooted concepts and is assessable according to accepted criteria. It assumes a commitment to these two principles. But these very principles are in fact fundamental to the pursuit of knowledge in all its forms, be it, for instance, empirical knowledge or understanding in the arts. The forms of knowledge are in a sense simply the working out of these general principles in particular ways. To give justification of any kind of knowledge therefore involves using the principles in one specific form to assess their use in another. Any particular activity can be examined for its rational character, for its adherence to these principles, and thus justified on the assumption of them. Indeed, in so far as activities are rational this will be possible. It is commitment to them that characterizes any rational activity as such. But the principles themselves have no such assessable status, for justification outside the use of the principles is not logically possible. This does not mean that rational pursuits in the end lack justification, for they could equally well be said to have their justification written into them. Nor is any form of viciously circular justification involved by assuming in the procedure what is being looked for. The situation is that we have here reached the ultimate point where the question of justification ceases to be significantly applicable. The apparent circularity is the result of the interrelation between the concepts of rational justification and the pursuit of knowledge.

Perhaps the finality of these principles can be brought out further by noting a negative form of the same argument. From this point of view, to question the pursuit of any kind of rational knowledge is in the end self-defeating, for the questioning itself depends on accepting the very principles whose use is finally being called in question.

It is because it is based on these ultimate principles that characterize knowledge itself and not merely on lower level forms of justification that a liberal education is in a very real sense the ultimate form of education. In spite of the absence of any metaphysical doctrine about reality this idea of liberal education has a significance parallel to that of the original Greek concept. It is an education concerned directly with the development of the mind in rational knowledge, whatever form that freely takes. This parallels the original concept in that according to the doctrine of function liberal education was the freeing of the mind to achieve its own good in knowledge. In each case it is a form of education knowing no limits other than those necessarily imposed by the nature of rational knowledge and thereby itself developing in man the final court of appeal in all human affairs.

As here reformulated the concept has, again like the original, objectivity, though this is no longer backed by metaphysical realism. For it is a necessary feature of knowledge as such that there be public criteria whereby the true is distinguishable from the false, the good from the bad, the right from the wrong. It is the existence of these criteria which gives objectivity to knowledge; and this in its turn gives objectivity to the concept of liberal education. A parallel to another form of justification thus remains, and the concept continues to warrant its label as that of an education that frees the mind from error and illusion. Further, as the determination of the good life is now considered to be itself the pursuit of a particular form of rational knowledge, that in which what ought to be done is justified by the giving of reasons, this is seen as a necessary part of a liberal education. And as all other forms of knowledge contribute in their way to moral understanding, the concept as a whole is once more given a kind of justification in its importance for the moral life. But this justification, like that of objectivity, no longer has the distinct significance which it once had, for it is again simply a necessary consequence of what the pursuit of knowledge entails. Nevertheless, liberal education remains basic to the freeing of human conduct from wrong.

CERTAIN BASIC PHILOSOPHICAL CONSIDERATIONS

Having attempted a reinstatement of the concept without its original philosophical backing, what of the implications of this for the practical conduct of education? In working these out it is necessary first to try to distinguish the various forms of knowledge and then to relate them in some way to the organization of the school or college curriculum. The first of these is a strictly philosophical task. The second is a matter of practical planning that involves many considerations other than the purely philosophical, and to this I will return when certain broad distinctions between forms of knowledge have been outlined.

As stated earlier, by a form of knowledge is meant a distinct way in which our experience becomes structured round the use of accepted public symbols. The symbols thus having public meaning, their use is in some way testable against experience and there is the progressive development of series of tested symbolic expressions. In this way experience has been probed further and further by extending and elaborating the use of the symbols, and by means of these it has become possible for the personal experience of individuals to become more fully structured, more fully understood. The various forms of knowledge can be seen in low-level developments within the common area of our knowledge of the everyday world. From this there branch out the developed forms which, taking certain elements in our common knowledge as a basis, have grown in distinctive ways. In the developed forms of knowledge the following related distinguishing features can be seen:

(1) They each involve certain central concepts that are peculiar in character to the form. For example, those of gravity, acceleration, hydrogen, and photo-synthesis characteristic of the sciences; number, integral, and matrix in mathematics; God, sin, and predestination in religion; ought, good, and wrong in moral knowledge.

(2) In a given form of knowledge these and other concepts that denote, if perhaps in a very complex way, certain aspects of experience form a network of possible relationships in which experience can be understood. As a result the form has a distinctive logical structure. For example, the terms and statements of mechanics can be meaningfully related in certain strictly limited ways only, and the same is true of historical explanation.

(3) The form, by virtue of its particular terms and logic, has expressions or statements (possibly answering a distinctive type of question) that in some way or other, however indirect it may be, are testable against experience. This is the case in scientific knowledge, moral knowledge, and in the arts, though in the arts no questions are explicit and the criteria for the tests are only partially expressible in words. Each form, then, has distinctive expressions that are testable against experience in accordance with particular criteria that are peculiar to the form.

(4) The forms have developed particular techniques and skills for ex-

ploring experience and testing their distinctive expressions, for instance the techniques of the sciences and those of the various literary arts. The result has been the amassing of all the symbolically expressed knowledge that we now have in the arts and the sciences.

Though the various forms of knowledge are distinguishable in these ways it must not be assumed that all there is to them can be made clear and explicit by these means. All knowledge involves the use of symbols and the making of judgements in ways that cannot be expressed in words and can only be learnt in a tradition. The art of scientific investigation and the development of appropriate experimental tests, the forming of a historical explanation and the assessment of its truth, the appreciation of a poem: all of these activities are high arts that are not in themselves communicable simply by words. Acquiring knowledge of any form is therefore to a greater or less extent something that cannot be done simply by solitary study of the symbolic expressions of knowledge, it must be learnt from a master on the job. No doubt it is because the forms require particular training of this kind in distinct worlds of discourse, because they necessitate the development of high critical standards according to complex criteria, because they involve our coming to look at experience in particular ways, that we refer to them as disciplines. They are indeed disciplines that form the mind.

Yet the dividing lines that can be drawn between different disciplines by means of the four suggested distinguishing marks are neither clear enough nor sufficient for demarcating the whole world of modern knowledge as we know it. The central feature to which they point is that the major forms of knowledge, or disciplines, can each be distinguished by their dependence on some particular kind of test against experience for their distinctive expressions. On this ground alone, however, certain broad divisions are apparent. The sciences depend crucially on empirical experiment and observational tests, mathematics depends on deductive demonstrations from certain sets of axioms. Similarly moral knowledge and the arts involve distinct forms of critical tests though in these cases both what the tests are and the ways in which they are applied are only partially statable. (Some would in fact dispute the status of the arts as forms of knowledge for this very reason.) Because of their particular logical features it seems to me necessary to distinguish also as separate disciplines both historical and religious knowledge, and there is perhaps an equally good case, because of the nature of their empirical concepts, for regarding the human sciences separately from the physical sciences. But within these areas further distinctions must be made. These are usually the result of the grouping of knowledge round a number of related concepts, or round particular skills or techniques. The various sciences and the various arts can be demarcated within the larger units of which they are in varying degrees representative in their structure, by these means.

But three other important classifications of knowledge must in addition be recognized. First there are those organizations which are not themselves disciplines or subdivisions of any discipline. They are formed by building together round specific objects, or phenomena, or practical pursuits, knowledge that is characteristically rooted elsewhere in more than one discipline. It is not just that these organizations make use of several forms of knowledge, for after all the sciences use mathematics, the arts use historical knowledge, and so on. Many of the disciplines borrow from each other. But these organizations are not concerned, as the disciplines are, to validate any one logically distinct form of expression. They are not concerned with developing a particular structuring of experience. They are held together simply by their subject-matter, drawing on all forms of knowledge that can contribute to them. Geography, as the study of man in relation to his environment, is an example of a theoretical study of this kind, engineering an example of a practical nature. I see no reason why such organizations of knowledge, which I shall refer to as 'fields', should not be endlessly constructed according to particular theoretical or practical interests. Secondly, whilst moral knowledge is a distinct form, concerned with answering questions as to what ought to be done in practical affairs, no specialized subdivisions of this have been developed. In practical affairs, moral questions, because of their character, naturally arise alongside questions of fact and technique, so that there have been formed 'fields' of practical knowledge that include distinct moral elements within them, rather than the subdivisions of a particular discipline. Political, legal, and educational theory are perhaps the clearest examples of fields where moral knowledge of a developed kind is to be found. Thirdly, there are certain second-order forms of knowledge which are dependent for their existence on the other primary areas. On the one hand there are the essentially scientific studies of language and symbolism as in grammar and philology. On the other hand there are the logical and philosophical studies of meaning and justification. These would seem to constitute a distinct discipline by virtue of their particular concepts and criteria of judgement.

In summary, then, it is suggested that the forms of knowledge as we have them can be classified as follows:

(I) Distinct disciplines or forms of knowledge (subdivisible): mathematics, physical sciences, human sciences, history, religion, literature and the fine arts, philosophy.

(II) Fields of knowledge: theoretical, practical (these may or may not include elements of moral knowledge).

It is the distinct disciplines that basically constitute the range of unique ways we have of understanding experience if to these is added the category of moral knowledge.

THE PLANNING AND PRACTICAL CONDUCT
OF LIBERAL EDUCATION

Turning now to the bearing of this discussion on the planning and conduct of a liberal education, certain very general comments about its characteristic features can be made, though detailed treatment would involve psychological and other considerations that are quite beyond the scope of this paper.

In the first place, as liberal education is concerned with the comprehensive development of the mind in acquiring knowledge, it is aimed at achieving an understanding of experience in many different ways. This means the acquisition by critical training and discipline not only of facts but also of complex conceptual schemes and of the arts and techniques of different types of reasoning and judgement. Syllabuses and curricula cannot therefore be constructed simply in terms of information and isolated skills. They must be constructed so as to introduce pupils as far as possible into the interrelated aspects of each of the basic forms of knowledge, each of the several disciplines. And they must be constructed to cover at least in some measure the range of knowledge as a whole.

In a programme of liberal education that is based directly on the study of the specific disciplines, examples of each of the different areas must of course be chosen. Selection of this kind is not however simply an inevitable practical consequence of the vast growth of knowledge. It is equally in keeping with what a liberal education is aiming at. Though its aim is comprehensive it is not after the acquisition of encyclopaedic information. Nor is it after the specialist knowledge of the person fully trained in all the particular details of a branch of knowledge. Such a specialist can not only accurately employ the concepts, logic, and criteria of a domain but also knows the skills and techniques involved in the pursuit of knowledge quite beyond the immediate areas of common human experience. Nor is liberal education concerned with the technician's knowledge of the detailed application of the disciplines in practical and theoretical fields. What is being sought is, first, sufficient immersion in the concepts, logic, and criteria of the discipline for a person to come to know the distinctive way in which it 'works' by pursuing these in particular cases; and then sufficient generalization of these over the whole range of the discipline so that his experience begins to be widely structured in this distinctive manner. It is this coming to look at things in a certain way that is being aimed at, not the ability to work out in minute particulars all the details that can in fact be discerned. It is the ability to recognize empirical assertions or aesthetic judgements for what they are, and to know the kind of considerations on which their validity will depend, that matters. Beyond this an outline of the major achievements in each area provides some grasp of the range and scope of experience that has thus become intelligible. Perhaps this kind of understanding is in fact most readily distinguishable in the literary arts as critical appreciation in contrast to the achievement of the creative writer or the literary hack. But the distinction is surely applicable to other forms of knowledge as well.

This is not to assert that 'critical appreciation' in any form of knowledge can be adequately achieved without some development of the understanding of the specialist or technician. Nor is it to imply that this understanding in the sciences, the arts, or moral issues can be had without participation in many relevant creative and practical pursuits. The extent to which this is true will vary from discipline to discipline and is in fact in need of much investigation, particularly because of its importance for moral and aesthetic education. But it is to say that the aim of the study of a discipline in liberal education is not that of its study in a specialist or technical course. The first is concerned with developing a person's ways of understanding experience, the others are concerned with mastering the details of knowledge, how it is established, and the use of it in other enterprises, particularly those of a practical nature. It is of course perfectly possible for a course in physics, for example, to be devoted to a double purpose if it is deliberately so designed. It may provide both a specialist knowledge of the subject and at the same time a genuine introduction to the form of scientific knowledge. But the two purposes are quite distinct and there is no reason to suppose that by aiming at one the other can automatically be achieved as well. Yet it would seem to be true that some specialist study within a discipline, if it is at all typical of the discipline, is necessary to understanding the form of knowledge in any developed sense. The study of a discipline as part of liberal education, however, contributes practically nothing directly to any specialist study of it, though it does serve to put the specialism into a much wider context.

A liberal education approached directly in terms of the disciplines will thus be composed of the study of at least paradigm examples of all the various forms of knowledge. This study will be sufficiently detailed and sustained to give genuine insight so that pupils come to think in these terms, using the concepts, logic, and criteria accurately in the different domains. It will then include generalization of the particular examples used so as to show the range of understanding in the various forms. It will also include some indication of the relations between the forms where these overlap and their significance in the major fields of knowledge, particularly the practical fields, that have been developed. This is particularly important for moral education, as moral questions can frequently be solved only by calling on the widest possible range of human understanding. As there is in fact no developed discipline of moral knowledge, education in moral understanding must necessarily be approached in a rather different way. For if it is to cover more than everyday personal matters this has to be by the study of issues that occur in certain particular fields of knowledge. The major difficulty this presents will be referred to briefly later. The important point here is that though moral understanding has to be pursued in contexts where it is not the only dominant interest, the aim of its pursuit is precisely the same as for all other elements in a liberal education, the understanding of experience in a unique way. What is wanted (just as in the study of the disciplines *per se*) is, basically, the use of the appropriate concepts, logic, and criteria, and the appreciation of the range of understanding in this form.

It is perhaps important to stress the fact that this education will be one in the forms of knowledge themselves and not merely a self-conscious philosophical treatment of their characteristics. Scientific and historical knowledge are wanted, not knowledge of the philosophy of science and the philosophy of history as substitutes. A liberal education can only be planned if distinctions in the forms of knowledge are clearly understood, and that is a philosophical matter. But the education itself is only partly in philosophy, and that is only possible when pupils have some grasp of the other disciplines themselves.

Precisely what sections of the various disciplines are best suited to the aims of liberal education cannot be gone into here. It is apparent that on philosophical grounds alone some branches of the sciences, for instance, would seem to be much more satisfactory as paradigms of scientific thinking than others. Many sections of physics are probably more comprehensive and clear in logical character, more typical of the well-developed physical sciences than, say, botany. If so, they would, all other things being equal, serve better as an introduction to scientific knowledge. Perhaps in literature and the fine arts the paradigm principle is less easy to apply though probably many would favour a course in literature to any one other. But whatever the discipline, in practice all other things are not in fact equal and decisions about the content of courses cannot be taken without careful regard to the abilities and interests of the students for whom they are designed.

Yet hovering round such decisions and questions of syllabus planning there is frequently found the belief that the inherent logical structure of a discipline, or a branch of a discipline necessarily determines exactly what and exactly how the subject is to be taught and learnt. The small amount of truth and the large amount of error in this belief can only be distinguished by clarifying what the logic of a subject is. It is not a series of intellectual steps that must be climbed in strict order. It is not a specific psychological channel along which the mind must travel if there is to be understanding. This is to confuse logical characteristics with psychological processes. The logic of a form of knowledge shows the meaningful and valid ways in which its terms and criteria are used. It constitutes the publicly accepted framework of knowledge. The psychological activities of the individual when concerned with this knowledge are not in general prescribed in any temporal order and the mind, as it were, plays freely within and around the framework. It is simply that the framework lays down the general formal relations of the concepts if there is to be knowledge. The logic as publicly expressed consists of the general and formal principles to which the terms must conform in knowledge. Coming to understand a form of knowledge involves coming to think in relations that satisfy the public criteria. How the mind plays round and within these is not itself being laid down at all, there is no dragooning of psychological processes, only a marking out of the territory in which the mind can wander more or less at will. Indeed understanding a form of knowledge is far more like coming to know a country than climbing a ladder. Some places in a territory may only be get-at-able by a single specified route and some forms of knowledge may have concepts and relations that cannot be understood without first understanding certain others. But that countries are explorable only in one way is in general false, and even in mathematics, the most strictly sequential form of knowledge we have, many ways of coming to know the territory are possible. The logic of a subject is relevant to what is being taught, for its patterns must be accepted as essential to the form of knowledge. But how those patterns are best discerned is a matter for empirical investigation.

School subjects in the disciplines as we at present have them are in no way sacrosanct on either logical or psychological grounds. They are necessarily selections from the forms of knowledge that we have and may or may not be good as introductions for the purposes of liberal education. In most cases they have developed under a number of diverse influences. The historical growth of the subjects has sometimes dominated the programmes. The usefulness of certain elements, the demands of higher specialist education, certain general 'psychological' principles such as progressing from the simple to the complex, from the particular to the general, the concrete to the abstract, all these factors and many others have left their marks. This being so, many well-established courses need to be critically re-examined both philosophically and psychologically before they can be accepted as suitable for liberal education. Superficially at least most of them would seem to be quite inappropriate for this purpose.

Though a liberal education is most usually approached directly in the study of various branches of the disciplines, I see no reason to think that this must necessarily be so. It is surely possible to construct programmes that are in the first place organized round certain fields of knowledge either theoretical or practical. The study of aspects of power, natural as well as social and political, might for instance be one element in such a scheme; or a regional study that introduces historical, geographical, industrial, and social considerations; or a practical project of design and buildings involving the sciences, mathematics, and visual arts. In this case, however, it must be recognized that the fields are chosen because together they can be used to develop understanding of all the various forms of knowledge, and explicit steps must be taken to see that this end is achieved. There will necessarily be the strongest tendency for liberal education to be lost sight of and for the fields to be pursued in their own right developing the techniques and skills which they need. These may be valuable and useful in many ways, and perhaps essential in many a person's whole education. (Certainly liberal education as is here being understood is only one part of the education a person ought to have, for it omits quite deliberately for instance specialist education, physical education, and character training.) But a course in various fields of knowledge will not in fact be a liberal education unless that aim is kept absolutely clear and every opportunity is taken to lead to a fuller grasp of the disciplines. Again some fields of study will be better for this purpose than others but all will demand the highest skill from the teacher, who must be under no misapprehension as to what the object of the exercise really is. Yet it is difficult to see how this kind of approach can be fully adequate if it does not in the end lead to a certain amount of study of the distinct disciplines themselves. For whatever ground may have been covered indirectly, a satisfactory understanding of the characteristically distinct approaches of the different forms is hardly possible without some direct gathering together of the elements of the disciplines that have been implicit in all that has been done.

Whatever the pattern of a liberal education in its later stages, it must not be forgotten that there is being presupposed a broad basic education in the common area of everyday knowledge where the various disciplines can be seen in embryo and from which they branch out as distinct units. In such a basic primary education, the ever growing range of a child's experience and the increasing use of linguistic and symbolic forms lays the foundation for the various modes of understanding, scientific, historical, religious, moral, and so on. Out of this general pool of knowledge the disciplines have slowly become ever more differentiated and it is this that the student must come to understand, not confusing the forms of knowledge but appreciating them for what they are in themselves, and recognizing their necessary limitations.

But is then the outcome of a liberal education to be simply the achievement of a series of discrete ways of understanding experience? In a very real sense yes, but in another sense not entirely. For one thing, we have as yet not begun to understand the complex interrelations of the different forms of knowledge themselves, for they do not only have unique features but common features too, and in addition one discipline often makes extensive use of the achievements of another. But we must also not forget that the various forms are firmly rooted in that common world of persons and things which we all share, and into this they take back in subtle as well as simple ways the understanding they have achieved. The outcome of a liberal education must therefore not be thought of as producing ever greater disintegration of the mind but rather the growth of ever clearer and finer distinctions in our experience. If the result is not some quasi-aesthetic unity of the mind neither is it in any sense chaos. Perhaps the most suggestive picture of the outcome is that used by Professor Michael Oakeshott, though for him it has more literal truth than is here intended. In this the various forms of knowledge are seen as voices in a conversation, a conversation to which they each contribute in a distinctive way. If taken figuratively, his words express more succinctly than mine can precisely what it seems to me a liberal education is and what its outcome will be.

As civilized human beings, we are the inheritors, neither of an inquiry about ourselves and the world, nor of an accumulating body of information, but of a conversation, begun in the primeval forests and extended and made more articulate in the course of centuries. It is a conversation which goes on both in public and within each of ourselves. Of course there is argument and inquiry and information, but wherever these are profitable they are to be recognized as passages in this conversation, and perhaps they are not the most captivating of the passages.... Conversation is not an enterprise designed to yield an extrinsic profit, a contest where a winner gets a prize, nor is it an activity of exegesis; it is an unrehearsed intellectual adventure....

... Education, properly speaking, is an initiation into the skill and partnership of this conversation in which we learn to recognize the voices, to distinguish the proper occasions of utterance, and in which we acquire the intellectual and moral habits appropriate to conversation. And it is this conversation which, in the end, gives place and character to every human activity and utterance.[8]

[8] Michael Oakeshott, *Rationalism in Politics and Other Essays* (London: Methuen, 1962), pp. 198–9.

V

TOWARDS A DEFINITION OF QUALITY IN EDUCATION

MARY WARNOCK

It must be agreed from the start that in this particular field there is no such thing as proof. It is a great mistake to reject conclusions in educational theory on the grounds that they cannot be proved. One must not, as Aristotle said, demand more rigour than the subject-matter is fitted for. The whole subject of education is practical. If there are theories, they must essentially be analytic of what actually occurs. Thus, if we are discussing what sort of education is best, we must take into account (again following Aristotle) what educated people think is best, and also, more importantly, whatever it is in education that people ultimately most enjoy, and therefore want.

That being said by way of preliminary, I want to defend the proposition that a good education must, above all things, be directed towards the strengthening of the faculty of imagination. To speak of the imagination as a faculty is doubtless misleading. I certainly do not wish to suggest that it is a power of the mind quite distinct from all other powers. But there have, historically, been certain uses of the expression 'imagination' which seem to me illuminating, and which, more or less, I wish to follow. Shelley spoke of the imagination as that which made love and sympathy possible. It was for this reason that he thought poetry so influential, simply because it appealed to the imagination. We may not assent to his views on the function of poetry; but his theory of imagination is independent of these. Again, Coleridge, in a well-known passage of *Biographia Literaria*, says of Wordsworth, 'It was the union of deep feeling with profound thought, the fine balance of truth in observing with the imaginative faculty in modifying the objects observed' ... it was this which made such a profound impression upon Coleridge. The imaginative faculty, then, in the sense in which I think of it, is connected with observation, and with thought. It is that which enables one to perceive things, not isolated, but connected, in a wider field. It is what enables one to see things as *significant*. It is not any part of my present purpose to go into the arguments, philosophical or psychologically descriptive, about whether or not the imagination has objects, whether or not we need to speak of images in order to speak of the imagination. We can admit that these questions may allow of different answers, and yet agree on a working *use* of the concept of imagination, whose edges need not be sharply drawn. There is, however, one further feature of the imagination, in whatever form it is conceived, which is crucial to my argument. The imagination is necessarily capable of being free (by necessarily, here I mean 'tautologically'—the concept of an imagination *not* so capable is a contradiction). That being so, the imagination is the faculty by means of which one is able to envisage things as they are not. This is the Sartrean concept of imagination, and it seems to me to be right. The imagination, though it may start from the observation of things, will not rest there, but will 'modify' them, will see how they might be different. Not only, therefore, will the imagination be that which enables a poet to see some objects of everyday life as symbolic of what they are not themselves— to see them as possessed of significance beyond themselves—but it will also be that which enables the reformer to see in what way things could be improved, since they are not inevitably fixed in the condition in which he finds them. None of these aspects of the faculty of the imagination is remote from the ordinary ideas of the imaginative or the unimaginative person, as we use these ideas from day to day. To demonstrate this would be tedious. But it is capable of demonstration.

Imagination, then, is that which will enable us to perceive things, as Wordsworth did, for their own sake, *and* for the sake of what lies beyond them.

If good education is the strengthening of the imagination, the question is how we are to set about this. We all know that in early childhood, and for a number of years thereafter, play is one of the most important ways of stretching the imagination and allowing it freedom. Play is what concentrates our minds, as children, on things *for their own sake*. But we also know that play without a certain amount of external stimulus is likely to be very frustrating for the players. It is extraordinarily difficult, in the case of young children, to know how much they need to learn to be imaginative about things which are familiar to them, and how much, on the other hand, they benefit from the introduction of ideas which are totally outside their normal experience. This problem, of course, arises acutely in the matter of their books, both those that are used as classroom material, and those which they will read for themselves. On the whole (though I know of no theoretical justification for this judgement) I am inclined to think that attempts to introduce totally alien material and familiarize children with it are not successful, and are misconceived. The greatest service of literature, whether for children or grown-ups, is to show how the apparently ordinary may be fraught with mystery or excitement. But this is by the way. One must not forget, in thinking of the education of the very young, that all the powers which I have ascribed to the imagination belong, in truth, to the intellect as well, if the intellect is that faculty whereby we abstract from the particular to the general, and by which we frame and operate with abstract ideas. It is nonsensical to suppose that human children are incapable of dealing in abstractions, and it is a relief to know that educational psychology is now beginning to accept as legitimate the beliefs which those of us who were neither education-alists nor psychologists had never given up. Whether one wishes to go so far as to say that children have an innate capacity for abstraction to enable them to learn so complex a thing as language does not very much matter for practical purposes. It is enough to recognize that any trend in education which would seek to deprive young children of the practice of abstraction is sadly mistaken. It is probably only later in life that some of us begin to quail before the abstract, and long to be Epimetheus rather than Prometheus.

One of the kinds of educational play which is much used at the moment is of course playing at research, pretending to find things out for oneself. This is certainly not a bad kind of play; but it is not good if it is continued at all beyond the age at which a child may begin to feel ashamed of playing, or embarrassed by it. It would be grotesque, after all, to try to deceive a child, whose only resources of research were the books in the classroom shelves, into thinking that what he was doing was real research. Up to a certain age, children may well be content with the 'project' as something they just do at school, and which may be quite interesting, without the idea having to be introduced of the difference between primary and secondary sources. But there does appear to be something humiliating to the pupil if the pretence is kept up for too long, as it is in some C.S.E. projects. Moreover, such play-acting may engender a kind of obstinate arrogance. We are all of us prone to think that what we happen to have seen with our own eyes constitutes the whole truth about a subject, forgetting that our eyes may be partial, prejudiced, or simply myopic. It is a pity to encourage people in this natural human failing. The imagination is better served in the long run by the vistas afforded by the work of other people better equipped than oneself to discover the truth. What we must not forget, in any case, in all discussion of learning through play (and this includes play-research) is the distinction between play-acting and reality. As long as this distinction is preserved no harm will come to the children.

We must turn now to the positive point in concentrating on the education of the imagination. It is only if the imagination is alive and active that the pupil will be able to *go on* with a subject, beyond the point at which the teaching stops. If there is any single feature to be picked out as a mark of a good education, I should say it was this, that the child who has benefited from it is able to leave his teacher behind. As a child grows up and leaves school, whether for a job or for further education, what he needs above all is the ability to go on, on his own, with whatever has interested him at school. There are two conditions jointly necessary for his being able to do this, both very obvious. The first is that there should be a subject in which his interest is fully engaged. The second, equally obvious, condition is that he should be equipped with the tools to go on if he should wish to. One can immediately draw one negative conclusion from this. Education should not consist in the accumulation of facts for its own sake.

But it is at this point in the educational argument that disputes about the examination system tend to obscure the real issue. It is said that fact-learning is necessary, because fair examinations can be conducted only on the basis of facts. If opinions were examined rather than facts, it is said, this would lead to the most frightful abuses and a total loss of comparability between results, such that the actual examination result would totally lose its value, especially to employers and universities. However, it seems to me that this is really a pretty low-grade kind of argument. There is, underlying it, an assumption that there is an absolutely clear-cut distinction between what is a fact and what is not, an assumption that many philosophers would wish to quarrel with. But worse than this, it must surely be putting the cart before the horse to argue for a certain kind of education on the basis of the examinations which are possible at the end of it. It would, surely, be better to devise the kind of education you want first, and then invent a kind of examination to fit. As a matter of fact, the whole connection between facts and examinations, which at present is a bugbear because it turns the examination into a feat of memory, could be radically changed for the better if there were more widespread use made of the habit of allowing notes, texts, dictionaries, and so on to be taken into the examination. Then the test would be less of memory and more of the intelligent power to choose and use material.

However, this, though it is a reform I should dearly love to see, is not really the point at issue. I wish to assert dogmatically and positively that in my experience intelligent people being educated at school in the way that for the time being we think it proper that they should, namely working in the sixth form towards three 'A' levels, feel passionately that they have not enough time to think about their subjects. They cannot, they feel, do them properly at all. It is true that the very same people also complain that they have to specialize too much. But if they could choose one reform, it would be that they should not have to take down so many notes; that they should have time to discuss the presuppositions of their subjects, or to speculate about what the consequences would be if something, assumed to be true without question, turned out, or were assumed to turn out, to be false. This is the kind of thing which they, rightly, feel would lead to understanding rather than just knowing. This is what would ensure that they would not forget the whole thing, that they could, if they wanted, *go on* with the subject on their own. The only way to come near to satisfying this demand, as far as I can see, is not *less* specialization in the sixth form but *more*.

There is, after all, nothing more inimical to the exercise of the imagination than boredom, and with the present system of teaching, many people who are perfectly intelligent and capable of thinking for themselves are treated as if they could not, and are bored by their compulsory three subjects, even though they chose them themselves. How much worse their plight would be if, like the French, they had to do a larger number of subjects, say five, and had almost no choice of what these five should be. (The ultimate absurdity of the French system is the teaching of philosophy, of all subjects, in this same mindless and uncritical way.) If it is barely possible, except with teachers of genius, to allow people to think about three subjects, because of the burden of facts and formulae, the situation would be far worse with five.

It is often argued that somehow 'in this modern world' it is absolutely essential for everyone to know a bit about everything. But I have yet to be convinced by any argument that it is better, better, that is, for the imagination, to leave school with a smattering of superficial jargon derived from economics, sociology, mathematics, and so on, rather than to leave with one genuine enthusiasm. Since in many ways this may appear to be the crux of the argument for or against specialization, perhaps one should stop at this point and look at the case rather more deeply.

There seem to me to be two quite different arguments, both of them fatal to the case of those who say that one ought not to leave school without some understanding of all subjects, and therefore one ought to specialize much less. The first argument is that, as is admitted on all sides, one cannot learn in detail about all subjects. Therefore, it is suggested, one ought to learn about the principles behind the subject (say physics) rather than the subject itself. One ought, in addition, to be primed up with some central examples of physical discoveries, as an illustration of the principles which one had learned. But there is, in this programme, the most sinister built-in possibility of dogmatism and indoctrination on the part of the teachers or syllabus-makers. If I know no physics, but only what someone has told me are the principles of physics, and if I cannot apply the principles, but know one instance which someone has chosen as an example of the way the principles have been applied, then the one thing I cannot ever be is a physicist. Neither have I any possible criteria by which to criticize the dogma of my teacher. This kind of learning, not of the subject but of some bastard meta-subject is of all things bound to be the most uncritically accepted learning—analogous only to learning the catechism or the thirty-nine articles in the past. However, this is not the argument which is relevant to my present thesis.

My main argument against the attempt to teach everyone a smattering of everything is the argument from boredom; and this goes right back to our initial definition, if such it can be called, of the imagination. Given that the imagination is that which enables our mind to rest upon a particular object or phenomenon and see in what way it is significant, see, that is, where it leads and what its point is, then the programme of nodding at this, that, and the other subject without stopping on any of them must be an anti-imaginative programme. Granted also that the imagination is infinite—that is, free—that by definition it is not bounded by what is before it, but is limitless in its capacity to go on, then the person who is exercising his imagination cannot at the moment when he is exercising it be bored. For boredom is the awareness of limits; it is the feeling of there being nothing to do. It seems to me that we are, educationally speaking, entering a period in which the combating of boredom may be seen as the main task of education. And I do not mean this frivolously. If there is more leisure, if there are more material goods for everyone, if, nevertheless, some jobs are inevitably bound to be alienating and unsatisfying, we must, as a matter of urgency, teach people to use their free faculty of imagination as their only source of freedom. We all know that a life of boredom is intolerable. We all know the desperate consequences of long-term boredom. We ought, therefore, to give serious thought to the precise question what makes a person believe that there is an infinity of things to do, an infinity of questions to be asked and answers to be sought. It certainly is not the case that being told what someone else's subject is like, though this may interest one for a bit, is the true way to produce either understanding or enthusiasm. It is only by considering a thing deeply and for its own sake, as Coleridge saw, that one can properly begin to enjoy or understand it. But of course there is a further task of education which must be equally insisted on in the curriculum, and that is the educating of the power of communicating what one sees.

For it is obviously no use to oneself or anyone else to be able to think beautiful thoughts, or to understand the most abstruse areas of chemistry or philology or astro-physics, if one is unable to discuss or expound these subjects and share them with others. Moreover, merely communicating information is not enough. One needs, in addition, to cultivate the habit of a genuine *exchange* of ideas. The imagination, if it is to work, needs to be perpetually on its guard against dogmatism. To have a closed mind is to have a mind that is imaginatively dead. Thus, it is a mark of a good education that a pupil should be constantly expected to argue, and to learn from a genuine dialectic, a genuine appreciation of the implications of what *other* people say. It seems quite obvious that the way to achieve this particular goal is not to insist on his learning parrot-fashion a large number of different things, but to let him, if he likes, concentrate on one, provided that within that one discipline he can genuinely learn to communicate and to receive ideas.

So far, everything I have said bears more closely upon education at school than upon education at university. But the same principles apply there as at school. Since the older a pupil is, the less he should be fobbed off with play and pretence, it follows that it is essential to avoid pretence of any kind in the education of university students. If they are following a line of inquiry which someone else has followed, if they are summarizing the critical judgements of other people in the field, then they must be absolutely clear that this is what they are doing. If, on the other hand, there is a chance for them to find something out genuinely for themselves, or make a real contribution to learning or criticism, then again they should understand that this is the case. Far the most important distinction between school and university seems to me to be this, that at university students should feel that they are in a place where real, not play, research goes on. (I know that some people at school have, with the help and encouragement of exceptional teachers, made genuine contributions to learning. But this *is* exceptional, and need not be thought of as a main purpose of school, or, probably, of polytechnics either.)

It seems to me inimical to all that a university stands for to invent special courses of French for physicists, or history of art for chemists, philosophy for linguists, and so on. Of course, if the physicists actually need or want to learn some French, then this is good, and they should be able to do so. But let them learn it definitely as a tool subject, or as something which they are doing on the side. Let it not be thought that they are *really* learning the subject in the way the specialists do. Thus, there seems to me to be a danger in some of the mixed courses offered at present by certain universities. It is not that there is anything wrong with combining different subjects. Notoriously, some combinations work very well indeed. But it is absolutely essential that, if a student is studying two different subjects, he should be taught both by people who are themselves experts. So, even if the student has little time to devote to the subject, he is at least aware of the kind of standards of learning that the subject demands. Too often, if a student is required, let us say, to submit one essay in science, while reading arts subjects, he has no sense of the complexity of the subject, and no means of achieving anything but a weak copy of opinions or facts which he has had put before him at a specially designed set of lectures. For an undergraduate course to be more than a mere extension of school, it is necessary that it should be taught by people who are themselves interested in advancing the subject; a university would be no better than a school if senior members of it did not engage in their subjects directly, that is, if they had no inclination for research. To attend a university in which those who taught had no interest except in teaching, and perhaps in getting their students through their examinations with good grades, would be like choosing pictures for one's house which had been painted with no end in view but the decoration of the walls of one's own room. At all costs, universities should not listen to students who demand that they be taught better—that is, by people who are more interested in teaching than in anything else.

All I have said so far amounts only to this, that quality in education entails learning about something, as they say, 'in depth'. This is not because it is undesirable to know about a great many different things.

On the contrary, it is certainly desirable. It is rather that, if the range of subjects is too great, it is simply impossible for the student's imagination to be fired in such a way that he can go on from what he has been taught to what he wants to think of or do for himself. And the purpose of all education is to seek this freedom to go on.

If the sign of quality in education is the degree to which the imagination of the student is nourished, then the practical question must next inevitably be raised, though certainly not answered. The practical question is this. Is the same kind of education nourishing for everyone, or is it possible that what may be good for one person may, at the same time, be bad for another? May we have to seek for quality by seeking for different kinds of education suitable for different kinds of people? This question is extraordinarily hard to answer, partly because all sorts of emotions immediately attach themselves to the terms used in posing or in answering it. But one should not be too much daunted by these difficulties. The suggestion that there are different types of people who may be suited by learning different types of things has an appallingly Platonic sound, and the question immediately arises as to how you tell *what* type a particular person belongs to. Do we have to have recourse to the mythology of the gold, the silver, and the bronze in order to get over the difficulty? Are we arguing necessarily in favour of an élitist education? It would be greatly to the advantage of educational theory at the present time if the word élite could be banned from the literature (along, perhaps, with certain other words). But, even without using that word, it is hard to avoid all emotive words whatever.

However, it is, perhaps, worth making once more the familiar point that what is objectionable in educational practice is not there existing different kinds of education, but there being some people who are debarred from one kind or another. Provided that, in principle, there is no reason why anyone should not enjoy any of the kinds of education that exist, there is no harm done. Having said this, then, I am at liberty to say that I do not think that everyone *should* have the same educational goals. More specifically, I regard the idea that everyone leaving school should take the same examination as little short of insane, and I cannot believe that anyone who has actually taught children could seriously think otherwise, unless they are blinded by the political desire to prevent differences. It would be a sad thing if fear of being thought right-wing should make it impossible to state the fact that some people are more academic than others—that some are straightforwardly cleverer than others. It is even sadder if the inability to say this should result in a refusal to allow the academic to pursue their bent, and allow their imagination to go forward freely in pursuit of what they can, if they are allowed, see as the distant frontiers of their subjects.

However, I am not suggesting that the academic and clever should specialize at school, and the non-academic should do a number of different subjects. Far from it. If anyone has got to do, let us say, five or six subjects until they leave school, the clever are likely to suffer less harm from it than the stupid, just as, presumably, the worst casualties of the baccalaureate are not the brilliantly able but the mediocre candidates who have to learn everything by heart. My belief is that there are some people whose main difficulty, intellectually, is in communicating with others, whether in speech or writing. I am absolutely certain that these people would find it much easier to learn to communicate, if what they were doing was communicating an enthusiasm, or sharing their own expertise. It would be far better, therefore, and far more effective if the non-academic at school were allowed to specialize fairly early, and to acquire the essential skills of writing and understanding through the medium of a chosen and congenial subject, rather than by means of a remote and abstract subject in which they may find it extremely difficult to get interested. It is surely better to leave school literate, even with a fairly limited range of knowledge, than to leave school barely literate, and never having been really interested in anything. I do not believe that the organizational problem of finding subjects, teaching and examining them, though they would be many, ought to stand in the way of a serious consideration of the merits of specialization for everyone.

To sum up these somewhat rambling remarks: quality in education is, in my view, measured by the degree to which the imagination is exercised. To exercise the imagination is to keep it in practice, by giving it to attend to, in detail, objects which are worthy of attention; and all objects are more worthy of attention in detail than superficially. The imagination, in the sense in which I have been talking about it, is identical with the capacity for free thought; so, if we neglect to educate the imagination, we shall, inevitably, restrict people's freedom. But education has always been intended to be the great instrument of liberation. If we aim at high quality in education, we aim to increase *everyone's* freedom by increasing their capacity to think for themselves. But this common aim does not entail that everyone must have exactly the same education as everyone else. Not everyone will wish, or be able to think freely about the same subjects. We must attempt to avoid dogmatism about which are the best subjects; but, at the same time, we must take great care not to be led by a passion for egalitarianism into adopting the kind of anti-intellectual attitude which would, in the end, be the ruin of our universities. For, if universities are to retain their role as places of learning and research, then it is absolutely essential that pupils at school should be, to some extent, prepared for them, and equipped with some of the tools that they will need to use when they become students. This, in its turn, entails that we must be brave enough to distinguish, while they are still at school, those pupils who will probably proceed to university and those who will not. It is idle to argue that everyone ought to have a chance to go to a university, and therefore that everyone ought to do the same things at school. If we seriously pursue this line, then, not only will numbers of clever children at school be held back or set to teaching their less able fellows, but also the universities themselves will have to take on the task of teaching students what they should have learned at school. This is the surest way to ruin, both intellectual and ultimately financial. There are, therefore, two arguments in favour of specialization at school. One argument is from the enriching nature of specialization in itself; the other argument is from necessity. We cannot afford to postpone specialization until after school. Both arguments, starting as they do from different places, lead to the same conclusion. To refuse to consider this conclusion is, it seems to me, to refuse to consider seriously what the quality of education should properly be.

VI

CURRICULUM INTEGRATION

RICHARD PRING

THERE is no doubt about the widespread interest in integrated studies or the integrated curriculum. Not only are teachers talking about it, they are 'doing' it, and more and more schools are changing from a curriculum divided by subjects to what is called an integrated approach. This has the backing of Plowden and Newsom; junior schools have their integrated day; secondary schools their interdisciplinary inquiry; colleges (especially in the junior–secondary courses) prepare students for integrated or interdisciplinary teaching; the Schools Council publishes examples of good 'integrated approaches'; and there is much talk of the 'seamless coat of learning', the 'unity of knowledge', or 'a single view of the world and of life', all of which, so we are told, can be reflected adequately only in an integrated curriculum. Admittedly any inspection of the different integrated approaches does reveal wide differences of interpretation, but they all have in common a disapproval of *fragmentation* of the curriculum which is said to typify the *traditional* school; that is, they disapprove of subject *barriers*, and the *compartmentalization* or *pigeon-holing* of knowledge with its accompanying specialization and frequent *irrelevance* to real problems. If muddle and confusion are to be avoided, there is need for a more critical appraisal of the many proposals for integrating the curriculum and, as a necessary condition of such an appraisal, a need also for a much closer examination of how the word 'integration' operates in educational discussion. Its meaning is not clear and its value is not self-evident.

I. *The Meaning of 'Integration', the Concern for Unity, and a Statement of the Problem.*

Generally speaking, 'integration' is an approval word. To call a programme integrated carries with it the sign of approval—the indication that what has been done is good. Integration implies unity, and unity is

From *Proceedings of the Philosophy of Education Society of Great Britain*, Supplementary Issue, Vol. 5, No. 2 (July 1971), pp. 170–200. Reprinted, with slight modifications, by permission of the author and Basil Blackwell Ltd.

to be preferred to diversity; the one is good, the many bad. In this respect one may liken 'integration' to concepts such as 'growth' or 'needs'; there is often an imperceptible transition from the descriptive meaning of these words to an evaluative meaning and it is rarely clear which meaning—the descriptive or the evaluative—is taking the lead. One might, for example, start with the general evaluative principle that an integrated programme is good and then search round for ways in which some semblance of integration might be given. Or one might start with the description of any one programme as integrated (and one would point to features of the programme to illustrate what one means) and then, without question, commend that programme simply because it is integrated.

Two things need to be examined therefore in any talk about curriculum integration, and both raise questions which, in their different ways, need some sort of philosophical treatment. Firstly there is need to examine the conditions under which 'integration' might be regarded as a *description* of what is going on—and this requires an inquiry into the different contexts in which the word is used. Secondly, there is need to examine why whatever is so described should be considered valuable or commendable. The first raises philosophical questions about the nature of knowledge; the second, philosophical questions about how one justifies one curriculum decision rather than another. In this paper I shall explore the first question, viz. what is being said about a curriculum that is described as integrated, and suggest more precisely the philosophical problems about the nature of knowledge that such a description necessarily raises. However, before it is possible to enter into these essentially epistemological problems, it is necessary to clear up some of the ambiguity about the application of this word and also to make a purely logical point about its use.

Let me illustrate immediately the ambiguities which surround the word 'integration' in an educational context. Professor P. L. Dressel, in his article 'The Meaning and Significance of Integration', describes how students drew upon both literature and social science to decide how Americans differ from Englishmen, and he describes how, in so doing, the students were engaged in an integrat*ive* experience. Later in referring to inquiries about the desirability of making certain scientific experiments (for example, the explosion of nuclear devices) and in referring to the different sorts of considerations that must enter into such inquiries, he talks about 'new integration of knowledge'. Later still, he speaks of knowledge as an 'organization (or integration) of experience'. He then goes on to distinguish between integrat*ed* experience and integrat*ing* experience. We have, therefore, *experiences* which are integrat*ive*, integrat*ing*, and integrat*ed*. We also have an integration of *knowledge* which is itself an integration of experiences. Clearly there is room for a bit of homework.

The teacher, according to Dressel, should provide not an integration of experience but rather those experiences which will enable the student to achieve 'his own' integration or organization of experience. Thus he says: 'We cannot impose an externally developed scheme of integration but rather must motivate the individual to make his own,' and earlier he says that 'our concern with integration then must be with the integrative process in which man engages as he strives to organize in meaningful fashion knowledge and experiences which at first seem largely unrelated'.[1] It is not clear (and here lies the major ambiguity) how Dressel can at one moment refer to the integrative process as striving to organize experience *and* knowledge while earlier referring to knowledge as an organization of experience. Certainly knowledge is *at least* that and, if so, it is difficult to see how the integrative process can be about the organization of this knowledge with experience—for the concept of knowledge includes that of experience organized or integrated in a particular way. If experiences were not integrated, there would be no knowledge. Knowledge would seem to presuppose some organization of experience in that in the very employment of concepts there is an integration, a structure, an organization of sorts. It would not make sense to talk of experience outside a conceptual system which related one happening to another. To have a concept is to have some principle of unity in what would otherwise be a series of totally unrelated happenings. Again, it is not immediately clear why Dressel should say that the integrative process strives to organize knowledge and experience in a meaningful fashion, as though it would make sense to talk of a person having knowledge that was not meaningful.

However, statements of this kind are made too frequently in the context of an integrated curriculum to be dismissed lightly. For, whatever confusions there may be in the way of formulating this point, behind many proposals for curriculum integration there seems to be concern

---

[1] P. L. Dressel, 'The Meaning and Significance of Integration', in 57th Yearbook of the National Society for the Study of Education, Part III, *The Integration of Educational Experiences* (Chicago: The University of Chicago Press, 1958), pp. 22, 23.

for the development of meaning. This concern for meaning in turn seems to be a request for greater unity, structure, and organization and the relating of otherwise unconnected experiences. Integration is identified with unity, singleness of view, wholeness, synthesis. And it seems to be contrasted with a collection or aggregate of *bits* of knowledge or of *unrelated* experiences.

None the less, it can be seen that the very application of the word 'integration' is ambiguous. And, unless this ambiguity is cleared up, what is being claimed by the 'integrationist' is limited. I say 'limited' because (to repeat) the insistence upon integrating *experiences* would seem, as such, to be asking for nothing more than what is contained in any learning situation in which knowledge is acquired. In any knowledge whatsoever there must be some sort of integration, of seeing otherwise unrelated events as events of a certain kind, of structuring our experiences by means of concepts. And therefore if this is *all* that is being claimed, then proposals for curriculum integration demand no more than that pupils should be helped to understand what they're taught—and that is a meek enough request.

Those, however, who advocate integrated curricula seem to mean more than this and one is forced, in justice, to look a little more closely at the specific cirriculum proposals and the specific arguments that are put forward. Unity, meaningful experience, interrelationship of parts may (taken literally) be precisely what the subject specialist claims to have been achieving in so far as these are characteristics of any claim to knowledge; but the 'integrationist' is insisting that knowledge calls for more integration or greater synthesis or profounder meaningfulness or more explicit interrelationship of parts. He may be putting his case badly but he certainly means something. Above all he means that in schools quite artificial limits to the development of knowledge are introduced. These limits prevent inquiry into areas that in some way are meaningful to the pupil. And these limits might be summed up in the words 'lack of integration'. In sorting out therefore the ambiguous use of 'integration' it becomes clear that the important problems concern the nature of knowledge. What meaning can be given to the unity of knowledge, to the integration of disciplines, to a balanced view of things, to seeing things as a whole? These seem to be the central questions in curriculum integration, and it is an examination of these that is introduced in the following sections.

Before beginning this examination, however, it is necessary to draw attention to one logical feature of 'integration'. The word itself means a unity of parts in which the parts are in some way transformed. A single grouping or adding of distinct objects or parts together would not necessarily create an integrated whole. There would have to be some formal characteristic of the whole from which the parts gained some new identity, this characteristic belonging only to the whole. Two or more types of judgement would be integrated where the conclusion from those judgements said something that was quite distinct from the premises and that could not be analysed out into them without loss of meaning. Thus, in the practical syllogism, proposition p, viz. 'All children ought to be obedient' and proposition q, viz. 'John is a child', entail proposition r, viz. 'John ought to be obedient'. But proposition r entails neither proposition p nor proposition q, for it is possible to have a valid entailment in which the premises are false yet the conclusion true. This is a logical feature of integration, to be contrasted with the sort of entailment where proposition r is entailed by proposition p and q, and in turn entails proposition p and q. For example, there is no integration where propositions p, viz. 'all children should be obedient' and q, viz. 'all children should be silent', entail the proposition r ($p.q.$) viz. 'all children should be obedient and silent', because r, viz. $p.q$, in turn entails proposition p or proposition q.

The foremost philosophical problem therefore in proposals for curriculum integration might be stated as follows. To talk of the *unity* of knowledge or of the organic interrelationships of particular areas of knowledge, or, on the other hand, to criticize the fragmentation of knowledge, or its pigeon-holing (as does Working Paper No. 11),[2] or its compartmentalization (as does the Plowden Report),[3] or of being imprisoned by the disciplines (as does Working Paper No. 22),[4] or, further, to talk (as in Working Paper No. 11) of 'overcoming subject prejudice',[5] is to talk of curriculum integration either with reference to knowledge as a whole or with reference to particular broad fields of experience; and this requires giving some coherent account of how particular claims to knowledge might be integrated in the sense that I have outlined. Such talk needs to show how any one claim to knowledge only makes sense or has meaning within a particular system of propositions

[2] Schools Council Working Paper No. 11, *Society and the Young School Leaver* (London: H.M.S.O., 1967), p. 27.

[3] Central Advisory Council for Education (England), *Children and their Primary Schools* (London: H.M.S.O., 1967), p. 198.

[4] Schools Council Working Paper No. 22, *The Middle Years of Schooling from 8 to 13* (London: H.M.S.O., 1969), p. 15.

[5] Working Paper No. 11, p. 24.

of which it is an integral part. Furthermore it needs to show that, in the cases where the integration crosses the boundaries of the disciplines, any claim to knowledge makes sense or has meaning only within a whole system of propositions that are logically or conceptually related even though they are not of the same formal kind. Thus one would, if one is to make the extreme claim about the ultimate unity of all knowledge, have to show that growth of meaning in any area of knowledge (for example in the sciences) would, even if in only a minute degree, necessarily affect the meaning that had been developed in any other area (for example, in one's conception of oneself and thus in moral knowledge and so on). Any philosophical analysis of curriculum integration would necessarily have to examine the extent to which this, viz. the unity of all knowledge—what I call the 'strong' thesis— might even make sense. That it *needs* to be examined however I would suggest, firstly because some such motive would seem to underlie (however implicitly) some proposals for an integrated curriculum and, secondly, because such a notion has some philosophical, if idealist, pedigree. I shall therefore look at the 'strong' thesis first. Secondly, at the more restricted level of humanities one would need to examine the extent to which the focusing of several disciplines upon, say, the subject of 'man' or upon certain practical problems constituted an integration of knowledge and not just an interdisciplinary inquiry. This latter—the unity of knowledge within broad fields of experience— I call the 'weak' thesis. Thirdly, however, there lurks beneath some claims to integration a theory about the unity of knowledge that does not fit my description of such claims in either the strong or the weak thesis. This I refer to as the 'inquiry' thesis in which the unity of knowledge is located in the particular inquiry of the learner. Fourthly, it would seem that the call for integration is often a claim for a closer examination of the logical interdependence of different disciplines while at the same time recognizing their distinctiveness. This latter claim is probably, in the current curriculum debate, the most interesting one to examine and the one to which philosophical analysis might most fruitfully make a contribution. I shall therefore suggest how such analysis might proceed, though clearly this is no place for carrying out such an analysis in detail.

The remaining part of this paper therefore is divided into four sections—each section making explicit the possible epistemological implications of proposals to integrate the curriculum: the 'strong' thesis, viz. the unity of all knowledge, the 'weak' thesis, viz. the unity of knowledge within certain broad fields of experience, the 'inquiry' thesis, and the interdependence of otherwise distinct disciplines.

II. *The Strong Thesis: the Unity of all Knowledge*

It is constantly stated in Schools Council publications and elsewhere that, through integrated work, the pupils come to a deeper understanding of the unity of knowledge. Various Working Papers and Government reports hint at what this unity might consist in. Working Paper No. 2 says that its 'view of the curriculum ... is therefore holistic.... It is suggested that it should possess *organic unity....* In all cases, however, the existence of an organizing principle for the curriculum as a whole is assumed.'[6]

In current appeals for a curriculum that is a 'whole' or is unitary or is holistic there seem to be different strands of thinking. On the one hand, there is the belief that, since the world or the knower is all one, so ideally is knowledge of that world or knowledge emanating from that 'knower'. Thus a recent report of a polytechnic states, apropos of its own programme of integrated studies, that 'and advantage of contemporary and environmental studies is that knowledge emerges as a whole. There is no conscious division into compartments since the environment is already a synthesis of the branches of knowledge.' Those who attempt to theorize about the curriculum might put this point as follows. '... because a person is essentially an organized totality and not just a collection of separate parts, the curriculum ought to have a corresponding organic quality ... the plan of study can best contribute to the person's growth if it is governed by the goal of wholeness for the human being'.[7] Wheeler talks of seeing the totality of man's knowledge as a unified system.[8]

On the other hand this unity is sometimes seen as balance between parts rather than a uniform system. Working Paper No. 11 says that 'it is sensible to keep a reasonable balance between the various branches of human knowledge'.[9] The Crowther report says of the sixth-former that 'as he sees how the facts he has been handling in his own subject *knit* together, he begins to wonder how his subject *fits into* the *whole*

---

[6] Schools Council Working Paper No. 2, *Raising the School Leaving Age* (London: H.M.S.O., 1965), pp. 52–3.

[7] P. H. Phenix, *Realms of Meaning* (New York: McGraw-Hill Book Co., 1964), p. 4.

[8] D. K. Wheeler, *Curriculum Process* (London: Athlone Press, 1967), ch. 2.

[9] Working Paper No. 11, p. 41.

field of knowledge. He reaches out for himself towards a wider synthesis.'[10] Again the report says that 'it is basic to our thinking that what is done in majority time should form a coherent whole, one subject continuously reinforcing another, so that teaching and learning may be enriched by cross-reference'.[11] The Newsom report is similarly concerned with how subjects 'fit in' with the whole field of knowledge. It says 'the separate lessons and subjects are single pieces of a *mosaic*; and what matters most is not the numbers and colours of the separate pieces, but what pattern they make when put together'.[12] The report is implicitly critical of the curriculum in which there is no 'total pattern', just as Crowther was critical of the curriculum without 'balance between parts'. However, it is difficult to see what sort of judgement it is that says which is a balanced or an unbalanced curriculum, or what constitutes a total pattern, as opposed to a collection of distinct parts. 'Coherence', 'synthesis', 'balance', 'pattern', raise epistemological questions about the unity of knowledge.

The appeal, however, to the essential unity of knowledge is not peculiar to the Schools Council or to American curriculum theorists. Unity in diversity has been a constant theme of educationists as well as of philosophers, and where it has been more than a slogan there would seem to be close links between the educational appeal for unity and particular philosophical theories.

The opening page of *The Education of Man* refers to: 'the all-controlling law [which] is necessarily based on an all-pervading energetic, living self-conscious, and hence eternal unity', and suggests therefore that 'a quietly observant human mind, a thoughtful, clear human intellect, has never failed, and will never fail to recognize this unity'.[13] Again, Bertrand Russell, in his essay on Dewey's logic,[14] accuses him of adopting what he calls a holistic view of knowledge. By this Russell would seem to mean an analysis of knowledge whereby all inquiry is ultimately a disguised attempt to analyse the entire universe, thereby implying the monistic idealism of F. H. Bradley in the sense that every judgement qualifies reality as a whole. Indeed in the frequent recom-

---

[10] Central Advisory Council for Education (England), *15 to 18* (London: H.M.S.O., 1959), p. 263.

[11] Op. cit., p. 273.

[12] Central Advisory Council for Education (England), *Half our Future*, (London: H.M.S.O., 1963), p. 29.

[13] F. Froebel, *The Education of Man* (London: Edward Arnold, 1902), p. i.

[14] B. Russell, 'Dewey's New Logic', in P. Schilpp (ed.), *The Philosophy of John Dewey* (Evanston, Ill., Northwestern University Press, 1939).

mendations to integrate the curriculum there might frequently be detected the emotional attachment to unity for unity's sake, and, by implication, the belief in some overriding unity of knowledge which would make such an attachment reasonable. Dewey acknowledges his debt to Hegel's thought in that it

supplied a demand for unification that was doubtless an intense emotional craving, and yet was a hunger that only an intellectualized subject matter could satisfy.... Hegel's synthesis of subject and object, matter and spirit, the divine and the human, was, however, no mere intellectual formula; it operated as an immense release, a liberation. Hegel's treatment of human culture, of institutions and the arts, involved the same dissolution of hard-and-fast dividing walls, and had a special attraction for me.[15]

One might object here that no description of a person's state of mind and no tracing of historical connection adds up to a philosophical argument. Dewey's 'intense emotional cravings', and his indebtedness to Hegel do not help in the logical analysis of what it means to know or to understand, nor do they provide valid justifications of this search for unity. None the less it is worth noting that there frequently lies beneath this search for integration an emotional attachment to unity which might arise from, or might even beget, the belief that knowledge is essentially one and undivided, and that it is this sense of unity which must be reflected in the curriculum of our schools. There is a tradition in philosophy which argues for the essential unity of knowledge and which sees the apparent diversity of knowledge, the independence of particular truths, to be an illusion; and at crucial places this idealism impinges upon educational thinking. Although it might be an ambitious and improbable task to attempt to establish links between current educational thinking and such philosophical beliefs, it would none the less be reasonable to say that those who hanker after this ultimate unity of knowledge or who (looking at the other side of the coin) see the diversity of knowledge—its manifestation in distinct forms or disciplines—as artificial or compartmentalized or fragmented might ultimately be forced into those philosophical questions raised by the idealists. And they might, if pressed far enough, be required to meet the criticisms directed against the idealist position. The point, put simply, is that you cannot tinker with the curriculum in so far as this is concerned

---

[15] J. Dewey, 'From Absolutism to Experimentalism', *Contemporary American Philosophy*, Vol. 2 (1930), p. 19.

with the development of knowledge or understanding without at the same time raising questions of central philosophical importance.

As a corollary of the 'strong' thesis one would, in any full treatment of curriculum integration, need to examine those claims for a unity to knowledge arising from the reduction of one 'form' of knowledge to another. Such a unity would be rooted in the belief that one particular way of conceiving things has priority and that other forms of thought can in principle be translated into this without loss of meaning. For example it might be argued (as it was by Comte) that all knowledge is characterized by its 'positivism' and is, in that sense, homogeneous. Within, too, the new 'positivist' ordering of knowledge it might be argued (as it was by Carnap) that priority could and should be given to a more basic 'physicalist' language. I can, however, in a brief paper refer only in passing to such a suggested basis for the integration of knowledge. It raises many issues that cannot be adequately dealt with here, and although it has very obvious implications for the organization of the curriculum it is in fact a philosophical position of historical interest that has very little, if any, impact on current educational thinking.

III. *The Weak Thesis: Broad Fields of Experience*

At the same time there emerges a less ambitious claim for integration in which a much more limited unity is sought. The Newsom report groups subjects together in 'three broad fields of experience', viz. practical subjects, the humanities, and maths and sciences.[16] It is chiefly within each 'broad field' that subjects will *support* one another, that similar situations will be approached from different angles, and that there will be cross-referencing. What precisely is meant, however, by 'field of experience' is not clear. On what grounds are maths and science linked together as a 'field of experience' and as such distinguished from the humanities? In what sense can history, geography, religious studies, and literature be regarded as a field of experience? Where would psychology go—in the sciences or in the humanities?

That there is need for much closer analysis of what constitutes a 'broad field of experience' is indicated by the quite different divisions of curriculum proposed by others within which integration is supposed to operate. For instance Denis Lawton talks of 'cores', rather than fields of experience, and suggests that there should be five rather than three—viz. maths, the sciences, humanities, expressive arts (which is to

[16] *Half our Future*, p. 126 and the following chapters.

include P.E.), and moral education.[17] Again it is not clear, nor is it stated, what the logical determinant of a 'core' is. Why, for example, is literature centred in the humanities rather than in the expressive arts? What concept of 'humanities' is at work here in that it is distinguished from moral education?

Clearly one cannot expect from a government report the sort of analysis of experience or of its division into 'broad fields' that would satisfy the critical appraisal of the philosopher. But the lack of clarity here is important because of the way in which the Newsom report has affected subsequent developments in what is being recommended and put into practice. 'Humanities' are taken to form a unity in a sense that the curriculum, as a whole, does not. But wherein lies this unity? In answer to this it is suggested that the unity lies not so much in the method of procedure or in the concepts employed or in mode of verification, but rather in the object with which different sorts of knowledge are most directly concerned, viz. man (in contrast with the sciences which would be concerned chiefly with inanimate objects or with man only in so far as he can be subject to scientific investigation). If this is the basis of the division it would in fact be hard to sustain. When, for example, Schools Council Working Paper No. 2 suggests that *interest in people* should be used as 'the central theme and motive for new curricula, pervading and *relating* all the separate courses, and *having its influence upon organization and methods*',[18] or when Working Paper No. 22 suggests that *organizing* themes should be such areas of study as 'man finds his feet', 'man and rivers', 'man the creator',[19] or when Working Paper No. 11, in giving basic considerations for a worth-while curriculum, says that a curriculum about man himself 'may mean less emphasis on the *barriers* (sic) between traditional subjects and more upon their interrelationship',[20] or when (as again in Working Paper No. 22) we are told that '"man and his environment" represents an integration of disciplines' and that one reason for integrating in this way would be that 'the environment around us is integrated and a child of this age does not classify what he observes on the basis of traditional classroom subjects',[21] then we are bound to ask in what way

[17] D. Lawton, 'The Idea of an Integrated Curriculum', *University of London Institute of Education Bulletin* (Autumn, 1969).
[18] Working Paper No. 2, p. 10 (my italics).
[19] Working Paper No. 22, pp. 50, 51 (my italics).
[20] Working Paper No. 11, p. 1 (my italics).
[21] Working Paper No. 22, p. 45.

does this theme or this area of study *itself* give a basis for structuring or organizing knowledge other than in the worked out disciplines of thought. How does a child classify what he observes if not within the conceptual scheme that owes its formal structure to the basic and differentiated forms of knowledge? In centring one's inquiry or study around man, how would one be asking questions other than those which depend for their form upon a particular conceptual framework and method of inquiry which we call a discipline? We need to ask in what way a theme or an idea or a subject of study, be it man or be it anything, can give structure to inquiry rather than simply a selective principle by which relevant material is chosen from the different disciplines of thought. It may seem in other words that, in studying man and his environment, one would be asking a range of questions that are formally of a different kind; and it may seem that these formally different kinds of question make sense only within an organization of thought which may in some cases be about man under some particular aspect but which are characterized by their own peculiar conceptual structure and mode of inquiry.

This is an important point that needs to be stressed, for it is a common practice of the Schools Council Working Papers to think of integration within the areas of the so-called humanities alone. Working Paper No. 11, for example, in a section entitled 'Raising the School Leaving Age—relevance and experience', says that 'as courses of the kind discussed in this report are developed there will be more work which crosses the frontier between individual subjects, such as English, Geography, History and R.E.'.[22] And the unity or synthesis or integration that is sought within the humanities is distinguished not so much by the form of judgement as by the subject of study—viz. man. The point is however that it is not clear how an idea, whether it be of 'man' or anything else, can give structure to the curriculum or to any part of it— even to an inquiry. None the less that it can give structure seems to be an underlying assumption. According to Working Paper No. 2 the curriculum 'should possess *organic* unity, and the *organizing principle* most likely to provide a sound basis for development is the study of Man and of human society, needs and purposes'.[23]

On the other hand we are told in Working Paper No. 11, with reference to 'an integrated syllabus in the humanities', that the 'ultimate goal is ... not to create a new subject of doubtful parentage, but to lay

---

[22] Working Paper No. 11, p. 37.
[23] Working Paper No. 2, p. 12 (my italics).

all the old subjects, and many of the newer disciplines, under tribute to answer real questions in which the pupils can be interested'.[24] This would not be integrated in the sense referred to and outlined above. There is, on the contrary, an acceptance of the distinct forms of knowledge and a denial that what is here being *called* integration is anything other than an application of this knowledge, in its diverse forms, to a particular range of questions. And the focusing of one's knowledge on a particular set of questions does not involve necessarily a new integration of that knowledge. There is not necessarily any new structure to that knowledge arising out of one's concern for a particular problem or question or theme. Or at least, if there is such a structure, then it would have to be demonstrated. It would have to be shown how the idea or the problem or the subject of study provided a logical, as opposed to a purely contingent, unity to different disciplines. It would have to be shown how the historical judgements one makes, for example, or how the religious concepts one employs are in some sense changed or modified in the unified study of man. If this cannot be shown, then it would seem that what we have is not an integrated but rather an *interdisciplinary* approach to a problem or an area of interest—and this distinction, viz. that between integrative and interdisciplinary, although usually blurred, is crucial because, if true, it saves us from many knotty philosophical problems.

Thus one must distinguish between, on the one hand, claims for an integration of knowledge in so far as this implies that knowledge has some sort of unity such that the *meaning* of any particular claim to knowledge can be grasped only within some totality of propositions (in so far, in other words, as this implies there to be a conceptual unity to our thinking which cannot be analysed out into particular conceptual structures without loss of meaning) and, on the other hand, the proposals for interdisciplinary treatment of some problems or topic which necessarily transcends the different disciplines. The two descriptions of the curriculum—integrated and interdisciplinary—are on different logical levels. That is, 'integration' raises certain questions in epistemology to which 'interdisciplinary' remains indifferent. The very notion of 'integration' incorporates the idea of unity between forms of knowledge and their respective disciplines. 'Interdisciplinary' on the other hand simply refers to the use of more than one discipline in pursuing a particular inquiry. It does not in fact raise questions about unity of knowledge, although further analysis of the logical form of inter-

[24] Working Paper No. 11, p. 40.

disciplinary thinking might very well show that such questions cannot be avoided.

An example of interdisciplinary inquiry is that of sex education, which raises questions straddling many disciplines. The biology teacher might give certain facts, but the English Literature teacher too has much to contribute. He might put forward a very good claim for educating the emotions and provide literary gems from D. H. Lawrence or, for that matter, from Jane Austen. And then, of course, the social studies teacher might wish to open up the whole subject from the perspective of different cultures or indeed of different social classes. Here we have an example of interdisciplinary approach to a series of practical questions. It is a further and distinct question to ask whether the treatment of these questions in an interdisciplinary way constitutes an integration of knowledge.

The conceptual distinction however between 'integration' and 'interdisciplinary' is frequently not made, and it would seem that it is integrated rather than interdisciplinary studies that are being ascribed to the humanities. It would seem that the authors of the Working Papers would, generally speaking, agree with Bernstein that '... when the basis of the curriculum is an idea which is supra-subject, and which governs the relationship between subjects, a number of consequences may follow. The subject is no longer dominant, but *subordinate to the idea* which governs a particular form of integration.'[25] The question to be asked is: in what sense can the idea which is supra-subject—the theme, the topic to be explored—*govern* a form of integration? Is not Bernstein here attempting (in the words of Working Paper No. 11) to create a new subject of doubtful parentage? As I have argued, if it is a new subject that is being created, then there would be need for closer analysis of the way in which the idea does govern a form of integration. This is of considerable practical importance for it is not self-evident what structure to inquiry an *idea* can give. The possibility of some such structure would seem to be presupposed by those schools and colleges of education that provide their students simply with a theme or a concept to explore as a basis for inquiry and collaborative effort. Even where direction to the inquiry is given by the teacher it is presupposed that the idea or concept itself gives some logical guidance. Working Paper No. 11 gives one or two examples of this—'shops and shopping', 'the family', and so on. The second report of the Goldsmiths Curriculum Laboratory talks of an idea 'fanning out' into a variety of problems,

[25] Bernstein, B., 'Open School, Open Society?', *New Society* (14 Sept. 1967).

etc.[26] It is thought that an idea or a concept could give *structure* to the curriculum. Given, however, only 'an idea', one would not know how to proceed. Yet it is precisely this sort of thing which a child is expected to do when told to explore 'transport' or 'communication'. But what particular questions are being asked about transport or communication? Only when these are clear does the instruction to explore or to make an inquiry into 'transport' or 'communication' become intelligible.

None the less, the 'integrationist' might still wish to argue that within certain broad areas—within the humanities, say—there is a conceptual unity which does transcend the boundaries of the disciplines. He might wish to argue that, since this is the case, any humanistic studies parcelled up into relevant disciplines would necessarily be impoverished by such divided treatment, for such would not respect the essential unity in our conceptualizing of man or of anything else and would not allow the free play of ideas between different areas of thought. In this connection it might be argued, as it was in the preface to recent proposals for integrated studies in a college of education, that 'many of today's spectacular advances in knowledge have come through the application of, for example, biological concepts to architecture and engineering' and that we need to incorporate into the curriculum the implications of this constant interplay of ideas and key concepts through all our understanding.

In pursuing this it might be argued, by those who see a more unified structure in knowledge, that the broad field of experience comprising science and mathematics is framed by such categorial concepts as measurability, cause and effect, substance; whereas the humanities are framed by such categories as intentionality and action. In other words the sciences would consider objects as material things that are intelligible simply within a conceptual scheme that is a refinement of the basic categories of substance, and of cause and effect, whereas the humanities would be interested in objects that are intelligible within a conceptual scheme of intentional activity. Man, as physical object that can be tinkered with, conditioned, treated, is the province of science.

[26] Report of Pilot Course No. 2, *The Raising of the School Leaving Age* (University of London Goldsmiths College Curriculum Laboratory, 1968), p. 15. The Curriculum Laboratory developed the notion of interdisciplinary inquiry. Mrs. Charity James, the director of the laboratory, would probably agree with the distinction made between 'interdisciplinary' and 'integrated'. See, in this connection, her book *Young Lives at Stake* (London: Collins, 1968), p. 138.

Man, as a purposeful being with conscious life and a will of his own, is the province of the humanities. This line of argument contains many difficulties, but it seems to me that it is along these lines that one must argue if one is to make the sort of curriculum divisions that Newsom and others recommend and if one is to establish the basis for a unified or integrated view of things within certain broad areas. In the remaining part of this section I shall show how one might argue for there being a more integrated conceptualizing of our experiences than is recognized by the subject-based curriculum.

There is a sense in which how we individuate objects, classify, and evaluate them is not given, as it were, but is one of the innumerable ways in which we might conceive the world. The distinctions that we come to make and the objects that we pick out in the light of those distinctions, the importance that we attach to them, will reflect not only an inherited conception of things embodied in a particular language but also will respond to the very practical needs of man in a particular set of circumstances. Above all there will evolve over a period of time a more refined philosophy of mind that will affect not only how one sees the world, but how one sees oneself acting within the world. The concepts, indeed the whole framework within which one views oneself and hence other objects and people interacting with oneself, are constantly open to revision in so far as they structure the feelings, events, needs, interests, that a man has at any one time. If one were to take, for example, the typical concepts for explaining human action—fear, ambition, pride, jealousy, envy, and so on—they would clearly correlate with emotion words. They would correspond closely with any list of virtues by reference to which one might evaluate the sort of person that someone is. There is a conceptual connection here between different forms of discourse—those in which one describes a person's state of mind, explains why he acts, approves of the sort of person he is—which may be an example of what could be meant by an integrated conceptual framework within, say, the humanities. This suggests that there is an underlying assumption in proposals for integration of knowledge within the humanities, viz. that there is a conceptual framework cutting across the traditional divisions between subjects, such that conclusions to problems raised within the humanities will arise from premises of quite different sorts; different considerations will be brought to bear upon the search for solutions. And the assumption would prima facie seem to be borne out by the nature of practical discourse. One might for instance argue that the conclusion of a practical syllogism, as with the conclusions of the syllogisms referred to earlier, would be a *synthesis* of premises that are different in form in that it is entailed by the premises but does not in turn entail either one of the premises.

The assumptions behind the claims for integration and behind the suspicion of subject boundaries would seem to arise from the close interrelationship of conceptual structures that defy precise analysis into distinct forms of knowledge, and the suspicion is greater in those areas of thought where the forms of knowledge may be more vulnerable if worked out in detail. In defining a form of knowledge one must distinguish between on the one hand those concepts which are categorial in the sense that they are the necessary schematic conditions for any thought at all and which define, as it were, the mode by which propositions of that sort might be verified, and on the other, those concepts which represent a particular, though dispensable, way of structuring experience. This distinction is crucial both for working out in detail the forms of knowledge and for locating the levels at which talk of curriculum integration makes sense. This can be illustrated within the area of science. Categorial concepts such as substance, cause and effect, motion, space, which provide the necessary framework for empirical judgements, must be distinguished from substantial concepts such as neutrons, electrons, etc., which are a particular though 'basic' structuring of our experience, but which are not logically necessary for the making of empirical judgements. In fact any one non-categorical structuring of experience is dispensable in the sense that it is always possible that at a very fundamental level there might be a total revision of our way of conceiving things.

One might argue that in the area of human action categorial concepts such as 'action' or 'intentionality' must be distinguished from the particular range of concepts through which one sees oneself and others at any one time. For example, it is inconceivable that in any culture man should not have seen himself as an agent in bringing about some state of affairs whether it be a simple matter of hunting animals, saying prayers, cooking meals, or passing on information. But the range of concepts through which this agency is seen and made effective will not remain static. It could be expressed in rather magical terms against a superstitious understanding of the world; or it could be in terms of role fulfilment; and so on. Again, in moral discourse, one must distinguish between such categorial concepts as 'ought' and the particular moral appraisal words such as 'humble' (a quality recognized by Christian ethics but not by Homer's heroes), theft (an evaluation that would be odd among those who held all things in common), magnificence (a moral quality picked out by Aristotle, but not part of our moral repertoire), and so on. It is central to the whole question of curriculum integration, especially in the area of what is commonly called the humanities, to recognize this distinction between categorial and substantive concepts, and to inquire further into the close interrelationship of concepts both within and across the broad fields established on the categorial level. I have illustrated what I mean here from the logical connection between (1) a range of mental concepts describing emotions and (2) the sort of explanations one would give of human action and (3) the way in which one approves of those actions. It would be worth pursuing this sort of analysis much further. It would be interesting, for example, to see how concepts which find their 'natural home' in a particular form of discourse, characterized by a particular range of categorial concepts, none the less depend for their meaning partly upon a form of discourse characterized by a quite different set of categorial concepts. 'Theft' or 'stealing', for example, is, within our society, a moral term and as such finds its natural home within a form of discourse in which one answers such questions as 'What ought I to do?' or 'What is to be approved of?' But clearly its meaning lies partly in a form of discourse in which the concept of property might be distinguished and hence in which distinctions might be made in terms of legal rights and duties. Or again, the concept of 'school' might require for its intelligibility an empirical schema in which it is possible to distinguish material objects. At the same time, its meaning cannot be grasped solely within the area of empirics but also requires a type of discourse, certainly not empirical, that makes *institutional* life intelligible.

Programmes for curriculum integration would seem to make assumptions about the complexity of our conceptual structuring of experience such that, within the limits set by logically necessary categorial concepts, it is doubtful that substantive concepts can be said necessarily to have a natural home within any one form of discourse or discipline, but rather are affected or developed by the distinctions or conceptual modifications made right through one's language. But to argue for this thesis or to show its untenability would require analysis which cannot be undertaken here. The point of this paper is to suggest what integration could possibly mean, what sorts of epistemological questions are being raised, and where therefore the philosophical homework needs to be done. And what I have said so far is that there is in this connection a 'strong' and a 'weak' thesis. The 'strong' thesis argues for the ultimate unity of all knowledge. The 'weak' thesis argues for integration within broad fields of experience. The line that I have adopted is that the unity which is built in, as it were, to the very concept of knowledge is manifest in the different disciplines and forms wherein knowledge is developed, and that this unity must find its logical basis ultimately in the 'categorial' structure that underpins, or provides the essential conditions for, any thinking whatsoever. A detailed analysis of these might provide a basis for a variety of ways in which we could in fact come to integrate our experience and it might also provide a basis for interconnections between areas of study which have developed independently of each other.

IV. *The Problem-solving Method, or Inquiry, as a Basis for Integration*

Curriculum integration would seem therefore to be a view about the nature of knowledge—that in some way knowledge either is all one or is unified within certain broad fields of experience—and that as such it must be distinguished from interdisciplinary inquiry. This would seem to complete the picture from the perspective provided by theory of knowledge. Not all talk of curriculum integration, of course, necessarily raises these questions. Often it may be a very loose way of talking about the integrated day, or interdisciplinary inquiry, or an integrating link provided by the interests of the child, or his needs, or the needs of society. Such talk would of course raise a host of philosophical problems about needs and interests—how one is to identify them and why they should be the basis of the curriculum—but as such they would not raise the epistemological problem about the nature and integration of knowledge.

It may be, however, that behind the claims for interdisciplinary inquiry, behind the concern for the interests and needs of the child, there is a theory of knowledge which gives further grounds for proposing an integrated curriculum in an epistemologically important sense. Mrs. Charity James says that interdisciplinary inquiry is not primarily a method but is rather the acceptance of the natural human process of exploration; that it has a heuristic basis—it serves to train children to find out for themselves.[27] It is interesting in this connection to see how two schools, both claiming to offer integrated studies, might have quite

[27] Charity James in *Ideas*, No. 3 (University of London Goldsmiths College Curriculum Laboratory, 1967), pp. 2 ff.

different conceptions of what exploration could mean.[28] In accordance with the analysis in the previous section, School A would work out beforehand what the different subjects might contribute to the understanding of a particular theme. It is assumed that 'to understand a theme' is to have it explored from these different angles in a preordained way and to see the interconnection of these different contributions which the teachers have marked out. In other words, the understanding of a theme requires an integration of the contributions from different disciplines; this integration is planned beforehand by the teachers and, as such, is 'handed on'. School B, however, would argue that School A is simply creating another subject of 'doubtful parentage', and that the integration to be sought must be based upon the child's own inquiry. Truth cannot be prepackaged in an integrated form and, as such, handed on to the pupil. The pupil must integrate his own experiences; he does this through his own inquiry; and the teacher's job is 'to spark him off' and to be an adviser, a collaborator, but certainly not an instructor. In the case of School B, the child's own individual inquiry is a focal point of curriculum organization. Because the inquiry will not respect the boundaries of subjects, these boundaries must disappear. Rather will the timetable be unstructured, whole periods of time blocked for the inquiry, and open arrangements made so that the child might benefit from the 'experts' and the facilities in different parts of the building. The argument in this section is that the stress given by School B to the inquiry and problem-solving approach can be seen to spring from a different theory of knowledge; it is not just a simple appeal for interdisciplinary inquiry.

In mapping out the different sorts of knowledge Aristotle saw the distinction between the theoretical and the practical to be fundamental.[29] Through the theoretical sciences one came to know the world as it really is—one got at the essences of things—and particular statements would be either true or false in so far as they were correct or incorrect ac-

[28] The caricatures represented by Schools A and B are based on experience, and are intended to represent distinct approaches to 'Exploration' or 'Inquiry' which are to be found in schools.

[29] See Aristotle, *Metaphysics* (Everyman Library, London: Dent and Sons Ltd., 1956), *passim*, but especially A. 1, 2 (pp. 51–6), E. 1 (pp. 153–6), a. 1 (pp. 361–2), and *Politics* (Penguin Books, Harmondsworth: 1962), Books VII and VIII, *passim*, where Aristotle distinguishes between speculative and practical reason, and suggests that the education of the rulers is to be directed at the development of speculative reason which should ultimately be pursued for its own sake.

counts of that reality. Systematic accounts of reality would be handed on to those who wished to learn and, if these students did in fact learn them, they would be in possession of a body of knowledge, i.e. of a set of statements that were either true or false irrespective of whether they provided answers to practical problems. There was a sense in which it was both meaningful and valuable to be in possession of the truth, even if that truth had no practical use. It would be possible to value the truth in itself irrespective of its practical use, and to believe in the possibility of understanding even where the person (who is to understand) sees no problem to which this 'truth' is related. This view would seem to have its roots in Aristotle and to be embodied in so much of our educational thinking.

Dewey, however, had a different theory of knowledge and much current criticism of the more traditional, academic curriculum would seem to be based upon implicit agreement with Dewey's criticism of Aristotelian epistemology and indeed to stem historically from his writings. Dewey denied the distinction between the theoretical and the practical.[30] The theoretical was but an offshoot of the practical; knowledge arose primarily from past problematic situations and was directed towards the settlement of problems. A proposition was true in so far as it was relevant or helpful to the settlement of problems. The value of knowledge therefore lay not in itself or for its own sake but in the degree to which it served the purpose of inquiry. I am however concerned here not so much with the value of knowledge as with what it *means*, and (according to Dewey) the service knowledge provided towards the pursuit of inquiry was a determinant not just of its value but also of its meaning. Dewey's position would seem to be this:[31]

(i) One is in a problematic situation—i.e. one sees things, while pursuing some action, in such a way that one is disturbed, and the source of this disturbance lies in not knowing what means will lead to a particular goal.

[30] In this, as in other criticisms of previous philosophy, Dewey argues that error lies in a dualistic way of conceiving things, viz. of knower *and* that which is known, of theory *and* practice, of body *and* mind, of authority *and* freedom. Dewey's analysis of social problems in general and of educational problems in particular was an application of his theory of experience, a central feature of which is an attempt to root out dualisms of any kind.

[31] The position outlined here is my summary of the theory of inquiry to be found in J. Dewey, *Logic: the Theory of Enquiry* (New York: Holt and Co., 1938).

(ii) In settling this uncertainty, so that one may proceed, one sets up an inquiry, this inquiry being aimed at achieving equilibrium or satisfaction where previously one was disturbed.

(iii) Knowledge lies therefore in seeing things in such a way that the source of disturbance (the obstacle to action, the failure to see what means will achieve a desired end) is removed. Such a way of seeing things (such knowledge) is called 'warranted assertion', i.e. it has been found so far, and in practice, to meet the practical needs for which it was established in the first place.

It can be seen that there is a quite different notion of truth at work here, and one which, if accepted, would provide a different basis upon which one might describe what is meant by curriculum integration. For if knowledge is an assertion which is warranted by virtue of its practical value in answer to a practical problem, then the description of the problem must enter into the very meaning of any claim to knowledge, and moreover the knowledge itself is relative to its value in pursuing some course of action. Problems are more than the focus of interdisciplinary inquiry; they must provide a very real integrating link in the account one must give of knowledge—for such an account would only make sense in the context of certain problems. There is no body of truths as such; there are only assertions which are warranted in so far as they are instrumental to the satisfactory achievement of some desired end.

What Dewey says in places *would seem* to point to a purely psychological account of truth and falsity—viz. a statement is true if it leads to a state of equilibrium. 'Equilibrium' however must not be understood in purely psychological terms. The *warrant* of the assertion lies not so much in a state of feeling as in the possibilities opened up intellectually or imaginatively to proceed towards some desired end. None the less no one position is either true or false as such—it is true in so far as it continues in conjunction with other propositions to be instrumental towards some end, and it is always possible that it might fail to be of this instrumental value. There are degrees of truth therefore and Dewey quotes C. S. Peirce in saying that 'the opinion which is fated to be ultimately agreed to by all who investigate is what we mean by the truth, and the object represented by this opinion is the real'.[32] Truth therefore is relative to its usefulness in inquiry, and (I suppose in order to avoid 'disturbance') this inquiry must include the contribution from quite different investigators. One never arrives at *the truth* if this

[32] J. Dewey, op. cit., p. 345.

is to be understood in some absolute sense, and thus there is no such thing as *the truth* in an absolute sense—rather is it what is agreed upon at any one moment in the pursuit of some inquiry, and will continue as the truth so long as it furthers the purpose of that inquiry. In so far as inquiry is conducted openly by several people together truth will preserve its essential public character.

There is, however, behind the notion of truth a pragmatic theory of meaning. Any proposition or part of a proposition needs to be interpreted by the person who is listening. His interpretation will take place within his own framework of symbols which in turn will need to be interpreted by others. Everything that we say is open to interpretation, for that is what it *means* to use symbols. In a sense, therefore, no two people inhabit the same world of meaning. The language that each uses will need to be interpreted, and the interpretation will be within the context and the associations and experience of another person. The child lives in his own world of meaning within which he accommodates the 'cues' given by the teacher. There will be adjustment—development, if you like—but it is logically impossible for anything to transcend the essentially personal nature of any one's understanding of a situation. In inquiry the constant accommodation to, and assimilation of, one's social as well as one's natural environment takes place as new experiences need to be integrated into the individual's conceptual scheme. Only in this way is there respect for the child's point of view, for the proper process of learning (viz. the accommodation to, and the assimilation of, new experiences), and for real understanding (viz. the interpretation of new experiences within the existing system of symbols).

A full statement and a critique of this position is important for any analysis of certain proposals for an integrated curriculum. In the context of proposals for inquiry or problem-based curricula statements about the need to make the curriculum more *meaningful* and more *relevant* to the pupil do present a puzzle. There often seems in such proposals more than just an interest in motivation; rather they seem to have implications for what it means to understand something. Hence, such statements are followed by attempts to construct the curriculum around the practical interests and problems of the pupils, because only then would it have meaning, rather than be a collection of inert knowledge that had meaning for different people at different times in answer to different problems. But quite clearly this is no place for such a critique. I have tried to show that a certain conception of curriculum integration, which can be distinguished from others by very clear features such as school organization and teaching method (illustrated in my caricature of School B), has certain underlying assumptions about the nature of meaning and knowledge. And the consequence of this is that any critique of this view of the curriculum would first have to make much more explicit what such a theory of meaning and truth is. My point here is simple. Talk of the problem-solving method or the method of inquiry as the organizing link in knowledge introduces an instrumentalist view of knowledge. If one holds that view then one must face the consequences. It imports a notion of truth quite foreign to our normal usage and such a notion incorporates logical difficulties that would have to be met at a philosophical level.

V. Interrelationship of Disciplines

In Schools Council Working Paper No. 12 Professor Hirst says, apropos of the autonomous forms of knowledge, that we must hang on to two things, viz.

there are distinct schemes; the concepts of maths, say, are not of the same logical kind as those of morals or even of science. Yet the sciences use mathematical concepts, moral judgements can depend on scientific evidence, and so on. We must, therefore, also hang on to the complex connections between the different domains.[33]

The view one has of curriculum integration depends upon the meaning one is to write into such a phrase as 'hang on to the complex connections between the different domains'. If one is to see these complex connections to be *conceptual* such that over a wide range of concepts it is not possible to say that they have 'a natural home' in any one discipline, then what is meant by integrative and by 'complex connections' will be the sort of thing referred to in my treatment of the 'weak' thesis, and the philosophical justification for this position will be along the lines that I suggested there. But if one holds the view that there is no *conceptual* relationship between autonomous forms of knowledge and that concepts have a 'natural home' within a particular form, then there is need to examine how judgements in quite distinct forms of knowledge do relate to one another—how, for example, mathematical concepts are employed in science, how religious concepts are employed by morals, how empirical considerations enter into aesthetics.

It is difficult to see how such interconnections can be established without admitting a much more complex conceptual interconnection than

[33] Working Paper No. 12, p. 80.

the holders of this view would allow. None the less, it is true that such advocates of integration are claiming precisely this, and it is important therefore to examine what form in general terms the analysis of the connections must take. I say 'in general terms' because the detailed analysis of the connections can only be done by those who are expert within the relevant disciplines.

It would seem that the general form in which propositions of distinct logical types might interrelate are as follows:

(i) propositions of type 'A' being *constitutive* of propositions of type 'B';

(ii) proposition of type 'A' being *instrumental to* our grasping of propositions of type 'B', but not being constitutive of them;

(iii) propositions of type 'A' being *evidence for* proposition of type 'B';

(iv) propositions of type 'A' being *necessary conditions* of propositions of type 'B', where however the truth of propositions of type 'A' does not entail the truth of propositions of type 'B'.

Examples of what I mean here would be:

(i) mathematical propositions are *constitutive* of scientific propositions in so far as mathematics constitutes part of the 'grammar' through which scientific propositions are structured and expressed;

(ii) biological forms of thought in Aristotle were instrumental to grasping a metaphysical view of things; similarly, in religion, analogous use of moral and aesthetic language is frequently *instrumental* to the grasping of an essentially non-moral and non-aesthetic view about the universe as a whole;

(iii) empirical judgements about a state of affairs, about a person's behaviour and about the social conditions in which someone lives might be *evidence* for moral judgements about ascription of responsibility;

(iv) psychological judgements about a person's state of mind may be *necessary conditions* for making moral judgements about that person, although a correct psychological judgement would none the less not be a sufficient condition for the moral judgement being correct.

Any analysis of the interconnection of disciplines, where this precludes the possibilities analysed in the previous sections, would have to be of this nature. The detailed way in which such an analysis would proceed is however very unclear, but possibly it is in this area that philosophers interested in curriculum organization have the most useful contribution to make. What mathematical concepts are essential to various kinds of scientific inquiry? What is the complex relationship between moral and religious or psychological knowledge? What empirical understanding is relevant to different kinds of aesthetic appreciation? Until more work is done on these sorts of questions, appeals for integrating the curriculum will be so many calls for 'I know not what'.

VI. *Summary of the Epistemological Questions Raised*

(i) 'integration' is a necessary feature of knowledge in that knowledge entails a judgement that something either is or is not the case and, hence, a conceptual scheme within which otherwise unrelated happenings are organized or structured;

(ii) the proponents of curriculum integration are however making claims that go beyond such basic analysis of knowledge in that such an analysis is compatible with what they derogatorily call the 'fragmented syllabus' or 'pigeon-holed' knowledge;

(iii) they are therefore claiming either that knowledge has some over-all unity—a coherence, a synthesis—such that the meaning of any one proposition cannot be fully grasped without an implicit reference to an entire system of propositions;

(iv) or that knowledge has some sort of coherence or synthesis within certain broad fields of experience (e.g. the humanities);

(v) or that, in order to answer particular problems it is necessary to focus different sorts or modes of knowledge and inquiry upon a particular topic (this, as such, not necessarily committing one to integration, though integration is an expression frequently but misleadingly used);

(vi) or that any development of knowledge has built into it some reference to the inquiry or problems for which it makes possible a practical solution and which therefore are the source of integration;

(vii) or that the different disciplines, though incorporating distinct conceptual structures and modes of inquiry, do interrelate and that this interrelation needs to be made explicit in the teaching of the disciplines and in the curriculum as a whole.

This then is the foremost philosophical question to be asked about curriculum integration—viz. what it could mean, and what assumptions are being made about knowledge, the forms of knowledge, the inter-relationship between these forms, and the structural unity of language. It may be of course that one is chasing a chimera—that there is no real philosophical problem here, that curriculum integration is but a grandiose way of talking about interdisciplinary inquiry which, as such, entails no necessary synthesis; that synthesis is neither necessary nor possible between different disciplines. If so then, in pursuing this analysis, one will have devoted a great deal of philosophical energy to showing that there is no real philosophical problem, but then (to parody Wittgenstein) it might be argued that the chief job of philosophy is to do itself out of business—and if, at the same time, we do a few mistaken curriculum reformers out of business, this may be a good thing.

VII

CURRICULUM PLANNING:
TAKING A MEANS TO AN END

HUGH SOCKETT

Introduction

THERE used to be a lot of debate in educational circles about Education —its aims, content, and methods. Nowadays the curriculum is the thing. The curriculum, which used to pick out the content of education, has now developed content, methods, and objectives (if not aims) of its own. So we are told that the familiar educational exercise of planning a syllabus is outmoded: for a syllabus is merely a list of contents. Rather, it is said, we need a curriculum in which detailed lists of objectives are set out. Such objectives are to be the statements of what the learners are to 'think, act, and feel' as a result of a course of instruction. They must be precise, unambiguous, and measurable. To remove ambiguity and to facilitate measurement, the objectives must also be 'behavioural', that is, they must be stated in terms of what the learner can be observed to do. While there are other less dogmatic views on planning curricula by objectives than that contained in these stipulations, the dominant view of curriculum planning in contemporary Curriculum Theory is this 'behavioural objectives model' in which clear-cut means are to be taken to palpable and measurable ends.

Working with a particular view of rational action, such curriculum theorists and planners as subscribe to this model demand the clear identification of the 'real' ends as a necessary first step. Once these are fixed, empirical inquiry will reveal the most effective means to their achievement. The view of rational action embodied in this picture of planning has, of course, been attacked by Popper in his critique of Utopian Engineering, in the wider context of social theory. Oakeshott too, particularly in his essay on 'Rational Conduct', has pilloried this

This contribution is drawn from section II of my paper 'Curriculum Aims and Objectives: Taking a Means to an End', published in the *Proceedings of the Philosophy of Education Society*, Vol. 6, No. 1 (Jan. 1972). Reprinted by permission of Basil Blackwell Ltd. For his invaluable help both in the clear formulation of the distinctions in that paper and in the presentation of them in this collection I am indebted to Professor R. S. Peters.

conception of rational behaviour. But this type of philosophical critique has not yet percolated through to these educational theorists. Admittedly there appears to be some realization in the discussions between advocates of the model that the dogma has its limits, but the difficulties are seen as technical rather than philosophical: for example there is debate on just how far the demand for precise specification can go, what ought to be regarded as a 'real' end, and so on. In general, however, the conceptual framework of social engineering is unchallenged. There is a firm separation of values from facts, and of ends from means.

There are two further features of this approach. Firstly statements of objectives are seen as statements of value, with the corollary that, since philosophers talk a lot about values, it is their task to reconcile value-conflicts. In this way a firm basis for the objectives chosen can be established. The possibility that philosophers might also help with the epistemological or methodological aspects of the undertaking does not seem to be taken into account and there is little sign that the difficulties raised about the enterprise at a philosophical level (e.g. by Popper and Oakeshott) have been considered. The philosopher then remains splendidly isolated, engaged on what Oakeshott calls the 'independent premeditation of ends'. Secondly, however, once the values have been sorted out, the curriculum technologist takes over in the more mundane (logical) task of formulating the objectives in the desired behavioural form. The way is thus clear for the empirical psychologist to examine and develop means to these scientifically sterilized ends. We are thus led to expect a host of empirical hypotheses derived from this curriculum data. Unfortunately, as recent critics[1] have pointed out, such hypotheses are conspicuous by their absence in published work in Curriculum Theory to date.

Throughout such curriculum literature there runs intermittent talk of taking means to ends, and, of course, the relationship between means and ends is conceived of as contingent. This is part and parcel of the positivist picture of curriculum planning. My thesis, in this paper, is that this picture is altogether too simple. Scant justice is done to the complex interrelation of fact and value in education, and to the ways in which we conceive ourselves as individual human agents taking means to ends. In this paper I do not propose to enter into complex questions about facts and values. Instead I propose to tackle the much more neglected task of examining different types of 'means–ends' connections

[1] See I. Westbury and W. Steimer, 'Curriculum, a discipline in search of its problems', *School Review*, Vol. 79, No. 2 (Feb. 1971).

which are possible in planning and rational action. I start from the view that our talk of taking means to ends in normal usage must be seen from the perspective of the agent, whether he be a member of an institution (e.g. a teacher in a school), a participant in an activity (e.g. a historian, scientist, or cricketer), or as is usual in the context of the school, both.

Taking a Means to an End

Intentional human action must stand at the centre of an account of curriculum aims and objectives. It is equally obvious that the notion of taking a means to an end is a form of intentional human action and thereby must be that of an agent's conception of what he is doing. Now there will be those who insist that the possibility of a cause–effect relationship which is testable empirically within the conception an agent has of taking a means to an end is the only proper sense in which we can appropriately use such talk. The housewife buys flour and yeast, as she puts it, to bake some bread. Given a common understanding as to what constitutes bread, flour, and yeast there are certain facts about the conjunction of materials when baked, i.e. heated at certain temperatures, such that the result will be a loaf or loaves of bread. In this case the relationship between the end and the means taken to achieve it is clearly contingent.

It does not seem particularly fruitful to argue, with this paradigm in mind, what is or is not to count as a means–ends relationship. It will be obvious that the interpretation here is liberal, since I will now claim that in addition to 1, the contingent relationship, there are four other possible connections which may be labelled

2. the logically necessary;

3. the logically constitutive where the means are to be seen as a *part* of the end;

4. the logically constitutive where the means are to be seen as an *instantiation* of the end;

5. the logically limiting where statements of certain ends logically preclude certain means.

1. The Contingent Connection

When a person takes a means to an end, there may be a variety of contingent relationships between the end he desires and the means he chooses. Notice that this is not a matter of distinguishing each and every empirical condition which must hold in the context, only those which are relevant to the way he frames his task. Say he wishes to get more light in his bedroom. To this end he fells a near-by tree. The desired state of affairs, the end, and the action which brings this about, the means, are contingently related in that

(*a*) as a matter of fact the removal of this tree does increase the volume of light in the bedroom, which is open to empirical test (and there may be innumerable other relevant contingent facts), and

(*b*) the agent chooses to fell the tree rather than put in brighter light-bulbs.

There are innumerable ways in which such contingent connections are important in teaching. A teacher's manner, his tone of voice, his use of exhortations, praise and blame, the forms of discipline he exercises can all be seen as means to the end of getting the children to learn. In an experiment with mentally handicapped children, for example, Lovaas has consistently shouted orders at them during treatment sessions to facilitate learning. Teachers feign anger to establish classroom order in which children can work more easily. It is widely believed that the way in which the desks or tables are organized in a classroom, in rows or groups, affects learning. Using different forms of classroom hardware may well be taking more efficient means to ends: the film cassette rather than the textbook, the overhead projector rather than the blackboard, carpeted floors not vinyl tiles, ballpoint pens rather than scratchy nibs and chalk-filled inkwells. In all these cases the teacher may see himself as taking means to ends, means which are in principle open to empirical test.

Furthermore as suggested by (*b*) above, there is a necessary element of contingency in some cases in what the teacher chooses to use. Thus as Hirst[2] points out, whether one adopts an approach through the disciplines or an approach through the 'fields of knowledge' as a means to achieving the aim of a liberal education remains a matter of choice, provided the aim is kept clearly in view. Whether sufficient control of the variables is possible to allow firm conclusions as to which is empirically the 'better' is another matter. But, given an agreed aim, one choice may be 'better' than another in that it may be more efficient.

[2] P. H. Hirst, 'Liberal Education and the Nature of Knowledge', see No. IV in this collection.

2. *The Logically Necessary Connection*

An example of this type of connection will help by way of introduction. Let us assume that it is a logical *precondition* of becoming a moral agent that one should understand the concept of a rule. It is of course possible to understand the concept of a rule without ever becoming a moral agent. It could be, perhaps in monastically secluded circumstances, that a novice was so morally inept that his moral tutor would say 'your trouble is that you'll never be a moral agent until you really understand what a rule is'. The novice goes away from the tutorial intent on mastering what a rule is so that he can be a 'proper' moral agent. The means in this case, mastering what a rule is, is logically necessary to the end (being a moral agent). Where X is a logical precondition of Y, if X is conceived as a means to Y, then X is logically necessary to Y. In this case x (mastering the concept of a rule) is logically necessary to y (being a moral agent).

Yet consider another example. A man hears a moving performance of Beethoven's Violin Concerto and is determined to play it like that some day. So he sets about learning to play the violin. But *learning* to play the violin is not logically necessary to being able to play the violin concerto, as the ability to play the violin might be innate or acquired at a flash of lightning, unless we make it logically necessary that being able to play the violin presupposes learning. In this case therefore he is doing p (learning) as a means to x (being able to play the violin) which is a logically necessary condition of y (playing the violin concerto). Apparently therefore we have two cases: [3]

(i) x (mastering the concept of a rule) as a logically necessary means to y (being a moral agent), and

(ii) p (learning) as a means to x (being able to play the violin) which is a logically necessary condition of y (playing the violin concerto).

But if we do consider it a contingent fact that a person learns X rather than that X-ing comes to him in a flash of lightning, (i) must be unpacked to resemble (ii) in form thus:

p (learning) as a means to understanding the necessary condition of y (being a moral agent).

This is correct within means–ends talk for this reason. In (ii) and the amended (i) the x's (being able to play the violin and understanding the concept of a rule) cannot be described as means for they are not being

[3] I am grateful to Ray Elliott for pointing out this distinction.

used in a task sense, but in their *achievement* sense. They are themselves ends, albeit ends which are preconditions of other ends, but not means to these other ends. In this case of learning therefore a person is taking means contingently related to achieving an end which is a logically necessary precondition of some other end.

However, if *teaching* is 'the intentional activity of bringing it about that another person intentionally learns X'[4] are there means which a teacher might take which are logically necessary to certain ends? The point is that teaching is governed as an activity by the character of what is being taught. Thus if within the context of what is being taught there are certain logically related elements of knowledge or skill such that possession of one logically presupposes the possession of others, then it makes sense to say of a teacher that he is taking logically necessary means to ends in teaching the one in order that the pupils may learn the other. A teacher who wanted his pupils to become moral agents would have to teach what a rule is (given certain variables) for them to become moral agents. The moral tutor is taking logically necessary means to ends in trying to bring it about that the novice should understand the concept of a rule as a means to his becoming a moral agent.

'The appropriate sequencing of the units of content [of a curriculum],' writes Gagné, 'can be based on empirical evidence. It doesn't have to be a matter of speculation about what the students are capable of learning, on the one hand, nor a matter of elegance of logical derivation, on the other. The pedagogical correctness of a sequence of content units can be tested by successively applied trials of what students can actually achieve.'[5] In the light of what has been said about the logically necessary connection, two points arise. Firstly, while there will be areas certainly in which there is nothing much to choose on logical grounds between different sequences, how could such a sequence be constructed in the first place without attention to the logical coherence of the units? Without that as a guide, the choice of sequence would either be random, or be based on other psychological evidence, thereby reducing the logical relations between things we say to matters of fact about what we say. But secondly, in the sequencing, it is difficult

[4] See P. H. Hirst, 'What is Teaching?' *Journal of Curriculum Studies*, Vol. 3, No. 1 (May 1971), which appears as No. VIII in this collection.

[5] See R. M. Gagné, 'Curriculum Research and the Promotion of Learning', in *AERA Monograph Series on Curriculum Evaluation*, Vol. 1 (New York: Rand McNally, 1967), pp. 34-5.

to understand how, where there are units with logical priority to others, these could be interchanged: presumably a child must understand the concept of number before he can understand the concepts of plus and minus. There is an impression, perhaps widespread, that a programmer working out a unit for a teaching machine selects the order of content simply on *psychological* grounds. But the logic of the unit, the demands made by the content, must be respected: indeed they will form the basis on which such units are devised. Now just what *are* the logical preconditions of this kind, and just what *are* the contingent matters is open to inquiry. Perhaps sitting down in one's armchair to plan units of this kind is a sensible way of trying to tease out what the logical relations are. But that is not doing psychology.

In fact the absence of established philosophical work in this area may make this point seem trivial and obvious. For to argue that being able to play the violin is necessary to being able to play the violin concerto, or that being able to read and to understand the meaning of certain words is logically necessary to understanding and appreciating *Daniel Deronda* is hardly a spectacular claim. (Even if one could add that clause analysis was not, as traditional teachers of English appear to have thought, logically necessary to such appreciation as is understanding the meaning of words.) More significantly, however, there is the point that in the construction of a curriculum, where knowledge is at stake, very complex and non-trivial logical and epistemological considerations are of paramount importance: and these are matters for the philosopher, the 'subject' expert, or the curriculum technologist for that matter, provided he wears the epistemological hat. For while there are obviously empirical issues of importance, what can be empirically investigated in this area depends on and is limited by the range of logically necessary connections that can be ascertained. There is, for instance, the extremely important and relevant difference between a strict logical connection and what Hamlyn calls a conceptual connection.[6]

3 and 4. *The Logically Constitutive Connections*

Consider two further cases in which the connections are logical but which do not conform to the pattern of the examples just considered. A man whose legs are paralysed from birth declares that if he recovers

[6] See D. W. Hamlyn, 'The Logical and Psychological Aspects of Learning' in R. S. Peters (ed.), *The Concept of Education*, which appears as No. IX in this collection.

he will try to run the 10,000 metres at the Olympics. At the age of 18 his paralysis is miraculously cured. Now is it logically necessary that he be taught to walk as a means to his declared end of running—eventually in the 10,000 metres? Two possibilities are open. First we can declare that there is no logical reason why a man should not run before he can walk. Secondly we could declare that, since we define running as a kind of accelerated walking, a man who wishes to run must logically learn to walk since the notion of running entails that of walking. Certainly the paralytic's statements are means–ends: but is the connection, if not contingent, logically necessary (i.e. as a precondition)? Consider another case: a performative. The man who says 'I will' in a marriage service might be said to be saying 'I will' as a logically necessary means to marrying the bride. But clearly in saying 'I will' he *is* marrying her, though of course he may be marrying her, by saying 'I will', to get his hands on her property. The point is this. If we assume that there is a logical connection between walking and running such that we define running as accelerated walking, then walking is not a logical *precondition*, but a logical *constituent* in the notion of running. The notion of a constituent is carried too far in the case of the performative for in this case it makes little sense to speak of taking means to an end.

In addition therefore to the contingent and logically necessary connections there are logically constitutive relations. The first of these, as in the walking–running example, is where the means are a *part* of the end. Among many things Mill suggests in Chapter IV of *Utilitarianism* he gives an account of the pursuit of happiness which could be regarded as a quasi-psychological account of a man who sets out on this road. He sees wealth, for example, as a means to happiness; such a means 'besides being means, [is] a part of the end'.[7] He then argues that 'from being a means to happiness' (wealth, power, and fame) they 'have become principal ingredients in the individual's conception of happiness', 'the means have become a part of the end and a more important part of it than any of the other things they are means to'—a somewhat elliptical remark. For the pursuer of happiness therefore, it is not that wealth is contingently or of logical necessity related to the end—happiness: it is a *part* of it, though still sensibly described as a means.

The second of the logically constitutive relationships between means and ends is where the means are an *instantiation* of the end. A man's aim is to get political power. He sets out on a political career which

[7] *Everyman Edition* (London: Dent & Sons, 1960), pp. 32–4.

leads to his eventual appointment as a Cabinet Minister. He might say 'I am trying to become a Cabinet Minister as a means to political power and influence.' Being a Cabinet Minister is not a part of political power but an *instantiation* of it, and in that sense is a constituent in his notion of political power. Or consider a doctor whose end is to relieve suffering: he cures a patient to relieve suffering, as means to his end. Curing the patient is thus an *instantiation* of the relief of suffering.

Thus, if a teacher accepts Hirst's view of liberal education as 'achieving an understanding of experience in many different ways', the objectives which the teacher sets himself from day to day, namely getting the children to master the concepts, logic, and criteria of the different disciplines, are not contingently related to the end, his aim. Nor are they logical preconditions of the achievement of the aims, and they cannot therefore be seen as logically necessary means to ends. Rather they are constitutive of the aim: they are part of the end, and in that sense logically constitutive means to ends.

The major point brought out by the notion of means as constitutive of ends is, however, that value questions are not themselves just questions of ends. The objectives that a teacher of history has will include not merely that his pupils should master certain historical facts, but that they should develop a historical imagination as well as mastering certain procedures necessary to giving adequate historical explanations. Yet within what is being respectively taught and learnt the teacher will have to respect the evidence, follow the procedures, use his own historical imagination as means to his end—getting the children to understand history. Means may be constitutive of ends in such activities, in that certain values are embedded in the activity, its content, and procedures: these may be attitudes which are part of what is learnt (and what is being taught) as well as part of the method of teaching. Peters has written that a teacher of mathematics to be an educator must be concerned for elegance of proof.[8] A teacher must see this as an end—something his pupils come to appreciate, and as a means—something that he must show in dealing with the context as part of his method. Such are the kinds of complex interrelations in an educational situation.

---

[8] This point was more elaborately argued by Peters at the end of his contribution to the Ontario symposium which is printed at the beginning of this collection. [See 'Aims of Education—A Conceptual Inquiry', reprinted above. —Ed.]

There is, however, a second point of some significance. Teachers have frequently regarded the social life of an institution as a means to the cultivation of desirable qualities in children, sociability, fraternity, leadership, etc. But of course the social life of an institution is shot through with values. A complex institution like a school could not conceivably review each course of action on the model of rational action outlined: its social life would disintegrate. Value decisions are made which become precedents or traditions, which become 'the way we do things here'. From this social life, as Jackson and others have argued, innumerable things are learnt. The social life of the institution as a means therefore instantiates the ends the institution seeks to achieve. It is interesting to note in this context that much of the vociferous criticism from teachers of the behavioural objectives model is precisely that it neglects the particular character of individual institutions.

5. *The Logically Limiting Connection*

One last possible uninteresting relationship is that where the description of the end logically precludes certain means. The man who wishes to fell a tree, so that its end can be described as the 'tree felled', is logically precluded from using such means as tactical nuclear weapons or bulldozers or a pen-knife, for what is meant by 'felling' is the use of an axe or a saw. This might be regarded as uninteresting because in the end as stated 'the tree felled' the means are contained within the statement of end, even though it is contingent whether he chooses an axe or a saw. However, this may be of importance in education in that some 'ends' may exclude certain 'means', e.g. the teaching of science may demand the use of certain methods, and in distinguishing the different relationships relevant in education, such a case is worth noting.

Indeed curriculum reform in science, as exemplified in the Nuffield projects, has been largely influenced by considerations of how scientists work, and the curriculum and the teaching is considerably shaped by these factors. Similarly it would be *logically* curious, given our current conception of philosophy, to provide as teachers no opportunity for discussion work or seminars if we want our pupils to understand philosophy. The means that we take to getting pupils to understand the activity are limited by the character of the activity: it is not a matter of opening up all possible means to empirical inquiry. Generally, therefore, where a teacher, anxious to give his pupils a liberal education, selects appropriate objectives from Hirst's analysis, the methods he uses will in part be influenced and restricted by the methodology of the discipline he is teaching.

Conclusion

I have made five distinctions about the relationship between means and ends where a person sees himself taking a means to an end, and put them in an educational context. The distinctions may very well be incorrectly drawn and they certainly require detailed criticism and further exemplification. They are not merely to be seen as part of a negative rebuttal of a fundamentalist dogma, but as an attempt to contribute positively to the philosophical groundwork necessary for planning a curriculum rationally. I have argued that the contingent relationship alone, which is at the heart of the dogma, is inadequate since it simply does not do justice to the range of interconnections of significance in the educational enterprise. I have suggested that the distinctions illustrate the importance of epistemological considerations in curriculum planning, and that there may therefore be quite severe limits on the kinds of empirical hypotheses which it is possible to generate from Curriculum Theory: from a Curriculum Theory, that is, which has such an unsophisticated conception of education. This paper, therefore, provides an example of the sort of work that it is appropriate for philosophers of education to do in curriculum theory in addition to the task which is usually assigned to them, namely that of clarifying, reconciling, and justifying 'independently premeditated ends'.

TEACHING AND LEARNING

VIII

WHAT IS TEACHING?

PAUL H. HIRST

THE question with which this paper is concerned is simply 'What is teaching?' How do we distinguish teaching from other activities? This is, I think, a very important question for at least four reasons. First, a lot of new educational methods are now widely canvassed in which the significance of teaching is far from clear. Repeatedly one finds an almost exclusive emphasis on certain activities of the pupils, say those of inquiry, discovery, and play, not on the activities of the teacher. In the discussion of such methods it seems to me there is much misunderstanding of what teaching is and therefore of what it involves, and this not infrequently leads to a very distorted view of the whole educational situation. Secondly, people are now aware of a range of activities, some of them thought to be morally undesirable, whose relation to teaching is by no means clear: activities like indoctrinating, preaching, advertising, and propagandizing. There are many terms that are as it were in the same logical band as 'teaching', and we are I think rightly getting more sensitive as to whether or not the activities these terms label ought to go on in school. If we can get clearer about the nature of teaching it will surely help us to see the character of these other processes and their interconnections. Similar problems are raised by the use of teaching machines and other devices, not to mention sleep-teaching.

Thirdly, we are clearly in need of a great deal of carefully controlled empirical research on the effectiveness of different teaching methods. But without the clearest concept of what teaching is, it is impossible to find appropriate behavioural criteria whereby to assess what goes on in the classroom. Most teaching methods new and old are advocated or defended on little more than hunch or personal prejudice. What we need to know are some relevant empirical facts, but these we cannot find if we are uncertain how to identify cases of teaching anyway. And

From *Journal of Curriculum Studies*, Vol. 3, No. 1 (May, 1971), pp. 5–18. Reprinted by permission of the author and Collins, Publishers.

finally, being clear about what teaching is matters vitally because how teachers understand teaching very much affects what they actually do in the classroom. If it is the case that our activities depend on how we ourselves see them, what we believe about them, then if we have crazy, fuzzy ideas about teaching, we will be likely to do crazy and fuzzy things in its name. One of the most important things for a teacher is surely to be clear about the nature of the central activity in which he is professionally involved. And if that is true for teachers in general, it is certainly true for the teachers of teachers in particular.

The question then is how do we characterize the activity of teaching so as to distinguish it from all other activities? How, for instance, on entering a classroom can one tell whether the teacher is in fact teaching? What exactly has to be going on? To begin to answer the problem here we must surely distinguish two obviously different senses in which we talk about teaching. In the first sense we talk about teaching as an *enterprise* in which a person may be engaged for a long period, say all afternoon. In this sense, a teacher spends the afternoon not in shopping, sunbathing, or taking the dog for a walk, but in fact in teaching. The term teaching is here functioning at a very general level, labelling a whole enterprise which may be broken down into many much more specific activities. And if indeed we look at these more detailed elements of the enterprise, it is perfectly plain that many of them are not activities we would in a more restricted sense of the term wish to call 'teaching' at all. Opening the window to let in more air, sharpening a few pencils, preventing a squabble between two pupils, all these may be legitimate parts of the enterprise of teaching as a whole. But we do surely use the term teaching in a much more specific sense whereby we can say that these activities are not the activities of teaching. In this second sense then we can speak of specific teaching *activities* which do not include in their number the sharpening of pencils, the opening of windows, and all other such activities which might form a legitimate part of the teaching enterprise as a whole. In the rest of this paper I am not concerned with the enterprise use of the term and would add only one point about it. Clearly for an enterprise to be that of teaching at all it is necessary that it must contain certain specific teaching activities. If a teacher spent the whole afternoon opening windows, sharpening pencils, cleaning her glasses, and so on, she would do no teaching in any sense at all. It is necessary therefore to the teaching enterprise that it should include specific teaching activities, and all other specific activities are part of that enterprise only because of their relation to these.[1]

But how are specific *teaching* activities to be distinguished from all other specific activities? Why exactly is opening a window or sharpening a pencil not teaching? Manifestly teaching is no one specific activity readily identifiable in general circumstances like, say, walking or running or riding a bicycle. There are an enormous number of specific activities which may in fact be teaching. One might be describing a historical situation and this could be called teaching. One might on the other hand be saying nothing at all, but be drawing on a blackboard, or doing a chemical experiment in front of the pupils. All these would seem to be teaching activities in a specific sense, so that there is no one immediately recognizable activity which the term teaching picks out. Is there then a limited number of specific activities which constitute teaching, so that to be teaching at all one would have to be carrying out one of these? A teacher would then have to know how to question, how to prove things, how to demonstrate, etc. If this were what teaching involved, it would greatly simplify the business of teacher training and indeed it seems to me that there is a large grain of truth in this idea. Such an approach is, however, too simple-minded, if only because many, if not all, of the specific activities which occur within teaching, also occur when one is certainly not teaching. One can tell a story to a child who knows it backwards but who just simply enjoys hearing it over once more. One might demonstrate something to entertain a night-club audience. In proving something, one may be actually discovering the proof, not teaching someone else. One may be translating something, without teaching anything to anybody. None of these activities implies that teaching is taking place at all. It therefore seems to be the case that we cannot hope to get clear what teaching is simply by producing an exhaustive list of activities of this kind.

Nevertheless, teaching is what is technically known as a polymorphous activity; it quite literally takes many different forms. Its parallels are thus activities like work and gardening, and explicit comparisons with these might help in the process of clarification. What does a person have to be doing to be working? Driving a truck, working a lathe,

---

[1] I am here using terminology which is in part the same as that used by B. Paul Komisar: 'Teaching: Act and Enterprise', in C. J. B. Macmillan and T. W. Nelson (eds.), *Concepts of Teaching* (New York: Rand McNally, 1968). In spite of certain similarities in both terminology and approach, however, our accounts are clearly in radical disagreement over the precise relationship between teaching and learning, and the necessary characteristics of at least certain of his 'teaching acts'.

solving mathematical problems, drawing beer, all these activities constitute somebody's work. Indeed any activity would seem to be in principle a possible form of work. On the other hand, gardening is much more limited in what it embraces. Digging, mowing the lawn, pruning are activities of gardening, but one cannot be doing *anything* as one might in the case of work. What then about teaching? Is it in this respect more like work or like gardening? Looked at one way teaching can take so many different forms that, like work, there seems pretty well no limit to the activities it can involve. Standing on one's head could in fact be part of teaching something, so could driving, working a lathe, solving a problem. Provided one looks at the whole range of things that can be taught, it would seem that any activity might occur as a teaching activity. Which activities might be involved in any particular instance will depend on exactly *what* is being taught. Yet it might be insisted that though teaching, say, to drive, might *involve* driving, when teaching one must in fact do more than merely drive. One must, say, *demonstrate* driving. This would seem to imply that though any activity might be subsumed under the notion of teaching, for that to be the case it must be carried out in some special way. And this in turn suggests that all the legion activities that can figure in teaching, to figure in that way, must be seen as occurring within a framework of the kind of specific activities mentioned earlier, such as demonstrating, proving, telling, etc. This view is I think correct and the analogy between teaching and other polymorphous activities would seem to be most helpful at the level of, say, gardening rather than at the level of, say, work. Yet the parallel with gardening is strictly limited. Activities like pruning and mowing the lawn are necessarily forms of gardening and that concept may be exhaustively analysable in such terms. Yet it was insisted above that demonstrating and proving are not necessarily forms of teaching and it is by no means obvious that, limited though the range of activities of teaching may be, there is an exhaustive list of distinct activities into which the concept of teaching could be even partially analysed. I conclude therefore that we cannot hope to characterize specific teaching activities simply in terms of the activities of proving, demonstrating, telling, etc. Rather, teaching must be characterized some other way which will make it clear to us when these activities are indeed involved in teaching and when involved in, say, entertaining. It will perhaps also make plain why these activities are peculiarly important in teaching.

How then are we going to characterize specific teaching activities at all? I think the answer to this is that they can only be characterized in the way in which we fundamentally characterize all human activities, by looking at their point or purpose. It is by clarifying the aim, the intention of what is going on, that we can see when standing on one's head to demonstrate something, or any other activity, is in fact teaching and not, say, simply entertaining. The difference here is in the different, overriding intentions involved in each case. What a particular activity is, what a person is doing, depends crucially on how he himself sees the activity. To take a standard example, if a person is seen to place a glass of liquid to his lips and slowly drain it, what is he doing? He may be quenching his thirst, committing suicide, or engaging in a religious ritual. Which of these if any it is, depends on the point, purpose, or intention that lies behind the physical movements. Clearly the physical state of affairs can be described without knowing the person's intention. It can be seen that the glass is moved by a certain force so many inches towards his lips, and so on. But an account of what is observed does not tell us what the activity is. Perhaps in a particular context we may be able to infer very readily the most likely point of the movements and thus what activity is involved; nevertheless it is only by reference to the intention that we can describe the activity, and of course there is no guarantee that our external judgement of the intention, based upon our observation, is in fact correct.

Yet if a 'sufficient' characterization of an activity can only be given in terms of its intention and not in terms of its observable features, that is not to say that certain observable features are not necessary to many particular activities. Clearly not all observable events could be described as quenching one's thirst or celebrating Mass. Unless liquid of some sort is being consumed, a person cannot be quenching his thirst and on empirical evidence alone we can dismiss such a description of many of his activities. From observation we can rule out many possibilities of what a person is doing even if we cannot from observation say which of the remaining possibilities he is engaged in. The points here are fundamentally quite simple. First, any activity is characterized by its intention, but many intentions cannot, logically cannot, be ascribed unless certain observable conditions hold. Secondly, for a given set of observable conditions a number of quite different intentions may be ascribable. Thirdly, in so far as there are necessary observable conditions for a particular activity, they are necessary conditions for there being the intention concerned in this case. They are not conditions of a logically independent character.

What we want to know then about teaching is first, what is the intention by which its activities are picked out from all others and secondly what necessary observable features are there by which we can judge that some activities could not possibly be teaching, whereas others might well be, though we can never be certain from such external characterization alone.

A crude answer to the first of these questions is I think simple. The intention of all teaching activities is that of bringing about learning. But simple and banal though this answer might seem, it is I suggest an extremely important answer. It involves the claim that the concept of teaching is in fact totally unintelligible without a grasp of the concept of learning. It asserts that there is no such thing as teaching without the intention to bring about learning and that therefore one cannot characterize teaching independently of characterizing learning. Until therefore we know what learning is, it is impossible for us to know what teaching is. The one concept is totally dependent on the other. Because of the tightest conceptual connection then, the characterization and *raison d'être* of teaching rests on that of learning. If therefore a teacher spends the whole afternoon in activities the concern of which is not that the pupils should learn, but, say, the inflation of his own ego, then in fact he cannot have been teaching at all. In these terms it could be the case that quite a large number of professional teachers are in fact frauds most of their lives, because their intentions are never clear. Perhaps quite a lot of our work is misdirected because this necessary intention is lost in a welter of secondary intentions, by neglect, if not deliberately. Of course pupils may learn many things when a teacher is not in fact teaching. That is another matter. What would seem to be particularly important here is that in taking a job as a professional teacher one is presumably being paid to carry out this intention whatever else one is paid to do. If one is not going into the classroom to bring about learning, if that is not the intention, then one cannot, logically cannot, be teaching. That is not to say that one may not be doing many other things which are of value. There are many ways of occupying children's time, some of them profitable, but that does not make them teaching. I wish to maintain therefore that the notion of teaching is totally dependent for its characterization on the concept of learning and that this has important practical consequences for how teachers see their job and therefore for what they do in the classroom.

Before going further, two particular points need commenting on. First, there are two ways in which we talk about teaching activities in the classroom context. The most common relates to the case in which a person may teach in the fullest sense of that word and yet, in spite of the intention and the appropriateness of the activities involved, the pupils learn absolutely nothing. Here the notion of teaching is simply that of trying to get people to learn and no more. But there is another use of the word, which involves the implication that not only has there been the intention to bring about learning, but that the pupil has in fact learnt what was intended. To say that Mr. Brown taught me to ride a bicycle, usually means not merely that Mr. Brown tried to get me to learn to ride a bicycle, but that I have in fact succeeded in learning this. There is thus not only a 'task' sense to the verb to teach, where trying or intending alone is implied; there is also a 'success' or 'achievement' sense, where in addition to the intention, there is the implication that learning has in fact occurred. For the rest of this paper I shall be concerned with teaching in the 'task' sense only, and in this sense it is *not* the case that teaching necessarily implies learning. What teaching implies is merely the intention to bring about learning.[2]

Secondly, if teaching activities are intentional, what are we to say about all the learning that goes on in a classroom, or anywhere else, which is not intended by the teacher? Is there not such a thing as unintentional teaching after all? Certainly, we do sometimes talk in this way, when a particular situation has been the occasion for significant learning. What is important here is surely the recognition that no teacher intended the learning, though significant things might have been picked up in the context. It will be suggested later that it is because of certain important features in the context that make the situation similar to that in which there is the intention to bring about learning that we use the term teaching here, though in a somewhat different sense. In schools we are not primarily concerned with unintended learning. What we are concerned with is the task of bringing about learning because

---

[2] The commonplace distinction I am here making leaves unnoted a complexity which any full task/achievement analysis of teaching cannot disregard. If teaching is directed towards another activity, that of the pupil's learning, then the task and achievement uses of 'teaching' need to be carefully related to possible task and achievement uses of 'learning'. We are inclined to assume that both uses of 'teaching' are directed to the achievement use of 'learning'. It is, however, far from obvious that this is always the case. Just this problem arises again with activities like demonstrating and proving as Dr. Komisar shows very plainly (see note 1). I am, however, unhappy about his account of these activities, though I am far from certain that I have always understood him.

we believe there is much that we can do towards making learning more than a random business. Of course, taking the education of children as a whole, what they pick up in the context of our unintentional teaching may indeed be important. Still this does not alter the fact that in schools we are centrally concerned with intentional teaching and that as soon as we turn our attention to what has been unintentional teaching, we thereby necessarily change its character.

The characterization of teaching given thus far makes the concept entirely parasitic on that of learning. That being so, it would seem important in clarifying the notion further to look at what is meant by 'learning'. Even if teaching is not the label of one specific activity, is learning? The answer I think must again be clearly no. One may learn things by trial and error, by discovery or observation, by being told and by many other means. But if there are many different activities of learning, what makes them cases of learning? I suggest the answer is again found, as in the case of teaching, by looking at the intention of the activities concerned. If the intention of teaching involves a concern for learning, what in turn is the intention of learning? Fortunately the answer seems not to be another type of activity whose intention would in turn have to be clarified. The end or aim of learning is, I suggest, always some specific achievement or end state. There are many such end achievements: believing something which one did not believe before, knowing something one did not know before, being able to do something one could not do before, having a habit one had not got before, and so on. As a result of learning one may know a scientific theory, know how to ride a bicycle, know how to calculate a square root, know that Henry VIII had six wives, appreciate the symphonies of Beethoven, or keep one's engagements punctually. The achievements or end states with which learning is concerned are of enormous variety and not surprisingly therefore the activities of learning are equally varied. Learning like teaching is a polymorphous activity. If then learning is the activity of a person, say B, the intention of which is the attainment of some particular end, we can say that B necessarily learns something, say X, where X may be a belief, a skill, an attitude, or some other complex object that characterizes this end.

For the purpose of this paper there is no need to pursue the nature of learning further, though two particular points must be stressed. First, it is I think important to note that the end achievements of learning are new states of the person and that these differ radically from each other. We seem to be under a perpetual temptation to think that all learning results in knowledge. Clearly this is false. Along with this too goes the temptation to think that what we learn, X, is necessarily a truth or fact of some kind. Clearly this is also false. To thoroughly disabuse oneself of these myths is a first step towards getting rid of many common but quite fallacious ideas about the nature of learning and, as a consequence, about the nature of teaching.

Secondly, it must be noted that I have assumed learning to be an activity on the part of the learner. But just as we have a use of teaching to cover cases when there is in fact no intention to bring about learning, so we have uses of learning where the pupil does not in fact intend to achieve the appropriate end which he nevertheless attains. In this sense we can speak of non-intentional learning, where as the result of a causal process as in hypnotism, conditioning, sleep-teaching, or even the unconscious acquisition of something, the intention of the learner is not involved. It is important to recognize here that the term learning is being used for a quite different process, in this case causal and not intentional. Nothing is to be gained by trying to legislate one meaning for the term, cutting across general usage which now covers both these processes. Yet the distinction between them needs to be kept clear. Whether or not causal processes are educationally desirable is a matter with which I am not here concerned.

Putting together what has been said about learning with what was earlier said about teaching, we have the following account of teaching. A teaching activity is the activity of a person, A (the teacher), the intention of which is to bring about an activity (learning), by a person, B (the pupil), the intention of which is to achieve some end state (e.g. knowing, appreciating) whose object is X (e.g. a belief, attitude, skill). From this it follows that to understand what is involved in teaching, one must start at the other end of a logical chain of relations, with an understanding of the end achievements to which everything is being directed. From this one can proceed to understand what is involved in B's achieving such ends, in learning X, and then proceed to an understanding of what is involved in A teaching B, X. This logical dependence of teaching on learning, and learning on the nature of the achievements to which it is directed is thus once more no mere academic matter. If teachers are not clear what end achievements their teaching is concerned with, they cannot know what is involved in B's learning X. And until they know what is involved in B's learning X, they cannot know what is involved in A's teaching B, X. Any notion of learning which is not the learning of some particular X is as vague as the notion of going somewhere but nowhere in particular. Equally some particular person B is necessarily learning this X. Following the logical chain, it is therefore only in a context where both what is to be learnt and who is learning it are clear, that we can begin to be clear about teaching B, X. Just as a pupil B cannot simply learn, but must necessarily be learning X, so A cannot simply teach, he must be teaching B, and he must be teaching B, X. It is as much a logical absurdity to say 'One teaches children not subjects' as it is to say 'One teaches subjects not children'. Both of these phrases might have their slogan use, but the serious discussion of teaching ought surely to reject such slogans in the name of the simple logical truth, that one necessarily teaches somebody something. Not that of course one is necessarily teaching a 'subject' in the traditional sense, but there must always be an end achievement which somebody is learning. A great deal of discussion of modern educational methods seems in danger of going seriously astray because of a refusal to accept the full implications of this simple logically necessary truth.

I have so far argued that in its central use, teaching is the label for those activities of a person A, the intention of which is to bring about in another person, B, the intentional learning of X. In addition, there would seem to be uses of the terms when the intention on the part of A is missing, but the intentional learning on the part of B remains, and also uses when the intention on the part of A is present, but the intention on the part of B is replaced by a causal process. But even in the central case, the intention on the part of A to bring about the learning of X by B might be thought to leave the characterization of teaching activities too open. On this account, might not the strangest events count as teaching a pupil say to count, provided this was the intention of the teacher? This would indeed be the case if there were no necessary conditions which an activity must satisfy before it could possibly be described as a teaching activity. Just as not all activities could be gardening surely not all activities could be teaching? What then are the necessary features of a publicly observable kind which all teaching activities must possess? There are I suggest at least two. As it is necessarily the case that A teaches B, X, there is one necessary demand on the activities in relation to the particular X that is being taught, and there is a second necessary demand in relation to the particular person B concerned.

The first of these demands is far from easy to express. But I suggest that in so far as one is necessarily teaching X, the specific teaching activity involved must be what I will call 'indicative' of X. By this I mean that the activity must, either implicitly or explicity, express or embody the X to be learnt, so that this X is clearly indicated to the pupil as what he is to learn. In this way the teacher makes plain in his activity *what* he intends to be learnt. It is not I think at all the case that what is to be learnt must necessarily be explicitly discernible in the activity, yet it must be so available in some sense that the pupil's learning activity can be directed to this as its object. It is because activities like demonstrating, telling, and proving can provide such excellent means for indicating an X that it is intended the pupil will learn, that they play such a central part in teaching. Yet just because these activities are such effective means for expressly indicating a given X, they can be significant not only in teaching but in such other concerns as entertaining. It is only when such activities are used in a learning context, to indicate what is to be *learnt* that they can become teaching activities. The fact that specific teaching activities must indicatively express what is to be learnt also helps to make clear why at times we speak of teaching in an unintentional sense. We do this, I suggest, when certain features of a situation can be legitimately interpreted as indicatively expressing something to be learnt, though this in fact may not be anyone's actual intention. The situation is thus interpreted as a teaching situation by the learner, when in fact, from an intentional point of view, it is no such thing. First, then, specific teaching activities must be indicative of what is to be learnt and it is for this reason that the opening of windows and the sharpening of pencils could never be themselves the teaching of historical facts or of Pythagoras's Theorem.

In the second place, as a specific teaching activity is necessarily concerned with the teaching of X to a particular pupil B, it must be indicatively expressed so that it is possible for this particular pupil B to learn X. One might teach an undergraduate class in philosophy Wittgenstein's criticism of the idea of a private language, by reading to the students sections from the *Philosophical Investigations*. But to carry out such an activity with a class of average six-year-olds would, I suggest, not constitute teaching at all. Indicative though the activity might be, as the six-year-olds could understand practically nothing that was being said, this could surely not constitute teaching *them* Wittgenstein's views on private languages. There is a gap between the knowledge, skills, or state of mind of the learner and what he is to learn, which it seems to me any teaching activity must seek to bridge if it is to deserve that label. Teaching activities must therefore take place at a level where the pupil *can* take on what it is intended he should learn. It must be possible, and this seems to me a logical point, for learning to take place. This logical demand is for the teacher to have psychological and other knowledge about the learner, and it clearly means that many specific things cannot possibly be taught to a given pupil given his present state of knowledge, skill, etc. I conclude therefore that a specific teaching activity must necessarily indicatively express the X to be learnt by B and be so related to the present state of B that he can learn X.

It might be objected to my second necessary demand for teaching activities, that to misjudge the present state of the pupils does not disqualify a person's activities from properly being described as teaching. Surely he has taught X whether the pupils have learnt X or not. Certainly teaching does not necessarily imply learning, but it does necessarily imply the intention of bringing about learning by someone, and if from one's activities it is impossible for that someone to learn what is intended, it does seem very odd to describe such activities as teaching. One reason why we are inclined to think that there could be teaching even when the present state of the pupils is grossly misjudged, is I think that we spend so much of our time teaching classes, not individuals, and the condition I am insisting on seems to make almost impossible demands. Must it not be the case that in any class with a wide ability range, what is presented is in fact inappropriate for some of the pupils? If we are to stick to the individualistic model I have used, must we not say that in even the 'task' sense, only some of the class have been taught X, and not others? Strictly I think the answer to that must be yes. But perhaps it would be better simply to recognize that we do use the word teaching both for activities aimed at group learning as well as individual learning. In the case of a group, what a teacher does if he is teaching them all the same X is to work with an appropriate norm for the attainments of that group. What constitutes an appropriate norm cannot I think be generally stated; nevertheless it seems to me that without working to such a norm there could be no activities that could properly be described as teaching the group. It might of course be argued, and with some justice, that properly understood, teaching a group necessarily involves attention to the individual differences of the pupils.

As a final comment on the two criteria which I have suggested are necessary to any teaching activity, it is I think instructive to note that in these terms opposing virtues and defects have tended to characterize both traditional formal teaching methods and more contemporary progressive alternatives. Traditional teaching methods have above all concerned themselves with the indicative features of these activities, often meeting the present learning state of the pupils in an over-generalized and inadequate way. In reaction, more progressive methods have tended to cater extremely well for the present learning state of individual pupils, but at the expense of the necessary indicative features that teaching activities must embody. It is not that either group of methods is of itself necessarily deficient as teaching activity, and each might well have its place according to what exactly is being taught and to whom. What is important is that we come to realize that in all teaching activities both these necessary features need the fullest responsible consideration.

In concluding this paper I would like to return to the problem of clarifying the nature of such activities as indoctrinating, conditioning, preaching, training, instructing, and so on, as the characterization of teaching that I have outlined can I think help in this process. As here considered, teaching activities form a very broad category indeed, one which is in no sense restricted to those activities we think it appropriate for schools to undertake. I have been concerned with teaching and learning in general, whatever the ends concerned, be they bad habits, perversions, concepts, facts, physical skills, etc. In so far then as indoctrination and other activities involve the intention to bring about learning of some kind, they involve teaching and in so far as they are themselves processes for bringing about learning of certain kinds they are themselves forms of teaching. From all that has been said about teaching, different categories of teaching activity can clearly be distinguished in a number of distinct ways. The object or objects to be learnt can be of one particular kind rather than another. The activity of learning may be of a specific sort, or the activity of the teacher may be restricted in some particular way. Clearly there are likely to be labels for certain types of teaching which become important for specific purposes and it is, I suggest, by looking at the particular sub-class of teaching activities involved that we are most likely to distinguish indoctrination, instruction, and so on.

Indoctrination, for example, would certainly seem to be picked out, at least in part, by the distinctive end state of mind of the learner, to which the teaching is directed. An indoctrinated person would seem to hold certain beliefs unshakeably.[3] In this case what the person is intended to learn, the X, is distinctive here, though in exactly what way it is important to note. On this criterion, it is nothing about the beliefs themselves that distinguishes indoctrination, but some higher-order beliefs about their status, or some attitude to them. But however this characterization is given, it is expressible in terms of certain distinctive objects for learning. Some have suggested that there is in fact something distinctive about the beliefs themselves in that one can only indoctrinate in matters of opinion or doctrines. Again this is to distinguish the teaching activities of indoctrination in terms of *what* is being taught. It can also be argued that indoctrination is restricted to certain learning processes, or that unintentional indoctrination is a contradiction. My point here is not to decide exactly what is meant by indoctrination or any other of these terms, but rather to indicate how a clarification of them might be helpfully approached.

What is however plain from the work that has already been done on the concept of indoctrination is that most terms in this area are likely to be in some respects unclear, being used in a number of interrelated ways. What matters then is not what any 'correct' use might be, but rather the conceptual distinctions that arise in this area. If, for instance, the notion of 'believing unshakeably' is seen as a distinctive result of some forms of teaching, and we for our purposes call these forms indoctrination, then indoctrination is being sharply distinguished from teaching leading to the holding of beliefs rationally, which many regard as a necessary part of education. Once we know the possible meanings of these very tricky terms we know our way around their relationships much better. We are clearer too about the significance of many of the things we do when engaged in teaching.

The distinctive features of such processes as conditioning and sleep-teaching would seem to be that they involve causal and not intentional learning, or if it is intentional, it is intentional in some very particular sense. Whether or not these processes ought to figure within indoctrination or education will of course depend on one's account of these latter processes. Training and instructing on the other hand would seem to be concepts connected unmistakably with intentional learning, the difference between them being determined by the particular group of end achievements with which each is concerned.

And finally, what of teaching machines: can such machines be

[3] See J. P. White, 'Indoctrination', in R. S. Peters (ed.), *The Concept of Education* (London: Routledge & Kegan Paul, 1967).

properly said to teach? In terms of the analysis I have here given the idea that a piece of hardware can of itself teach is nonsense, for it itself can have no intentions and cannot engage in activities. But taken in the proper context I see no reason why a machine, properly programmed, should not be the instrument of a teaching activity. It is indeed the machine programmed so that it indicatively expresses what is to be learnt, in such a way that the pupil can in fact learn, because it meets his current state of mind, that must be thought of as the teaching agent. The appropriate programming of the machine is of course an essential part of the teaching activity as a whole. What the invention of books, let alone teaching machines, made possible, was a separation in time between the teacher's expression of what is to be learnt and the pupil's encounter with this. Nothing new in principle is introduced into the idea of a teaching activity. What is, however, available here to the pupil is a programme of indicatively expressive activities drawn up after expert consideration of the problems involved in pupils' learning that might be much better for the task than the live activities of the teacher available. As the teaching activities that involve the use of such machines must be completely predetermined, it is of course important that the details of the programme be constructed with the utmost care and that it be appropriate to the learning state of the pupils. It is of course only when these conditions are fulfilled that in using the machine these pupils could be said to be being taught.

Throughout this paper I have been concerned with mapping the features that distinguish teaching activities from all others. It has not been my concern to lay down the criteria for good teaching or even successful teaching. Successful teaching would seem to be simply teaching which does in fact bring about the desired learning. Good teaching, however, is much more difficult to discern. I am not even sure that successful learning is a criterion for good teaching. Certainly in a given particular case there is no contradiction in saying that a person was successfully yet badly taught. Yet in so far as this account of teaching is correct, it has at least indicated which activities we are concerned to study in a critical comparison of teaching activities. What is more it must have at least some important implications for the methods whereby such comparisons must be made. But what these are, will not be gone into here, if only because such elaboration would be rather premature when the criteria for what teaching is are not yet agreed. It is towards establishing what these criteria are that this paper has been primarily directed.

IX

HUMAN LEARNING

D. W. HAMLYN

THE two great classical theories of knowledge—rationalism and empiricism—bring with them not only different conceptions of knowledge, but also different understandings of the acquisition of knowledge. They also involve different philosophies of mind, at any rate to the extent that for empiricism the mind is, as Locke put it, like a great mirror which passively receives reflections from without, while for rationalism the mind is more active, involved in its own operations. Like any characterization in terms of '-isms', what I have said is a caricature of any actual philosopher, but the tendencies are undoubtedly there. If that is so, one would expect similar tendencies in accounts of learning and the acquisition of knowledge based on these theories of knowledge and mind. With the development of psychology as an empirically orientated science, accounts of learning inspired by empiricist ways of thinking have become the accepted thing, as was only to be expected. Charles Taylor has noted[1] that S–R theory can be construed as 'a mechanistic transposition of the traditional empiricist views on epistemology', and he has sought more recently (e.g. in lectures given at the University of London) to show how theories of human behaviour based on the ideas of computer simulation and machine analogies tend to reflect the atomism which is to be found in traditional empiricism with its apparatus of, for example, impressions and ideas. That atomism is there because a theory of behaviour must have as an essential part a theory of the acquisition of knowledge about the environment, in the light of which knowledge behaviour ensues. The theory of the acquisition of knowledge in question reflects traditional empiricist epistemology which is based on the idea that all knowledge is built up from

From *The Philosophy of Psychology*, ed. S. C. Brown (London: Macmillan, 1973). The paper was read at a conference at the University of Kent in Sept. 1971, and is reprinted by permission of the author and The Royal Institute of Philosophy.

[1] C. Taylor, *The Explanation of Behaviour* (London: Routledge & Kegan Paul, 1964), p. 143.

certain atomic elements derived directly from experience. I am not here concerned with the explanation of behaviour in general, but with the acquisition of knowledge, and theories of this might be expected to have a direct relationship to theories of knowledge themselves.

Some empirically minded psychologists might maintain that I have begged the question in speaking so easily of the acquisition of knowledge and in assuming that this is what learning is. Indeed there has been some tendency on the part of recent psychologists to take it that learning embraces any modification of behaviour in an organism as the result of experience, or even as the result of stimulation from the environment.[2] Some of the reasons for such a point of view lie in a preoccupation with animal, as opposed to human, learning; for it is thought that animal learning is hardly to be characterized in terms of the acquisition of knowledge, understanding, etc. Whatever may be said on that issue, human learning is of course much more complicated in many cases than animal learning, and it is true that many of the abilities acquired by animals through learning involve little or no understanding of what is involved. Nevertheless, I do not think that the account of the matter under consideration will do; the definition of learning implied by it is far too wide. It will not exclude, for example, sudden and apparently irreversible changes of behaviour brought about by certain experiences; it will not exclude, to take two quite different examples, the phenomena of imprinting described by ethologists—the tendency in certain animals for crucial experiences to produce far-reaching and more or less permanent effects when they occur at certain stages in the animal's development—or the onset of sudden madness as the result of very disturbing experiences. It is not even true that someone who has acquired a certain habit has thereby necessarily learned anything; *a fortiori* being conditioned is not a form of learning. I have maintained elsewhere, in discussing the irrelevance of conditioning to learning,[3] that learning must involve at least the *use* of experience, a notion which suggests a more active role on the part of the learner. But I am not now sure that this will quite do, unless 'use' is given an exceptionally wide sense. A person who has simply been given a piece of information may certainly be said to have learned

[2] Cf., e.g., A. E. Seabourne and R. Borger, *The Psychology of Learning* (Harmondsworth: Penguin Books, 1966), pp. 14 ff.

[3] D. W. Hamlyn, 'Conditioning and Behaviour', in R. Borger and F. Cioffi (eds.), *Explanation in the Behavioural Sciences* (Cambridge: Cambridge University Press, 1970), p. 149.

something; yet it would be hard to say that he has in this case *used* his experience, even if the idea of a person receiving all his knowledge in this way, without his performing any role himself, is scarcely if at all intelligible. Not all learning is like problem-solving. Still, this is not an objection to the thesis that learning must at least involve the acquisition of knowledge through experience and that changes of behaviour due to learning must be the result of the new knowledge. In many cases, but not all, the acquisition of the new knowledge will entail the learner's using his experience. At all events, on our ordinary conception of learning it would, I suggest, be impossible to suppose that someone could have learned something if he had not in some sense acquired new knowledge, whatever form that knowledge may take (and it may of course include skills as well as factual knowledge).

An objection of a different kind to my association of learning with knowledge[4] would be that there are forms of learning in which the end of the learning is not in fact knowledge. We can, after all, learn to see things in new ways, to accept things, to appreciate things, and so on. Does this learning involve new *knowledge*? Suppose that a man comes to see something in a certain way, even to appreciate it as it is and to have an affection for it; we may sometimes say that he has learned to do these things and in saying this we imply something about the relevance of the experience that he has acquired to his seeing it in this way, and so on. We rule out thereby any suggestion that his attitudes may have been brought about causally in ways that have nothing to do with experience. Similar considerations apply to such cases as having learned to treat someone circumspectly or to be tactful in certain circumstances. There is a whole range of somewhat disparate cases which may fall under the general heading of 'having learned to ...' These may not involve the acquisition of knowledge *simpliciter*. Yet I am still inclined to think that knowledge enters into the picture in other, more indirect, ways. If I have learned to love someone, rather than merely come to love them, my love follows upon and exists in virtue of what I have come to know. How this happens is another matter, and any account of this would be a complex one which I cannot enter upon here. Suffice it to say that the kinds of case that I have in mind here are in my view parasitical upon those cases of learning which do involve the acquisition of knowledge *simpliciter*; and while I recognize their existence I shall concentrate in the following on those cases of learning

---

[4] The objection has been made to me by Mr. J. M. Cohen.

which do straightforwardly involve the acquisition of knowledge. It should be noted, however, that that knowledge can take a great many different forms.

Theories of learning inspired by rationalist theories of knowledge have not had much of a press until lately. When Piaget, in various places in his writings, tries to place his own approach in the spectrum of theories of human development, he characterizes Gestalt Theory as rationalist in effect. While empiricism involves, he says, development or geneticism without structure, Gestalt Theory involves structure without development. I suppose that this is one way of looking at Gestalt-ism, although I do not think that the immediate origins of Gestalt Theory were in fact specifically rationalist. Piaget himself, as I have argued elsewhere,[5] seems Kantian in inspiration; like Kant he attempts a putative reconciliation between rationalism and empiricism. A more straightforward claim for a rationalist account of learning (or at any rate human learning) has been made by Chomsky, with his now notorious defence of the doctrine of innate ideas. Chomsky's claim that we need to espouse the notion of innate ideas was initially made in the context of language learning, but there are signs in recent writings that he thinks that the view has a wider application. Thus in *Language and Mind*, p. 64, he asks whether there are other 'areas of human competence where one might hope to develop a fruitful theory, analogous to generative grammar'. He suggests that 'One might, for example, consider the problem of how a person comes to acquire a certain concept of three-dimensional space, or an implicit "theory of human action", in similar terms.' It is noteworthy that the examples mentioned involve concepts where there is more than a *prima facie* implausibility about empiricism. Just as there is an immense difficulty, if Chomsky is right, in seeing how the notion of language, of how to talk, could be abstracted from experienced data, if the person concerned did not already know that these data were language-data, so there is the same difficulty, as Kant saw, in seeing how the notion of space could be abstracted from experience; and the same difficulty applies to the idea of abstracting the notion of action from observed bodily movements. There are, of course more general difficulties about the notion of abstraction as a source of concepts, but the difficulties emerge in a specially crucial

[5] D. W. Hamlyn, 'The Logical and Psychological Aspects of Learning', in R. S. Peters (ed.), *The Concept of Education* (London: Routledge & Kegan Paul, 1967), pp. 24–43. (This volume pp. 195–213.)

form in examples of this kind. As far as language is concerned, Chomsky's point seems to be that a child could not abstract the notion of language from the data available to him.[6]

There are serious objections to this way of putting it. In the first place, the fact that a concept cannot be abstracted from experienced data does not mean that it must be innate. In Kantian terms, a concept might be *a priori* without being innate (although I do not think that it is really helpful so to speak, since the notion of an *a priori* concept implies by its contrast with *a posteriori* concepts the very abstractionist thesis that is at fault). At all events the knowledge involved in having a concept might begin with experience without arising out of experience. It is somewhat surprising that Chomsky seems to suppose that the only alternative to empiricism is rationalism. Even while operating within the terms of reference supplied by traditional epistemology, there is the Kantian point of view. Piaget, who does adopt a Kantian point of view, does not suppose that the structures of the mind which he thinks it important to recognize are innate; indeed it is a crucial point for him that they *develop*. For him, as I have already said, rationalism involves structure without genesis, without development. I do not point this out because I think that Piaget's approach is the right one, rather to indicate that there are, within the terms of reference that Chomsky accepts, other possibilities than those which he recognizes. Chomsky's brief comments on Piaget in *Language and Mind*, apart from adducing putative evidence that may cast doubt on the validity of Piaget's actual findings—a strictly empirical issue on which it is scarcely open to a philosopher as such to comment, are to the effect that Piaget does not adequately explain 'the basis for the transition from one of the stages that he discusses to the next, higher stage'. This is an *ignoratio elenchi*, since for Piaget there is no basis in the sense that Chomsky seems to demand. It is in his view merely a fact about human beings in the sort of environment in which they find themselves that there are the stages that he distinguishes in their development. It is true that Piaget seems to make this more than a merely contingent fact; the reasons for this are complicated and I cannot go into them properly here, although I have discussed them to some extent else-

---

[6] Cf. N. Chomsky, *Language and Mind* (New York: Harcourt Brace, 1968), p. 74, where he speaks about the problems involved in the idea of the grammar of a language being discovered by the child 'from the data presented to him'; his point is that the idea of language itself with its deep structure could not be so discovered.

where.[7] Suffice it to say that for Piaget it is a kind of essential truth about the nature of the understanding, a kind of metaphysical truth about man in his place in the world. Or so I think. Yet whatever the status of Piaget's theory about the development of understanding in the individual, it provides a further possible view in addition to those recognized by Chomsky, and it is an *ignoratio elenchi* to force it into the mould of one or other of the initial alternatives.

But, as I have implied before, I do not think that any of these alternatives are really viable, and there are objections to Chomsky which are more fundamental than those which I have mentioned. Chomsky speaks of the child having to discover the grammar of a language from the data presented to him,[8] and thus seems to think that it makes sense to speak of there being data which the child has to survey. The term 'data' could be taken either as referring to sense-data or in a more ordinary sense where data are correlative with evidence. The two uses of the term are no doubt connected in that sense-data may be construed as incontrovertible pieces of evidence provided by the senses, while data in the more ordinary scientific sense provide evidence in a straight-forward way, though scarcely incontrovertible evidence in any absolute sense. But in the ordinary, scientific sense of the word something can be taken as datum only if it is already understood as such. In other words, if it is true that the child has to discover the grammar of a language from the data presented to it, the child must not only have a prior idea of what a language is, but have also a prior idea of what among its sense-experiences is relevant to the supposal that it is hearing a language being used. Data are data only relative to a prior question and thus to a prior understanding. Since this applies wherever reference is made to data, the inference to be drawn is that *any* discovery about the world, no matter what, presupposes a prior understanding of it. By this token we should need prior (innate) ideas not just of language, but of any feature of the world in which we find ourselves. The only way to short-circuit this argument would be to suppose that there are data which are absolute, which provide their own understanding without dependence on concepts. Such a conception is part of the traditional notion of sense-data, which thereby constitute pieces of information provided by the senses in a way that is independent of concepts. I shall

---

[7] D. W. Hamlyn, op. cit. and 'Epistemology and Conceptual Development', in T. Mischel (ed.), *Cognitive Development and Epistemology* (New York: Academic Press, 1971).

[8] N. Chomsky, loc. cit.

not rehearse the objections to this whole way of thinking; they have been made by a whole host of philosophers in many places. It is not clear, in any case, that Chomsky means to have recourse to such a notion. Without it, however, once the problem is posed in the way that Chomsky poses it, one is committed to the view that there must be concepts prior to any experience of data; and once one is on this road to innate ideas there is no obvious way off it again. This is the inescapable conclusion for a rationalist—that all ideas are innate—and Chomsky does not appear to see that it is so.

A point associated with the last, and one which is bound up with an issue in the philosophy of mind which is common to both empiricist and rationalist epistemologies, is that the child, and indeed any individual, is construed as set over against a world which he has to construct on the basis of what is presented to his senses. This point of view is a legacy of Cartesianism, which involves the identification of a person with his mind, which is thus separated from the physical world; that physical world is therefore 'external'. Given all this, unless the child has a world already made for him, it must be supposed that he has to construct it from what is given to him, from the data, as if he were a scientist working on a problem, but a scientist who in the nature of the case must work on his own. The child has thus to find his own way about the world, and there is no one to help him, since other people are part of that 'external world'. If this were so, it would be impossible to see how the child could ever come to a conception of the world at all, let alone the same world as we know. I shall not dwell on these absurdities; what I have said should be sufficient to indicate that any view which in effect construes the child as a solitary inquirer attempting to discover the truth about the world must be rejected. (What after all could be meant by 'truth' in these circumstances?) But it is a view of this kind that is implicit in Chomsky's way of looking at what is presupposed in language learning, or at any rate in some of the things that he says about this, such as his remark about the child having to discover the grammar of a language from the data presented to him. It is equally implicit in his views about learning of other kinds.

There is perhaps a tendency at this point to say to oneself 'But surely the child has to acquire knowledge of the world somehow; if it is not something like this how does he do it at all?' To think like this is to think of the child as on a par with an adult, as indeed a little adult with adult kinds of knowledge and understanding. It makes perfect sense to ask of an adult with a certain amount of knowledge and under-

standing how he can go about acquiring further knowledge and understanding; but it is that prior knowledge and understanding that makes
possible the acquisition of more of the same kind. If therefore one per-
sists in thinking of the child as a little adult, then if knowledge is to
develop at all it will be necessary to attribute to him prior, and there-
for presumably innate, knowledge. But the knowledge in question must
be knowledge of the world as *we* know it; the knowledge and understanding in question must be objective, not any kind of understanding
will do. But surely knowledge and understanding of this kind could
only be acquired. This is not to say that we are not born with equipment, physiological or otherwise, necessary for the acquisition of such
knowledge and understanding. It *is* to say that the suggestion that we
are born in possession of understanding, that this understanding is
objective, and that this is not a mere happy accident, makes no sense.
Some animals are of course born with ready-made dispositions to
react in appropriate ways in certain circumstances, dispositions that we
call 'instinctive'. But such facts are to be explained in evolutionary
terms, and in terms of whatever mechanics in the individual animal are
appropriate to the preservation of the species; this very fact, among
others, makes it inappropriate to say that they have innate knowledge
or understanding. In sum, I do not think that it is intelligible to speak
of innate knowledge and understanding, and therefore of innate ideas,
at least in any sense that makes the notion of any use for the explanation of the acquisition of the rest of our knowledge of a common and
objective world.

How, then, is knowledge acquired? The only reasonable response to
this question is to ask in return 'What knowledge, and by whom?' A
similar response is required for the question 'How does learning take
place?' It depends entirely on what it is that is being learned and who
it is that is doing the learning. Knowledge may take various forms, and
the ways to the various goals which knowledge may constitute are
likely to vary with the nature of the goal in question. Even within the
sphere of, say, skills, learning how to play the piano will be a quite
different matter from learning how to type, although both involve the
use of the fingers. I do not mean to suggest by this that there are no
similarities between skills and methods of acquiring them; but it is
equally important to stress the differences, and when one brings in
other forms of learning and other things to be learned the differences
become even more apparent. Psychologists, at any rate all those who
are not chained to one form or another of dogma, are well aware of

this, and references to forms of learning of differing kinds are now relatively commonplace in books on these matters. But the application of knowledge of these differing learning processes to actual educational problems involves knowing about the learners too. People obviously have different facilities for learning, but even within groups of people with roughly the same facility starting-points may also differ.

I mean by starting-points the previous knowledge and understanding of the persons concerned. Even if one can be fairly sure that a child of a certain age could not, given the general framework of educational processes within our culture, have certain forms of understanding and knowledge (a fact that no doubt underlies Piaget's notorious, and probably over-rigid conception of the stages of intellectual development, whether or not he would put it in this way), there is still room for great variety in the knowledge and understanding possessed by such children. Hence educational processes must always be a compromise and, I suspect, a question of hit and miss. (And one might add, for professional educators, that the educational processes that they often have in mind, what goes on in the school class, constitute a comparatively small part of the learning that goes on in everyday life.) Apart from all this, there is a large array of motivational and emotional factors which will clearly influence the way in which learning goes on, if they do not actually prevent it. I do not see how it is possible to say anything both significant and general about human learning processes, although there is nothing against the possibility of a kind of natural history of such processes, a rough classification of their species and of the forms that they may take. Moreover, a consideration of the goal to be attained in any process of learning may lead to a delimitation of the possible range of processes that are relevant to that goal. At the same time, it has to be said that people sometimes acquire understanding and knowledge, even knacks and skills, in surprising ways which could not be ruled out in advance; it would be foolish and unprofitable to undermine such possibilities *a priori*.

All this may suggest that we are thrown back upon an empiricist epistemology, according to which there are no prior limitations on what can be acquired through experience. It was not my intention to lead up to such a conclusion; nor do I think it the right one. For it is still necessary to meet the point that Chomsky, for example, makes against empiricist theories of language learning—how the business could even get off the ground if those theories were correct. For the possibility of learning *X* presupposes the existence of prior knowledge in terms of which X will make sense to the learner. In learning which involves a positive attempt to arrive at an answer to a question there must be prior knowledge of what sort of thing will count as an answer. (This is a point which Plato seems to me to be groping after in the *Meno* when he attempts to meet Meno's paradox, that we cannot carry on an inquiry since either we already know what we seek or we shall not recognize it when we reach it, by his doctrine of recollection. Plato's solution is clearly wrong, but he may have a correct sense of the problem.) But where the learning is more passive or is not a function of a positive search on the part of the learner, the prior knowledge may be more indirectly connected with what is learned. Yet, at all events, without a background of knowledge of some sort what is to be learned will not be made sense of and is in that case not a possible object of learning.

Does this lead back towards a rationalist epistemology? The answer is, I believe, 'No more than it leads to a Platonic doctrine of recollection.' The problem is real enough but not the solutions so far considered. It is not really a question of 'either an initial *tabula rasa* or an initial body of innate knowledge'. The '*tabula rasa*' conception implies too mechanical a view of the acquisition of knowledge apart from the other failings already noted; for it implies that the effects of external stimulation are simply imprinted on the soul, the mind, the organism, or whatever it is. The opposite conception implies too intellectual and perhaps too conscious an operation on our part; in all cases we have somehow to apply prior knowledge to what we now experience, like the application of a hypothesis to the data being acquired. But there is in any case no need for the prior knowledge which I have mentioned as necessary for learning to be *temporally* prior. This is a point that requires emphasis. The point that I was making was meant to be a conceptual point—it is simply that someone could not come to knowledge of X, if this is to be learning, without other knowledge. But this other knowledge does not need to have been acquired previously in time. The priority that is necessary is a logical priority only. Someone who has come to see that q is implied by p may be said to have learned that q, but it is not necessary for this that he should have come to see the truth of p before coming to see that of q; he may come to see both together. A slogan which would make my point would be that all learning is, in one way or another, connecting things, and it is in this way that experience develops. But the connecting may take many different patterns. Why, then, should learning be simply like either of the two processes implied by rationalist and empiricist epistemologies? Why should we be confined to the two alternatives—either mechanism or intellectual operations. Piaget maintains that intellectual operations, when on his view they eventually occur, have already been 'prefigured' in sensory–motor movement. Whether or not this particular suggestion is helpful, could we find in a suggestion of this kind a clue to an adequate solution to the problem how learning can get started?

What I mean by this is the following. Both the approaches so far discussed (as well as any approach that can be construed as anything like a straightforward compromise between them) seem to assume that we can consider the acquisition of knowledge by a person in isolation from the other factors that go to make up that person's life. It is true that there have been philosophers like Maine de Biran who have insisted that any adequate epistemology must bring in the will as well as sense-perception and the understanding. But the force of such suggestions has typically been that resistance to the will can simply provide extra pieces of information about the environment, information that could not be provided in any other way and certainly not in the merely passive reception of information that traditional empiricism presupposes. Similar things might be said of suggestions that *action* is necessary for the acquisition of knowledge and that a purely passive and sensory consciousness is an absurdity.[9] So it may be, and the necessity of activity has equally been stressed by Piaget (among others of whom one might perhaps mention J. J. Gibson in his book *The Senses Considered as Perceptual Systems*). I have no wish to underestimate the importance for the acquisition of some knowledge of exploration on the part of the learner, of trial and error, and of active experimentation. But, once again, without prior questions to be put to nature such exploration and experimentation cannot get a purchase, for the reasons already rehearsed. Hence it is not just this sort of thing that I have in mind when I say that the theories so far discussed do not pay attention sufficiently to the other factors that go to make up a person's life.

One thing that I have in mind is the point that an individual is not a solitary centre of consciousness for which the questions of which I have spoken have somehow to arise—and if so how? A person is a social being from childhood, and the knowledge that he has to acquire is equally socially determined in an important sense. For knowledge presupposes criteria of truth, and these presuppose the agreement

[9] Cf., e.g., G. E. M. Anscombe, *Intention* (Oxford: Blackwell, 1957), p. 67.

in judgements of which Wittgenstein spoke.[10] Hence learning on the part of an individual is as much as anything his initiation into a framework over which there is wide agreement, even if there is also plenty of room for individual deviations from the norm. For this to be possible there has to be, and is, a background of common interests, attitudes, feelings, and, if I may put it in these terms, cognitive apparatus. There must be, to use Wittgenstein's phrase, agreement in forms of life. By 'cognitive apparatus' I mean everything that makes possible a common and shared sensibility and ways of thinking—physiological make-up, sense-organs, etc. In animals, of course, much more than is the case for humans depends on this sort of thing, upon common and inborn ways of reacting to the world, ways of reacting that we call instinctive, the explanation of the persistence of which is, as I said earlier, to be found not in its value for the individual but for the species. But even in humans there has to be something of this sort of thing, and it was to this in part that I was referring in speaking of common interests, etc.— the need for food, comfort, etc. But the child has to be put in the way of things that will satisfy those interests; he cannot find them for himself, since he can have no conception of what will satisfy them or even of what it is for something to do so. The same is true of animals in a way; but there is in their case a natural disposition for the satisfaction of needs, due to a pattern of behaviour appropriate to the species, without which the species would not survive (cf. the patterns of behaviour investigated by ethologists such as Tinbergen, for example the tendency of a chick to peck at a spot on the mother's bill, so getting food from her). In humans there have to be some instinctive patterns of behaviour, e.g. sucking, but so much more depends on what the mother puts the child in the way of. Equally much depends on such things as expressions of love and affection and on the *rapport* that is normally set up between parent and child.

Thus the child is not a solitary but immature consciousness trying to make sense of a mass of data which come before it in the light of certain mysterious principles with which it is born. Awareness of objects, in the formal but not material sense of 'object', is something that we must presuppose in the child. What he is put in the way of will determine the ways in which the formal notion of an object is cashed for him, what objects, in other words, he takes to exist; in the end too this will determine that the ways in which that notion is so cashed are

[10] L. Wittgenstein, *Philosophical Investigations* (Oxford: Blackwell, 1953), I, 242.

roughly our ways. Psychologists have sometimes said that for the infant there is initially no distinction between self and not-self. If this is meant to be an empirical point it is difficult to know on what basis the truth of the claim is to be assessed. But one might contrast it with Kant's assertion in his 'transcendental deduction' that awareness of objects with an identity in space and time is correlative with awareness of oneself as such. If the psychologists' claim is correct the child has to get from a stage at which there is no distinction between self and not-self to a stage at which there is a correlative awareness of oneself and of other spatio-temporal objects with an identity. Whether or not the matter is happily so put, there is no intrinsic difficulty about a child's having to learn of his own identity as a person with a body as distinct from other bodies with other identities. He could not do this purely on the basis of experiences which are in a genuine sense private; but the child is in the world and a part of the world from the beginning and is put in the way of making these distinctions by adults. His attention is drawn to them by the circumstances of his upbringing, and in particular by the treatment that he receives from and the relations that he has with his mother. Differences between objects of awareness are thus forced upon him. Of vital importance in all this is the role of correction by adults. Only through this, I suggest, can something like the concept of truth emerge and in it the concept of judgement. I am tempted to maintain that it is an *a priori* truth that a baby left on a desert island would not survive; nothing would put it in the way of making the distinctions, etc., necessary to survival. Even 'wolf-boys' receive some initiation into a 'world'.

I have in the foregoing spoken often of the child being put in the way of things; I have not said merely that the child is taught things. The vital role that I have given to other people, and to the mother in particular, in the child's learning about the world is not merely that of a teacher; although in performing the correcting function to which I have already referred parents and other adults *are* in effect teaching or at least performing a necessary prolegomenon to teaching. For what they are doing is ensuring that the child takes things as we do. Yet the relation that exists between mother and child is, if not from the very beginning yet nevertheless soon, fundamentally a personal relation. It is a vital factor in the child's upbringing that parents and other people treat the child as a person and not just as a thing; there is a constant respect for feelings, care, love, and so on, which elicit responses from the child which are, if not the same, at any rate appropriate to the situation. Thus it is part of my thesis that early learning is very much a function of personal relationships that exist between the child and other human beings; without this or something like it, it is difficult to see how learning could go on at all, let alone make much progress. How much of this is also applicable to adult learning?

Psychologists such as D. O. Hebb[11] have made a distinction between early and late learning, the former being general in character and slow in development, compared with the often dramatic jumps that sometimes occur in late learning. The distinction was made, I believe, for, among other reasons, its relevance to the continuity/discontinuity dispute that occurred in the hey-day of the argument between strict S–R theorists such as Hull and others such as Tolman who thought of learning as occurring on occasion at least by other means than the slow piling up of associations or S–R connections. Whether or not the distinction has that particular relevance, it is real and important enough. One would expect early learning to consist of a slow sorting out of categories and distinctions[12] and the gradual acquisition of general principles. The application of these distinctions and principles to cases, even to new and previously unforeseen cases, might well be sudden and quick. If late learning is dependent on personal relations at all, it clearly must be so in a quite different way from that in which the earliest learning is so dependent. In the case of late learning factors concerned with personal relationships may enter the scene as providing motivation or the reverse, insight or the reverse, but they are not a condition of learning taking place at all. Initially in the life of the child I think that they do constitute such a condition.

How does this apply to the problem with which Chomsky is concerned—the acquisition and learning of language? Chomsky postulates an innate language faculty because it is for him inconceivable that the child should acquire familiarity with the idea of language merely from the noises that he hears from other people when they use language; Once given the idea of language itself it is more intelligible how the child should pick up the details of the language spoken by those in his environment. But this account of the matter not only presupposes the view of the child as a little adult having to deal with a problem, it also assumes that the child does it alone and *ex nihilo*, except what it is born with. But surely the idea of language is merely one idea that the child has to pick up in its early years and it is not an idea that lacks connec-

[11] D. O. Hebb, *The Organization of Behavior* (New York: Wiley, 1949).
[12] Cf. the learning that not all men are Daddy.

tion with other things. The point might be put in the following way. Chomsky's problem is that of how the basic categories and phrases of deep structure could be abstracted from the data available. The answer is that they could not be; but it is not entailed by this that they are in consequence innate in the child, since much has gone on before the ability to use and understand language emerges. In particular much has gone on in the way of communication, and communication itself has its foundation in the mutual emotional responses that take place between child and parent. Admittedly communication by language is something in many respects new when it emerges, and it would be very surprising if every aspect of the grammar of language at the level of deep structure had its counterpart in some aspect of pre-linguistic behaviour. On the other hand, from the earliest days when interchange of smiles, for example, is possible, communication is built into the web of behaviour that takes place in the context of personal relations between child and mother, and then child and other people. It is not language alone that the child has to catch on to and interpret, but a mass of behaviour which becomes meaningful to him in one way or another and which is all part of the form of social life into which he is being initiated and in which he comes to share. There is no question of his having to decide what language is all about unaided, any more than he has to reach all by himself the conclusion that some mobile bodies in his vicinity are people and that the movements that they make are actions.

I make this last point in view of Chomsky's remark, noted earlier, about the problem, parallel to that of the acquisition of the idea of language, of the acquisition of the idea of human action, so that just as generative grammar provides a theory relevant to language acquisition so there might be a theory of how people acquire an 'implicit theory of human action'. This in effect foists the other minds problem on to the child, since action is attributable in the primary sense only to things that have minds, and the question whether something is acting in the primary sense is therefore tantamount to the question whether it has a mind. Thus Chomsky's suggestion is that we have to explain how a child comes to understand that some things have minds and how he comes to attribute minds to the right things and not to others. But the child's relations to his mother and thereafter to other people are not so academic as this. Given the care and love that a mother devotes to her child (or if not this at least *some* attitude which is appropriate to a person) how could there even be a problem for the child about the difference between people and things? Indeed one might expect that if there were a problem it could be how it can be, in effect, that things are not people. Consider in this connection the animism of children that Piaget and others have emphasized.

At all events, in the various ways that a child may have his attention drawn and in which he may draw the attention of others, in the various mutual responses, in what happens in the context of everyday life, there is much that prefigures the essential functions of language (functions, for example, such as reference and description, to which are tied the grammatical categories of subject and predicate). We should, however, expect, that the original development of linguistic competence will be a very different thing from either the development of such a competence later in life or the application of the originally acquired competence to the learning of new languages with different surface structure. Every indication is that such expectations are correct. Such cases of 'wolf-boys' that have been recorded indicate that the acquisition of language at a later than ordinary age and where the usual mother–child relationship has been lacking (or at any rate some personal relationship) is extremely difficult if not impossible; while cases like that of Helen Keller reveal the difficulties for those for whom ordinary means of communication in similar or analogous personal contexts are drastically curtailed. This goes together with the claim that I have been making from the beginning that what learning consists in and how it takes place varies considerably according to what it is that has to be learned, who it is that is doing the learning, and in what circumstances. If an analysis of the task to be performed may make it possible to work backwards setting out the steps to be followed rationally in order to reach the goal, the application of such a construction to any educational context must involve making vast assumptions which may or may not be fulfilled to any appreciable extent. Any teacher must make such assumptions in applying his knowledge of what has to be taught; but they are assumptions nevertheless and teaching must for that reason remain an art. It is perhaps fortunate that so much comes out in the wash.

What I am left with is what I suggested at the outset—there are a number of differing kinds of learning process which are more or less fitted to the differing kinds of knowledge, competence, skill, or what have you, that may be required of human beings. Careful analysis of the goal to be attained and the circumstances in which the attempt to reach it is to be carried out may provide guidance on what form of learning is appropriate when. Consideration of the abilities, personality, and character of those doing the learning may provide extra guidance on the ways in which the principles obtained by the analysis may be applied to given individuals. But in the end, as I have said, it is likely to be a matter of compromise and art, and this inevitably imposes limits on education as a discipline in its own right.

X

THE LOGICAL AND PSYCHOLOGICAL ASPECTS OF LEARNING

D. W. HAMLYN

It is, I suppose, obvious enough that some children learn better when there is a smile on the face of the teacher, just as it is conceivable that others may learn better when it is all done in time to music. Some learn better when they are happy, others perhaps when the conditions are austere or comfortable enough not to be distracting. The study of such individual differences is clearly a matter for psychology, since it will be a study of the psychological processes which bear on the facility with which individuals learn. It is even possible in principle to produce generalizations in this field, statements which may apply to people in general, though it may be doubted whether these will in fact amount to more than platitudes—that people learn better in general when encouraged or rewarded, when they are given opportunities for practice, when they are given material in digestible amounts, and so on. Nevertheless, these would certainly be *psychological* generalizations if not very exciting ones. But there are questions about learning which are not psychological questions—questions such as what learning is and what is implied when it is said that someone has learnt something. To answer such questions we have to clarify the concepts which we employ in this sphere, something that requires both reflection and some familiarity with the subject-matter to which those concepts apply. Investigations of this kind are not so much a matter for the psychologist as for the philosopher.

What, then, is it to learn something? In fact, this is a question which I shall, in effect, shelve for the time being, and it may be that I shall have nothing very illuminating to say about it directly. But I shelve it quite deliberately. One might of course say that to learn something is to acquire knowledge of it through experience; but this, although correct as far as it goes, is not likely to be enlightening because, apart from other vaguenesses in the formulation, much depends on the 'something'

From *The Concept of Education*, ed. R. S. Peters (London: Routledge & Kegan Paul; New York: Humanities Press, 1967), pp. 24–43. Reprinted by permission of the author and publishers.

in question. To learn a list of words or a set of formulae, to learn to play the piano or to ride a bicycle, to learn a language or a technique, and to learn a subject or a discipline are all very different things. Although they all involve the acquisition of knowledge, that knowledge is of quite different forms. To learn a list of words, simple rote-learning, as it is called, is nothing more than to memorize that list, and the knowledge involved is merely the knowledge of the words in their appropriate order. In skills such as that involved in riding a bicycle 'knowing how' comes to play a role, and the acquisition of such skills may involve practice as much as does rote-learning, even if in a different way. But here too other things begin to emerge; for few skills could be acquired by practice alone in the most rudimentary sense of that word, and few are in any way independent of some understanding of the issues involved. You could not play the piano without some such understanding, and practice in this case, if it deserves the name, must be intelligent practice. The existence of such understanding may indeed be implied whenever we speak of knowing how to do something, and this, among other things, distinguishes knowing how to do something from merely being able to do it. When we come to learning a language or a technique, and even more so with learning a subject, the appreciation and understanding of the subject and its principles comes to the fore. With the understanding of principles goes the ability to use certain concepts. If there is a distinction to be made between my two last categories, it is that learning a language or a technique is inevitably a practical matter in a way that learning a subject is not so obviously so. But this is a matter of emphasis only; technique and intellectual understanding, theory and practice cannot be completely divorced from each other.

What I have said so far is meant to show the complexities involved in any general discussion of learning. Fortunately, for educational purposes, it is surely unnecessary to go into all this. Rote-learning and simple practice may or may not be adequate tools for educational purposes, but they cannot in any way constitute anything in the way of the essence of education. This last, I suggest, is nothing unless it brings with it understanding and appreciation of principles, their relevance, and their interconnections. Understanding, moreover, involves and presupposes the acquisition and use of concepts. One can understand nothing of a subject unless one has the concepts in which that understanding is to be expressed. Hence, the process of learning a subject goes hand in hand with the process of acquiring the relevant concepts, the concepts in terms of which the subject-matter and its principles are to be formulated. I shall try to say something by way of elucidation of this in the following. But my main concern will be with two points, both of which seem to me comparatively simple. They are as follows.

(1) The subjects into which knowledge is conveniently divided are not block entities laid out, as it were, in a Platonic realm. There is an inclination, I believe, to think that there exists objectively something called, to take one example, mathematics, and that it is the aim of education to bring the learner to a confrontation with it. Subjects are, on this account, ideal entities available for contemplation. Given this, one can then argue about the best way of bringing about this contemplation, since the subjects are too complicated to grasp all at once. Is it better to concentrate on those parts of a subject which are somehow logically prior to others or on those which are psychologically easiest to grasp? The snag about this is that it is not immediately clear what the question means, what the distinction amounts to. Certainly, I think the question what is easy to grasp is not a matter for psychology. On the other hand, the notion of logical priority is perhaps obscure and it has different implications according to the ways in which it is interpreted. I shall enlarge on these points directly.

(2) No one could be said to have come to understand a subject, to have learned it, without some appreciation of general principles, some idea of what it is all about. But knowing and understanding general principles is not just a matter of being able to recite the relevant general propositions. Nothing is contributed by way of understanding when people are made to recite general propositions, even if these are fundamental to a subject. Thus, to present a very young child with, say, the general principles of number theory or algebra would be a futile business; for, he must be capable of cashing such general principles in terms which mean something to him, if understanding is to follow. There is in the growth of understanding of any subject an intimate connection between principles and their applications or instances. Principles must always be seen cashed in their instances, but instances must themselves be seen as cases to which principles are relevant. Thus an appreciation of general principles implies in the full sense an appreciation of how they are to be applied. My point is analogous to one which could equally well be made about concepts; it may be expressed in Kant's famous or notorious slogan that 'thoughts without content are empty, intuitions without concepts are blind' (where by 'intuitions' Kant means something like the reference to instances). To present a

child with little bits of information without reference to general principles at all is a sure way of preventing the development of understanding; such a child would be intellectually blind. But to go to the other extreme and concentrate on principles alone is another way of producing an equally unsatisfactory end-product; the child's thought, if this could be brought about, would be empty—without reference to any particular cases through which the general principles could mean something to him. There must always be a delicate balance between principles and cases; but since there are degrees of generality it is clear that the attainment of full understanding at one level of generality must presuppose something of a balance attained at a lower level of generality, a balance between an understanding of principles in general terms and an understanding of their relevance to particular cases. Otherwise, there is little hope of the relevance of the more general principles being seen. What is the point of presenting to children the principles of set-theory if they are not capable of understanding what it is for something to be a set? This has an obvious relevance to any discussion of Piaget's 'stages', especially to the distinction between concrete and abstract operations. Indeed, I suspect that Piaget is an essentially Kantian thinker in many respects.

I shall discuss my two points in turn. They are not of course unconnected. I have said that it is a superstition to think that subjects exist as block entities, the contemplation of which should be the goal of the learner. I do not mean by this that there are no differences between, for example, history and physics. The historian may be distinguished from the physicist by, among other things, his interests, his methodology, and the concepts which he brings to his subject-matter and in terms of which he thinks about it. There are also differences between the modes of explanation which the two employ—between historical and scientific theories. All these differences—and no doubt there are others—are important. But to suppose that the real difference is that there is one body of knowledge, expressible as a set of facts, called 'history' and another called 'physics', which the two are out to discover betrays a quite erroneous conception of learning. It is to suppose that learning consists merely in the acquisition of knowledge of a set of facts, the contemplation of a set of propositions. At its lowest, it reduces learning to simple rote-learning. But it cannot be anything like that in fact. Even at the simplest level the acquisition of knowledge of facts goes hand in hand with understanding. Even in rote-learning it is essential to understand what is going on, and in higher forms of learning understanding is much more important still. Thus words like 'history', 'physics', and 'mathematics' are not just the names of bodies of knowledge, in the sense of sets of true propositions; they are, if anything, the names of approaches to facts of generally different kinds. At a certain level, perhaps, we cannot even say that; distinctions between subjects tend to break down, they become an administrative matter only, or a question merely of the differences in the background of interests on the part of those who are concerned with them.

I may be thought to be labouring the obvious. Surely, it may be said, no one really thinks that subjects exist in *that* sense. Perhaps so, but I detect suggestions of this sort in certain discussions which imply that learning should start from what is logically prior in a subject, and even perhaps in those who deny this and insist that psychological priorities are everything. Let me explain what I mean—and the best way to do this is to indicate and explain one sense of the words 'logically prior', a sense which I shall directly come to repudiate in this context.

Explanatory theories, e.g. scientific theories, have a logical structure in the sense that the propositions of which the theory is constituted can be arranged in a certain order, so that certain propositions can be derived from others. It is indeed the fact that from general laws and statements of initial conditions it is possible to derive conclusions—the fact to be explained—that provides the basis of scientific, and no doubt other kinds of explanation. We thus expect that with the help of reference to the general we shall be able to deduce the particular. It is because of logical relationships of this kind—relationships of entailment—that we can speak of the theory having a structure, and we may say, as Aristotle said, that the general is logically prior to the particular. The same sort of thing applies in mathematics. In so far as it is true to say that set theory provides the basis of arithmetic it is because arithmetic can be explained in terms of set theory. Set theory furnishes the more general point of view under which arithmetic can be subsumed. Hence, we might say that the notion of a set is logically prior to that of, say, a number, because the latter can be explained in terms of the former, but not vice versa. The direction in which explanation must proceed, and the logical relationships which go with it, thus determine what is logically prior within a discipline.

This, however, only applies where the discipline in question constitutes a theory—to parts of science, the foundations of mathematics, and so on. Where questions of explanation do not arise and do not have a place, then this sort of consideration has no place either. It is difficult to see how large parts of history or literature could be said to have a structure in this sense. But even where it could be said that this is so—where a subject admits of the formulation of a theory of it— this could have few implications for education. Even if there is *a* sense in which someone could not be said *fully* to understand arithmetic without understanding set theory, this is only in the sense in which it might be said that someone could not fully understand, say, the movements of billiard balls without understanding the principles of sub-atomic physics. And no one, I take it, would suggest that children should be introduced to physics *by that route*. The most fundamental concepts of a subject, from the point of view of explanation, are not likely to be the most familiar. To concentrate on such concepts may hinder the understanding of how the more familiar concepts are to be applied—a matter which is just as important for complete understanding. But, to repeat the remark which I made earlier, there are subjects for which none of this makes sense, since questions of explanation do not arise within them, or do so only to a minor extent.

If this is accepted, it may be suggested that the only remaining position is that, as far as learning is concerned, the only priorities are psychological priorities. For, from the point of view of learning, the priorities that the structure of explanation provides are not relevant. That is to say that the only possible procedure for an educationalist is to find out empirically what parts of a subject are the easiest to learn and to insist that learning should start from there. For there is now no question, it might be thought, of having to start from those elements which are logically necessary if anything else in the subject-matter is to be seen as it is. There is no question of having to see the subject arranged in its proper logical order. There are no logical conditions for a proper understanding of a subject; there are only psychological conditions, e.g. that no one could grasp the difficult parts before grasping the easy ones. So it might be said. To come to this conclusion would, I think, be far too quick a deduction from what has already been established, but there is in any case something very odd about the suggestion that the easiness or difficulty of a subject or a part of a subject is a matter for psychology. It is clearly enough a matter for psychology that something is easier for one person to learn than another; for, the question why this is so could be answered only by an investigation into the people concerned. The conditions under which individuals learn something more easily is also clearly enough a matter for psychology, as I indicated at the beginning of this lecture. It is not so clear that the same thing holds good of the question why one subject or part of a subject is easier than others.

In what ways might one subject be more difficult than another? It might demand knowledge of more facts (so I have heard it said about psychology in comparison with philosophy). It might be more abstract (so I have heard it said about philosophy in comparison with psychology). It might demand knowledge of skills, procedures, or ways of thinking not demanded by the other, and it might even presuppose the other in one way or another. Factors like abstractness and complexity loom large here, although these factors may arise in many more ways than one, and I would not claim that these are the only factors at stake. However, abstractness and complexity are obviously very important and I shall concentrate on them in what follows. It may be thought that these factors are relevant because of the truth of psychological generalizations such as that people generally find the abstract and the complicated more difficult to understand or grasp than the specific and the simple. But is this just a psychological generalization? *Could* a man find the abstract easier to grasp than the specific, and the complicated easier to grasp than the simple? Would this indeed make any sense? If not, then we are confronted here, not just with empirical psychological generalizations, but with some sort of *a priori* or necessary truth. That is to say that in that event abstractness and complexity will be *criteria* of difficulty; if one subject is more abstract and complex than another then it will follow necessarily that the one is more difficult than the other. I do not claim that it is always obvious whether some branch of a subject *is* more abstract or complicated than another, and to discover the truth on the matter may require investigation of a kind. The way in which this might be done is by turning what I have said on its head. Given that people normally find X more difficult than Y, this will be a reason for saying that X may be more complicated or abstract than Y (depending on the exact nature of the difficulties reported). The idea of what is normal is very important here, and I shall return to it later in an analogous context. The point is that if a subject is difficult people may be expected normally to find it so— just as, if something is red it is to be expected that people will normally see it so. When I say 'normally', I do not mean 'generally'; I mean 'in normal conditions'. It is this notion of what is normal which provides the link between what something is and how it appears to people or how they find it. Thus, if abstractness and complexity are criteria of difficulty we may expect that people will normally find the abstract and complicated difficult; and conversely, if people normally find something difficult, this will be an indication of its abstractness or complexity.

We need, however, to look further at the idea that there is some kind of necessary connection between the notion of difficulty and those of complexity and abstractness. Can we even conceive of a man finding the complicated or abstract easier than the simple or specific? There are of course people who feel more at home with the complicated than the simple—people of whom we say that they cannot see the wood for the trees; and there may be people who are similarly more at home with the abstract than the specific, people who fail to bring issues down to earth. But this indicates something about their habits or qualities of mind; it indicates nothing directly about the comparative easiness of the subject-matter. The man who cannot see the wood for the trees may indeed find the simple too easy for his taste. It may come to be that the simplicity of a thing constitutes an obstacle to his understanding, just because of his cast of mind; we might perhaps say that for some reason he shuts his eyes to the simple. But his case provides no grounds for denying that the complicated is normally more difficult for people than the simple. Indeed, the special explanation that is required indicates that the case is not normal. The indications, then, are that we should expect people normally to find the complex difficult. Indeed, the connection between complexity and difficulty seems to turn on certain things about the concept of understanding. The complicated may, in fact, be described as that which puts a certain kind of demand on the understanding. To grasp a complicated whole is to grasp the simpler components in their relationship with each other; hence this kind of understanding presupposes the understanding of the simpler; and where a man appears not to find it easy to take in the simple by itself, we need a special explanation of the fact. The same is true of the relation between the abstract and the concrete or specific, although this raises considerations to which I have already referred under my second heading and to which I shall return later. I conclude, however, that factors like complexity and abstractness are in fact criteria of difficulty, and that it is thus not just a psychological truth that people find the complicated and abstract difficult.

These considerations, however, open up once again the question whether there are any priorities in a learner's approach to a subject which are more than psychological. (And that there *are* psychological considerations I have no wish to deny, since, for example, personality differences between people may make one way of putting over a subject more rewarding in one man's case than in another's. Factors relative to the learning of something on specific occasions and by specific individuals are always psychologically relevant.) Now, I think that there are priorities in learning which *are* more than psychological, and they might be described as epistemological, or logical in another sense from the one already discussed. In the growth of knowledge, certain things must be done before others. Not only is it the case that certain facts must sometimes be known if one is going on to make sense of others, but it is also the case that sometimes certain things must be understood, certain concepts grasped, before progress can be made at all. For example, in arithmetic it is essential that one should understand the notion of an ordinary integer if one is to understand that of a fraction. This is quite apart from such general considerations as the priority of the simple to the complicated, to which reference has already been made. The appreciation of certain subjects demands a certain order for knowledge. That this must be so is indicated by the existence of general principles for the establishment of curricula, and if it were not so any suggestion that programmes could be laid down for teaching machines would be impossible. What I am now saying is that such programmes, such principles of order, could be established only by decisions on what is the appropriate order for the development of the knowledge and understanding of a subject. To reach such decisions demands that very knowledge and understanding of the subject itself, plus an ability and willingness to reflect upon the exact relationships between the concepts presupposed within it. This is not a matter for psychology. I would emphasize this point.

Let us consider in some detail an example which brings out the kind of consideration which I have in mind. As is perhaps well enough known, Piaget and his associates have carried out a number of studies, which have become known as 'conservation studies', concerned with the child's appreciation of such general principles as the conservation of matter, size, and weight. It has been brought out that children at a certain age do not always appreciate such principles and even appear to apply them inconsistently. Moreover, they do not come to accept them all at the same time. There appears to be a general assumption in Piaget's approach that they perhaps *should* do so, and that it is surprising that they do not. There is also perhaps a sense of surprise that children should fail at all to accept the principles, despite the fact that in the actual history of thought some of these principles were not formally established until comparatively recently, at any rate during the last three or four hundred years. These studies might be represented as concerned with the understanding of concepts which fall within the general field of physics, and may thus be described as studies in the child's understanding of elementary physics. The question that arises is what could be discovered about the situations under investigation merely by reflecting about them. Let us take a specific and simple case of a Piagetian type: we have, let us suppose, a definite quantity of liquid of a specific colour, which can be poured from a wide transparent container into a similar narrow one. When the liquid is poured from the wide container into the narrow one, a child at a certain stage of intellectual development might well say, because of the comparative depth of the liquid in the containers, that there is more liquid in the narrow one. This may be so even though he sees the liquid being poured from the one container into the other. What are we to suppose has gone on here—what concepts employed and how?

Many sorts of consideration are relevant. We, who know the right answers, know that change of place and container does not affect the identity of the liquid or its volume, and that volume is not a simple function of depth. But these are not factors which we can take for granted in a child, and it does not take a great deal of reflection to see that we cannot. Moreover, the notion of the identity of a liquid (or of any other object) is not necessarily an obvious one. After all, we allow some changes in things without thereby denying that they retain their identity. Liquids expand when heated without becoming thereby different liquids. If we were to maintain that the identity of a liquid has something to do with its mass, this is obviously by no means a simple notion, and is not one that could at all be taken for granted in a child. What *does* identity depend on for a child? I am anxious here only to raise such questions for consideration, and to bring out the complicated relationships that may exist between the concepts which we use even in situations which may seem obvious to us. *We* tend to take notions like that of identity for granted (even when we cannot give an account of them); but there is no saying that a child does. Nor should we expect insight into these relationships to emerge all at one time; for some of them are more complicated than others. The notion of volume, for example, is a more complicated notion than that of depth—it introduces another dimension. The volume of a liquid is therefore necessarily more difficult to estimate than its depth. Hence, the apparent relationship between the identity of an object and its depth or height may well seem more obvious than that between the identity of an object and its volume. All this should be evident to one who is prepared merely to reflect about the situation, provided that he has the requisite concepts.

Furthermore, it is not surprising that at a certain stage of development a child may be pulled in different directions: it is the same object for him to the extent that nothing has apparently been done to it which could cause it to change its volume or indeed change at all; yet it is different because its apparent depth and therefore apparent volume have changed. In the development of the 'right' view of things social influences obviously play a large part—a point very much under-emphasized by Piaget. Similar considerations apply to the part played by the acquisition of linguistic tools. In other words, the facility with which a child may come to see the proper relationships between such factors as volume, depth, and the identity of the object will depend on the extent to which he is subject to social influences of a certain sort and on his ability to formulate the relationships in words.

I have no wish to draw any other general moral than the one which I have already mentioned, i.e. the need for reflection on such situations. I certainly do not believe that it is possible to lay down any general law of development which the child must follow in acquiring concepts and coming to see the relationships between them. I would, however, point to the fact that concepts vary in complexity and abstractness, and that this determines certain general priorities. In considering how education should proceed one has to start from a knowledge of the concepts which a child possesses and the goal to be attained, and work out the intervening steps in the light of such general considerations as I have mentioned. This, I would emphasize again, can be done only by one who knows the subject and is prepared to reflect about it. There is no short cut, but that certain things must come before others in any process of this sort is a matter of logical necessity of a kind. How exactly, how precisely the priorities could be worked out is a matter for speculation, and the steps to be followed in the teaching of any given child will obviously depend on where that child is already, on what concepts he already has, and on what relationships he already appreci-ates. For this reason, any generalized programme for teaching children of roughly the same stage of development must inevitably be a matter for compromise; but that *some* general principles can be laid down for the development of knowledge within any given sphere is of course a presupposition of any educational programme. In some disciplines the steps to be taken by the learner are comparatively easy to establish; hence their amenability to instruction by teaching machines. In other disciplines, any programme of teaching must inevitably be a hit and miss affair. It is all a question of the complexity of the relationships which exist between the concepts in terms of which the subject-matter is to be understood. An assessment of these relationships can come only from one who knows the subject. It is not a matter for one who has specialist psychological knowledge alone.

I may have given the impression that while subjects are not block entities, in the sense explained earlier, they nevertheless have a fixed order of development, and that learning consists in finding out what this is and following it up. I do not think that this would be the correct account of the situation. This is not just because it is unrealistic, not just because finding one's way may involve going down many blind alleys. Wittgenstein once described coming to understand the nature of mathematics as trying to find one's way round a strange town, and this is not a bad description of any attempt to learn a subject. Moreover, it may be that in the end one of the best ways of coming to understand the geography of a town is to get thoroughly lost and have to find one's way home despite this. The apparently blind alleys may turn out not to be blind after all. Sometimes too the best first step may be to acquire a habit of going in a certain direction; habits can always be adapted later, as long as they do not become ossified. All this is true, but it does not get to the root of the problem. The analogy may or may not work even at the most abstract level of a subject, although the idea of a settled geography to be discovered may be one to be retained at any rate as an ideal. But the child in a school is not so much learning the geography of an area as acquiring the tools and techniques by which he may eventually come to make a map of it. A tool is of little use until it is decided what purposes it may be used for. Maps also may be constructed for different purposes and with different projections.

The point of this analogy is that concepts too can be thought of as tools of this kind. In making a map one has to know not only the features of the terrain to be represented on it, but also what counts as a feature of a specific kind. Similarly, concepts may be thought of as instruments for the task of attaining a familiarity in thought with some range of facts and also for attaining an understanding of what counts as a fact of a given kind. And just as the map has a purpose, so too concepts may be regarded as devices for thinking of the facts in a way which may be useful for some further end. That is why I said earlier that in considering how education should proceed one should start not only from a knowledge of the concepts which a child already has but also from a knowledge of the goal to be attained. What is the goal to be attained in teaching a young child elementary arithmetic, the salient facts of an historical period, or the rudiments of English grammar? Until questions of this sort are answered it is impossible to say how we should proceed or in what order concepts should be invoked. It has, in sum, to be decided what is the goal of any given inquiry. The problem is a well-known one in connection with the learning of Classics. Until the goal to be attained in studying Classics has been decided it is pointless to argue about how to go about studying it —whether, for example, the doing of Latin proses or the study of Ciceronian cadences has any utility. Concepts are, to change the analogy, like keys too; they open doors, but if they are to be of any use one must know what door each opens, whether the door leads anywhere, and whether there is any point in opening it.

I have spoken of concepts long enough without really explaining the term. I must now say something of what it is to have and acquire a concept, and this will bring me to my second main topic, about which I have in effect said something already. It must now be made explicit. The connection is this: I said earlier, in presenting my second main point, that it turned on what was involved in understanding principles. The notions of a concept and a principle are interconnected; to have a concept of something is to know the principle in accordance with which things are said to be of the relevant kind. To have a concept of, say, man is to know the principle whereby certain things may be collected together—those things, namely, which we call men. It is thus to know what it is to be a man. This entails not only being able to give an account of what sorts of things men are but also thereby to recognize men as such. To acquire a concept thus involves acquiring this knowledge and this ability. Of course, someone may have a *certain* understanding of a concept without being able to recognize the things which fall under it. There is a sense in which a blind man may be said to have some understanding of the concept of redness. He may be able to tell you that it is a colour, and he may be able to give a formal account of what a colour is, e.g. that it is a property of the surfaces of objects that is accessible only to vision. He may indeed be able to give some account of the structure of colours and of the relation of red to the other colours. All this is possible without sight, and therefore without the experience necessary to a full understanding of what it is for an object to be red. Such a full understanding requires both the ability to give a formal account of redness and the ability to recognize instances. A concept thus gives one a principle of organization for a subject matter. If one has a given concept one has knowledge of that principle. That is why I have already talked of the understanding of a subject as a matter of appreciating certain concepts and their inter-relationships.

It is a dogma of empiricism that one acquires a concept by reviewing a number of particular things and seeing what is common to them. This cannot be the correct view of the situation if only because in order to do this one must be in the position to regard those particular things *as instances*. It is necessary to know what things it is relevant to collect together for this purpose. Thus it might seem more pertinent to speak of applying concepts to things rather than abstracting them from things. The truth is what I have already said—that we have the concept in question only when we are both able to see a range of things as falling under the concept and also in the position to know what it is for them so to fall, what it is that makes them instances. For this reason, there is inevitably in the process of acquiring concepts a delicate balance between a kind of abstract understanding of what it is to be an *X* and a knowledge of what things conform to this criterion. In learning—that is to say, in the growth of knowledge and understanding of a subject-matter—there must at every stage be achieved a balance of this sort if progress is to be maintained. Habits of mind, habitual ways of thinking, however useful when considered merely as stages in a transition to greater understanding, become intellectually dangerous if allowed to ossify. But there are other dangers also, those which I referred to earlier. There is the danger of becoming too concerned with particular things to the extent that it becomes just one damned fact after another. There is also at the other extreme the danger of spinning out connections between concepts without stopping to ask for their cash value.[1]

These points which I have made are, as I indicated earlier, essentially Kantian. They are to be found also in a sense in Piaget, although in his case they receive a strange biological dress. A strictly philosophical point is tricked out under the guise of a rather vague and certainly misleading psychological or biological theory. I refer here to Piaget's

---

[1] I ignore here the possibility of *a priori* concepts, but these would be intelligible only in some sort of connection with concepts which do have the application discussed above.

notions of accommodation and assimilation and the balance to be achieved between these processes. What Piaget has in mind is the idea that our knowledge of objects is partly determined by what these objects are in themselves, partly by how we regard them. This comes down to the point which I have already set out, concerning the relationship between concepts and instances. But to use the notions of accommodation and assimilation to express the point is harmful in two ways at least.

(1) The idea that perception and the acquisition of knowledge generally involve accommodation and assimilation amounts to the idea that in this context there is a mutual modification of subject and object. (A parallel for this idea can again be found in Aristotle, in his view that perception consists in an actualization of the corresponding potentialities of sense-organ and sense-object.) But this sort of view depends on analogies which are supposed to exist between perception and other situations in which there is a reciprocal causal relationship. Such reciprocal causal relationships exist often enough in biological situations, where the attainment of a balance is the function of an organism. Thus the proper working of the body depends on the existence of physiological balances of one kind or another. The stimuli which affect certain bodily organs are themselves affected and modified by a process of feed-back when the balance is disturbed. But the relationship which comes to exist between concept and object in perception is not a causal relationship at all. A concept is not the sort of thing which can have a causal relation with an object; it makes no sense to suppose so. For, concepts are not things of this kind, as should be clear when it is remembered that, as I have already said, to have a concept of X is to know what it is for something to be an X. Correspondingly, the growth of knowledge is not itself a causal matter (however much it may depend on causal factors of a physiological kind, i.e. on bodily conditions).

(2) If the employment of a biological model is misleading in giving us an incorrect understanding of what the acquisition of knowledge consists in, it also has misleading implications of a more directly philosophical kind. It suggests that the balance to be attained is one between something about the individual which is essentially subjective, i.e. the concept, and something about the world around us which is clearly objective, i.e. the object. Knowledge is thus a blend of the subjective and the objective. But the relationship to which I have pointed as existing between concept and instance is not one between the subjective and the objective. It is not up to an individual to organize in

thought what he is confronted with in any way he pleases—or if anyone shows signs of so doing we think of him as mad. I have already said more than once that to have a concept of X is to know what it is for something to be an X; hence, to see something as an instance of X is to see it as something to which this knowledge is appropriate. There is nothing subjective about this. In fitting something to a concept we are not imposing on it a subjective point of view; for, given what I have said, to have a concept can be as much an objective matter as anything else. The objectivity of a concept is bound up with the idea that it must be inter-subjective, interpersonal, just as knowledge is. Hence, it is impossible to look on the growth of knowledge as some kind of transaction between an individual and his environment, as if social, interpersonal, factors had not part to play. I have commented already on the serious underestimation of the social in Piaget's thought. This is borne out by his adoption of this curious biological model, which effectively rules out the social factor, and thereby undermines the objectivity of knowledge. It is most important to note the extent to which notions like that of knowledge and concepts are social ideas, and the extent to which objectivity depends on this point. For the same reason it is impossible to think of education and learning at all except from a social point of view.

An important truth nevertheless remains in all this—that a balance must be attained between the formal understanding of the principles of a subject and an appreciation of what counts as instances to which those principles are to be applied. Unless this balance is attained, one cannot be said to have a proper understanding of the concepts involved. Hence, being aware of the general principles of a subject, which itself presupposes having the concepts, the particular forms of knowledge, in which the subject-matter is to be formulated, implies also attention to instances. Of course, this is of itself to take an over-simple view of the situation, since concepts do not come by themselves, and any subject will involve connections between concepts of one degree or another of abstractness. To be made to learn these connections without any prior understanding of their relevance to instances would be to be given knowledge which was formal only, and therefore empty; the lack of understanding would make the learning equivalent to rote-learning. It would be the learning by rote of empty phrases. It is perhaps arguable that in certain spheres of knowledge progress might be better made by instilling the formal knowledge and then cashing it in instances than by building up from instances in the first place. But this is merely to make the point which I have laboured all along—that at every stage in the development of knowledge a balance is required between formal knowledge of principles and appreciation of what counts as instances, and that it is of less importance which one invokes first than that a balance should be attained. Nevertheless, it is clearly futile to expect a child to move from one extreme to the other, and the concrete and particular is clearly more obvious than the abstract and general. Is it, therefore, any surprise that what Piaget calls the stage of concrete operations must in general precede that of abstract operations? As Aristotle said, while in knowledge the general is prior in itself, the particular is prior relative to us. This is what Piaget's point comes down to.

What do I mean when I say that the concrete and particular is more obvious than the abstract and general? I do not present this as a mere fact of human psychology. It seems to me a consequence of the situation in which human beings find themselves, of the nature of human experience. The possibility of creatures who come to knowledge of, say, the principles of physics before knowledge of their immediate surroundings is a science-fiction conception, but it corresponds to nothing human. In so far as our concept of knowledge is really a concept of *human* knowledge, it is doubtful whether the possibility which I have mentioned is even one which is intelligible to us. The development of human knowledge may be represented as an enlargement of experience, an enlargement of the individual's intellectual environment. (The part played in this by social factors is obvious.) The things which are the individual's immediate and original concern are particular and concrete. As experience is widened and enlarged, as too it becomes more interpersonal, so it must inevitably become more general and abstract.

Given all this, what seems at first sight to be merely a natural transition from the concrete to the abstract in the development of human thinking emerges as some sort of necessary principle. It is necessary because this transition is just what, as we conceive it, the development of human experience must consist in. That development can of course fail to take place, but it can have no other order; otherwise it would not be *development*. But, it may be said, has not Piaget shown by empirical investigations that the concrete comes before the abstract as a matter of fact? How can something which is supposed to be a necessary truth be discovered by empirical investigations? We must be careful here. Let us consider what Piaget's response might be to hypothetical counter-examples to his thesis. Presumably, if children did not develop from the concrete to the abstract at all, he would have to say that they were not normal children—and we would agree. If the development occurred in the reverse order, would he not have to say, as I have already indicated, that they were not human? The presumption in his investigations is that he is concerned with normal human children. One thing that he may be said to have discovered is that the subjects who at one stage employ concrete operations and only later abstract operations are indeed normal human children. What else should we expect to happen in such circumstances? The situation is similar to the one which I mentioned earlier in stressing the connection between abstractness and complexity on the one hand and difficulty on the other. If there is a way of establishing the abstractness and complexity of a subject, this is *eo ipso* a way of establishing that people normally find it difficult, and vice versa. Similarly, if there is a way of establishing that children are normal human children, that their experience is what is normal, then this will *eo ipso* establish that their intellectual development will be along certain general lines, and vice versa.

It seems to me that Piaget's discoveries here are like discovering that circles when presented to people in a frontal plane look round to them. To insist that they generally do would be to labour the obvious. The point is that this is the normal case, and it is by reference to it that the application of concepts like 'roundness' is established; it is the norm for what counts as round. If circles presented in a frontal plane did not normally look round our understanding of notions like that of a circle and roundness would be completely different; indeed, we should not know what to think. Hence, given that the people and the situation are normal, it could not be otherwise. It needs no empirical investigation to discover that circles seen in the frontal plane look round in normal conditions. Analogously, I do not claim that the stages found in Piaget's subjects are not there as a matter of fact; I do claim that *if his subjects are normal human children*, we could not conceive it otherwise. Hence, the priority of the concrete to the abstract is something that all normal human beings could discover by reflection on what they know about the nature of human development, of human learning; it needs no further empirical investigation. On the other hand, of course, it does need empirical investigation to discover *when* John or Mary pass from one general stage of development to another, and whether they do so at roughly the same age. But such findings of course presuppose our present educational and cultural set-up; there is no reason to suppose that the norms are unalterable. Hence, what needs even further investigation is whether what is true of John and Mary is also true of Fritz, Ali, and Kwame, i.e. we need to know the effects of different cultural and perhaps genetic backgrounds on the general development of children.

Finally, let me say again that if it is thought desirable that the process of intellectual development be accelerated (something that is perhaps arguable, considering that *intellectual* development is not the only thing), then the best people to provide the answers how this is to be done are those who have reflected most deeply on what is involved conceptually in their own subject, what is best understood first, and so on. That is to say that the best person to say how the teaching of, say, mathematics should proceed is the mathematician who has reflected adequately, and perhaps philosophically, on what is involved in his own subject (especially, in the first place, in its application to experience). Of course, here again the difficulties in the way of coming up with any firm answers may be insurmountable; in which case, the only hope is to find out empirically what courses of learning children do as a matter of fact normally find most easy. For, as I have said, easiness goes with concreteness and simplicity of subject-matter, and this provides a clue to what should come first and what second in learning.

My intention in what I have had to say has been above all perhaps to delimit the roles to be performed by philosophy and psychology in this field, and to emphasize the differences between empirical and conceptual inquiries here. Psychology has much to tell us about learning— about, for example, particular cases and individual differences. It can also tell us about the effect on learning of all those factors in people which we can call psychological—personality traits, intelligence, and so on. What I have been urging is, amongst other things, that there is also required proper reflection on what learning and education are, and what they involve in consequence. For, only in this way can we be rid of misleading models which may inhibit our understanding of intellectual development and education.

THE JUSTIFICATION OF EDUCATION

XI

EDUCATION, DEMOCRACY, AND THE PUBLIC INTEREST

PAT WHITE

DRAINS, defence, and *Don Giovanni* are most frequently produced in inquiries as to what can be pronounced with certainty to be in the public interest. Drains and defence are offered as solid candidates to which no reasonable man could object and *Don Giovanni,* or opera generally, is held up as an example of a highly doubtful candidate, which, if at all, only the most subtle argument will allow under this rubric. I want to take up this argument and ask specifically whether in a democratic society there *must* be any agreement on what is in the public interest.[1] In other words is a democrat *compelled* to regard some things as in the public interest? Eventually I hope to show that he must regard one thing under this aspect—an appropriate political education —and that this finding, when elaborated, has some important implications for the general school curriculum. On my way to establishing this claim I shall make a number of points about the term 'the public interest' which have a more general relevance to discussions about educational policies and the public interest.

I

The first step must be an attempt to understand this complex term 'the public interest'. There is a sense of 'acting for the common good' or 'in the public interest' which comes fairly readily to mind, where this means something like acting after due weighing of all relevant interests. It is important to note that in this sense of the term, which

From *Proceedings of the Philosophy of Education Society of Great Britain* Vol. 5, No. 1 (Jan. 1971). Reprinted by permission of the author and Basil Blackwell Ltd.

[1] In what follows I shall equate the terms 'public interest' and 'common good'. There are differences between them but they are not significant for this discussion. For a discussion of these differences, see B. Barry, *Political Argument* (London: Routledge & Kegan Paul, 1965), chapter xi.

Benn and Peters and H. L. A. Hart[2] mention, it is quite possible that the course of action finally decided upon favours one particular interest, or set of interests, as against another. For instance, a government considering how best to distribute educational resources at the higher education level and considering the various institutions making claims on it, e.g. universities, colleges of education, polytechnics, etc., might decide to favour university expansion at the expense of the other institutions. After due consideration one set of interests is preferred to others. And the government might, if necessary, defend its action by saying that it had acted in the public interest, meaning, in this instance, that it had acted fairly or impartially. But this is only one possible meaning of this phrase and Barry[3] has even suggested that it is misleading to use the term in this way. We already have perfectly good terms for describing this kind of behaviour, namely 'acting impartially', 'acting fairly', 'giving equal consideration to all', etc. The notion of 'acting in the public interest', he suggests, is a rather different one. For a government to justify an action or policy in this way is for it to draw attention to a different range of considerations from these. It is this other range I want to explore now, in an analysis very much influenced by Barry's work in this area, whilst at the same time radically differing from it at certain points.[4]

Let me first recapitulate certain fairly familiar points about the notion of interest and put out of the way two senses of interest not relevant here. Not relevant is the occurrent sense—'I was interested in what was going on in the flat opposite yesterday morning'—meaning 'My attention was attracted by what, etc., etc.' Equally irrelevant is the related dispositional sense, where one talks of one's interests in wild life, ancient civilizations, or knitting, meaning something like one's hobbies. To say x is in A's interest (where A may be a single individual, or a group, or the public) is not necessarily to say that A is interested in x in either of these senses. It may be in my interest to scour all the local supermarkets looking for the best bargains but I may not be in the least interested in doing so—at any particular time or as a hobby!

---

[2] See S. I. Benn and R. S. Peters, *Social Principles and the Democratic State* (London: Allen & Unwin, 1959), p. 272; and H. L. A. Hart, *The Concept of Law* (Oxford: O.U.P., 1961), pp. 162–3.

[3] B. Barry, 'Justice and the Common Good' in *Political Philosophy*, ed. A. Quinton (Oxford: O.U.P., 1967).

[4] This exploration will also suggest why 'acting in the public interest' is often used to mean 'acting impartially/justly'. There is, it seems to me, a link between these different uses of the same phrase. See below, note 12.

Some writers equate 'x is in A's interest' with 'x is a means to what A wants'. Barry, for instance, says 'an action or policy is in a man's interest if it increases his opportunities to get what he wants'.[5] But we can and do say 'x is a means to what A wants but it is not in his interest', as, for instance, in the case of a man who is left sufficient money to indulge all his wants—which happen to be drinking, smoking, and taking drugs. (We may of course be *wrong* in saying that having the money is not in his interests. But it is not necessary to pursue this substantive issue, since the concern here is only with what is implied in making the distinction between what is in someone's interests and what is a means to what he wants.) In an attempt to cope with the sort of objection raised by this example Barry introduces a distinction between want-satisfaction now and want-satisfaction later:[6] even though having money is a means to what A wants now, it is not a means to what he would want in the long-term. In such a case, Barry argues further, we do not talk merely of what is in a person's interests but what is in his best interests.[7] One could raise the question here whether Barry is justified in arguing that in this sort of case (i.e. where one person says of another that, although x is a means to what A wants, x is not in his best interests) A's long-term wants would necessarily be different from what he wants in the short-term. But that possible objection aside, it seems to me that there is not in any case sufficient support in the language to draw Barry's distinction between 'in a person's interest' referring to short-term wants) and 'in a person's best interests' (referring to long-term wants). If this is granted, then what is in a person's interest can be what satisfies one want rather than another and something's being in a person's interest cannot, therefore, be defined purely in terms of wants. Indeed it is presumably the partial recognition of the need for a distinction here which forces Barry to introduce the short-term/long-term wants and the in a person's interest/best interest distinctions, because he clearly has to take account of the fact that, however one describes the situation, in such a case the satisfaction of one sort of want is seen as *better* than another. This introduction of a welfare notion as distinct from a want notion in fact *compels* one to formulate a second sense of in A's interest, distinct from Barry's original one.

In this second sense, x is in A's interest if it is a means to something which is *good* for A, or which he ought to have. This is not to say

---

[5] Barry, *Political Argument*, p. 176.
[6] Ibid., pp. 184–5.
[7] Ibid.

that there are any neat answers as to what *is* good for a person: views on this will be as numerous as those on the good life for a man. Further, one will not necessarily even be able to equate what is good with what a person wants. For this reason it is a sense which has particular application to children. Cod-liver oil and regular hair washings may be in little A's interest even if he does not want them. Benn[8] mentions this sense of interest and points out that in *educating* a child we may be acting in his interests, even if not necessarily doing what he wants. Barry attempts to dispose of this claim by suggesting that ' "acting in the interests of a child" involves very special contexts' and that educating children is 'a different notion from "acting in their interests" '.[9] However, this attempt to deny a second sense of interest fails, it seems to me, because Barry does not show that educating children could not be one instance of acting in their interests. That one is more likely to come across this phrase, as Barry claims, when a local authority is checking on foster parents to see that they are not exploiting children in their care or when a court is deciding whether the executor of a will leaving property in trust to a child had managed the estate 'in the child's interest' may well be true, but this alone cannot show conclusively that it has no application to the education case, for this would be to allow the application of concepts to depend on the contingencies of what people actually have occasion to put into words. Therefore, since this second sense—*x* is in A's interest if it is a means to something good for A—seems to me an intelligible one, with particular application to children, I shall rely on it in what follows.[10]

It is not however the unqualified notion of 'interest' I want to pursue but the '*public* interest'. In political and social life generally when we talk about something being 'public' there is usually an implied contrast at least with what is 'private'. Meetings may be public or private, theatre performances may be public or private, restricted, for instance, to the members of a club; again there are public parks as opposed to private estates and public footpaths as opposed to private ones. In the case of private amenities, like these, to call them private is to say that they may only be rightfully used by some determinate, specifiable

[8] S. I. Benn, 'Interests in Politics', *Proc. Arist. Soc.*, Vol. 60 (1959–60), pp. 130–1.

[9] Barry, *Political Argument*, p. 185.

[10] However, even if this second sense of 'in a person's interest' cannot be maintained, the main argument to the conclusion that a political education must be in the public interest in a democracy still has relevance to Barry's sense of 'in a person's interest'. See below, note 18.

class of persons. For instance, only members will be allowed to attend theatrical performances if the theatre is run as a club, only members will be allowed to attend meetings of a given society, and only members of the family and its retainers will be able to enter the estate without fear of prosecution for trespassing. Public amenities are so called not because they are actually visited by every member of the community but because they are open to all without discrimination. Anyone may go to the meeting, or the theatre, stroll in the park, or use the footpath.

It follows therefore that 'the public interest' picks out what is in a person's interest as a member of a community, of a public, as distinct from what is in his interest as a member of a *section* of the community, as, e.g. a theatre club member, an estate owner, an old age pensioner, or a teacher. To illustrate: it might be claimed, say in a government educational report, that it would be in the public interest to have more girls taking some science to 'A' level. Recommendation might be made to the effect that more scientists should be recruited to the teaching profession, more courses should be put on in schools, and girls should be encouraged in various ways to opt for these courses. The implementation of this policy might in fact not be in the interests of some *particular* sections of the society at all. Suppose a highly successful science-for-girls campaign draws girls away from the traditionally popular girls' subjects, like modern languages, this may mean a drastic change in the career prospects of teachers of these subjects. Again, more scientists coming on to the labour market may mean that the salaries of present scientists are depressed or at least that their prospects are not quite as rosy as they were. However, such a policy can still be in the public interest; for to claim this is to claim that it is good for everyone as a member of the public, perhaps because, by promoting the country's economic growth in various ways, it leads to an increased, though not necessarily equally increased, standard of living for everyone. Even the now prospectless modern-language teachers must benefit marginally under the aspect of members of the public. This may be cold comfort to the man who was dreaming of running three language laboratories and enjoying a large responsibility allowance, but that is not the point. If this is properly a public-interest policy he must be benefiting, along with everyone else, as a member of the public.

All members of the public benefit, then, from the implementation of public-interest policies and, it is important to note, all benefit under the same description, i.e. as members of the public. By contrast, it is possible to imagine other, not strictly public-interest policies which benefit all members of a community under different descriptions as, e.g. parents, businessmen, actors. It is perhaps just conceivable, for instance, that some educational policy might benefit all members of a given community under different descriptions, but nevertheless benefit them all. For instance, to take an only slightly far-fetched example, a new curriculum project may give children a better understanding of history, it may increase the profits of textbook publishers, it may boost government revenues as large numbers of children are taken to view ancient monuments, and it may give parents an easier time in the school holidays, as the children, enthralled by history, occupy themselves making models, amassing data, and so on. In so far as one could call such a policy a public-interest policy it would be in a different and, one might say, much diluted sense, since it benefits everyone only because it happens to satisfy a whole number of disparate individual and sectional interests. The public interest, in the strong sense intended here, is a truly corporate interest in that each member of the community benefits under the same description—member of the public.[11] In what follows, therefore, any reference to a public-interest policy will always be a reference to a policy which benefits everyone of a given public under this description.

This is still not to have said, however, what 'the public' is, where, so to speak, its boundaries are. Sometimes the context makes this apparent. In the example of the science-for-girls campaign, for instance, the writers of the government report obviously had the national community in mind in talking of what was in the public interest. But there is no logically necessary link between 'the public' and the members of a nation-state. 'The public' is a purely formal notion and people could debate policies in the 'public interest' with very different 'publics' in mind. One might be thinking of the national community alive at the moment, another the national community and yet unborn generations of it, a third could be thinking of mankind generally and in time to come 'the public' might include all persons in our universe. The importance of knowing who is included in a given public is obvious if any assertion that a policy is in the public interest is to be open to

[11] In this connection it would be interesting to explore empirically the effect, if any, of the implementation of public-interest policies on the promotion of feelings of fraternity and social equality in a community, since if people are benefiting in the same way there would be a ready basis for the development of feelings of kinship to others. Alternatively, it may be that something like the converse is the case: public-interest policies can only be successfully carried through in communities already characterized by fraternity and social equality.

rational examination. This will become apparent when we consider educational policies which might be held to be in the public interest.

To pull these various threads together now, a policy in the public interest is one which benefits every member of a given public under the description member of the public.[12] It is not necessarily the policy which is best for any individual considered as an individual.

II

So far this has been an attempt to explore what might be meant by the term 'public interest' in which educational policies have only come in by way of illustration, but now I want to show that this notion is directly relevant to the critical consideration of educational policies in three ways:

(i) If a policy in the public interest is one held to be *good* for everyone as members of the public, determining what is in the public interest in the educational sphere cannot be left to experts, to be worked out much as the value of the gross national product is calculated. There are certainly highly technical points in such a judgement which *are* matters for expert calculation, for to determine whether a given policy is in the public interest, it is necessary to calculate whether all members of a given public benefit under the description member of the public. Also presupposed, however, in all judgements about public-interest policies is the value judgement that the policy is a means to something the public ought to have. This value judgement element cannot be calculated by experts. This seems obvious and yet in some educational literature it seems to be implicitly assumed that what is in the public interest is entirely a matter for expert calculation. Some basic educational textbooks on 'the social foundations of education', for instance, suggest that although the child must be educated as an individual and be encouraged to express himself in his own way, develop his own point of view, and so on, educators must also have regard to the needs of society, to the public interest. One of the needs of an industrial society like ours, it may be pointed out, is to have the right kind of manpower coming on to the labour market at the right time. Here the right kind of manpower and the right time will be regarded as

[12] There is a link here with the other sense of acting for the common good. (See above, note 4.) Both senses employ the notion of impartiality. In the Benn & Peters and Hart sense the emphasis is on the use of impartial *procedures* to arrive at a decision. In the sense developed here the *decision itself* must be an impartial one, in the sense that it must benefit all.

matters for the experts to determine. Perhaps expert calculation will suggest, for instance, that educational institutions must increase the number of skilled technicians they are producing. In this case it seems that the educational expert *is* saying that it is in the public interest to have more skilled technicians, but qua educational economist or sociologist he cannot do this. He can make the technical judgement, of course, that to maintain a certain type of economy more skilled technicians are needed, but whether this type of economy is good is a value judgement outside the realm of economics or sociology.

It might be objected at this point that this argument neglects an obvious fact, namely that in most communities there will exist some sort of moral consensus about such broad aims of the economy as are being considered here. Therefore the expert's suggestions about manpower needs will be suggestions for efficient means to moral ends and will be therefore suggestions about what is in the public interest. If this objection is taken at face-value and it is allowed that the ends are moral ones this, far from being an objection, seems rather to reinforce the point made above—that the judgement that a given economic system is in the public interest is not a straightforwardly technical one. It is a moral judgement to be supported by moral argument.

(ii) An understanding of the 'public interest' also supplies a kind of built-in test for policies advanced with this backing. One can ask of a given proposal put forward on the grounds that it is in the public interest, i.e. good for everyone under the description member of the public, whether in fact it is good for everyone under this description or whether rather it benefits only a section of the community. For instance, one argument sometimes advanced for retaining private schools is that they are a good testing ground for all kinds of educational experiments and it is to the benefit of the whole educational community, and ultimately of the wider community, too, that there should exist a private sector of education where parents can pay for their children and so make possible such experiments. Whether this claim is true would depend on whether *in fact* these experiments *do* benefit all members of the public. If they do, this might be *one* reason, on public-interest grounds, for having fee-paying schools. (Although it might of course be outweighed by other considerations.) But investigation may reveal that the public-interest argument is merely a smoke-screen and in fact private schools merely benefit a section of the community. This might be the case, for instance, if they never undertook any really significant educational experiments, whilst providing the kind of education which enabled their exclusive clientele to obtain access to highly rewarded positions in society.

This test might also be used in connection with claims made for training for leadership programmes.[13] In so far as it is claimed that these élite training programmes benefit all members of the public by, for instance, providing dedicated and responsible personnel for top governmental and Civil Service positions, these claims can, in principle at least, be tested.

(iii) It is possible to ask of any proposal put forward on public-interest grounds whether the 'public' envisaged is a morally defensible one. If, for instance, a national government decides that it is not in the public interest, meaning here the national interest, to continue a policy of reduced fees for students from developing countries (and, to avoid complications, let us assume that as far as the national interest is concerned, they are right) it might be criticized for considering too small a public in this instance. Whether or not this would be a justified criticism would clearly depend on various factors. But in general it is always to the point to ask how defensible it is to advocate a policy on the grounds that it will benefit a *given* public.

III

In suggesting that a judgement about whether or not something is in the public interest is a moral judgement and that in educational policy-making such judgements must be scrutinized to see whether the public to be benefited is sufficiently inclusive, I have implicitly assumed that there will be educational policies in the public interest. Now I want to return to the question raised at the start and ask specifically whether in a pluralistic democratic society there *must* be any policies in the public interest. Some may even doubt that there *could* be any. They might argue that in such a society some people may feel that their children should have an education with a certain kind of religious bias, say, Christian, Hindu, or Moslem, other groups will favour a wholly secular general education, others will want a high-powered scientific training, and others may want general education underplayed in the interest of some specialist artistic training, say, music. All of these proposals will be advanced in the interests of the children, conceived as for their good, but the point about such a society is that different

---

[13] See *Governing Elites: Studies in Training and Selection*, ed. R. Wilkinson (London: O.U.P., 1969), particularly 'Elites and Effectiveness' by Wilkinson himself.

groups will hold different views on what is in a child's interest.[14] It is hard to see therefore at first sight how any educational policy could be in the interests of the whole society.

It might seem that this scepticism can be met by arguing that in such a society an obvious policy in the public interest is the establishment of educational institutions which cater for all the various activities wanted by different groups. This, however, is not a policy in the public interest in the sense that it benefits all members of the public *as* members of the public. It benefits everyone certainly but it benefits them under different descriptions (see pp. 221–2 above). This does not mean, though, that such a policy could never be in the public interest in the strong sense. It could be, if all members of the society happen to value living in a pluralistic society and seeing around them a great many different styles of life. If they do, this policy benefits everyone under the same description, as members of the public, because it promotes the variety they all desire. The important point to note, however, is that there is no sense in which citizens of a pluralistic society are *obliged* to value variety. Living in a pluralistic democracy obliges people to *tolerate* variety but they do not have to positively value it. Therefore the promotion of the various different activities does not *necessarily* benefit everyone as a member of the public.

There *can*, then, be policies in the public interest in a pluralistic democracy but it seems more doubtful whether it is possible to establish that there *must* be. It is often suggested, as I mentioned at the outset, that policies which ensure the provision of such things as drains and defence—and one might add food and medical care—must be in the public interest. It is not clear, however, in what sense they must. It is not inconceivable that there could be a society where the good life for man is conceived as one of rugged independence. In this society everyone values adequate sanitary arrangements, defence, food, and medical care as necessary to survival, and therefore as things which men ought to have, but they also hold tenaciously to the belief that each should shift for himself where these things are concerned. A policy whereby it is ensured that they are provided for all is anathema to them. Such a policy, far from being in the public interest, in the sense that it benefits everyone, is a ruinous one, only likely to produce a decline in the quality of life, as they conceive it.

[14] Nothing is being said here about the *rights* of these groups to implement their views. The claim is simply that there will exist different views on what activities it would be good for children to be introduced to.

There is however one policy about which there can be no choice in a democratic state, whatever views are held as to the good life for man. The policy which must be in the public interest in any human democracy is the ensuring of the provision of a political education. This is necessary because for a democracy to survive the citizens must know how to operate the democratic institutions. Human beings are, however, born ignorant and unless they receive some education in political matters they remain ignorant of them. Therefore they must receive some political education, either through a formal education system or in some informal way, or by a mixture of both. It follows, therefore, that whatever views about the good life for man the citizens of a democracy have, if they value the democratic system, they must regard a policy which ensures the provision of a political education as in the public interest, because without it the system will collapse. However much, therefore, a democratic society values freedom and wishes to allow individuals to pursue their own concerns without interference (in, say, matters relating to health), it cannot refrain from 'interfering', through its appropriate authorities, to ensure that children get an adequate political education.

To say, however, that a democratic society, whatever views on the good life for man its citizens hold, *must* ensure the provision of a political education is not to claim that this is a matter of logical necessity, as Wollheim thinks it is. Wollheim argues that 'both Education and Toleration are essential not accidental attributes of a democracy', because citizens must understand the issues about which they are asked to choose and must have access to ideas relating to these.[15] But education cannot be one of the 'logical conditions of a democracy or the conditions whose instantiation is entailed by the existence of a democracy',[16] for there could be beings, in other respects like men, except for the possession of certain innate ideas and capacities constituting the knowledge of how to operate a democratic system. For these beings democracy might be a morally defensible type of government but the provision of a political education would be impossible. For *human* beings, however, given their present ignorance at birth, the ensuring of the provisions of a political education is a policy which must be in the public interest in a democracy. It must be in everyone's interest

[15] R. Wollheim, 'On the Theory of Democracy', in *British Analytical Philosophy*, ed. B. Williams and A. Montefiore (London: Routledge & Kegan Paul, 1966), p. 266.

[16] Ibid.

because it is a means to the kind of government the public ought to have.[17, 18] Everyone is similarly benefited since it is to everyone's advantage that all fellow citizens respect and abide by democratic procedures. And there is no indefensible limit on the public, since there is no necessary limit on it at all; democratic government could be extended, via international organizations, to cover the whole world. In this way the ensuring of the provision of a political education in a democracy is a policy in the public interest in the way in which a political education in a fascist state could not be. Both might be equally necessary in order to perpetuate each state, but on the assumption that the fascist state, unlike the democratic state, could not be regarded as the kind of government the public ought to have, a fascist political education could not be in the public interest.

IV

Given, then, that the provision of a political education in a democracy is a policy which must be in the public interest, to determine in detail what this involves we need to find out what an appropriate political education for a pluralistic democracy is. A *first* suggestion might be that each child, who will already be a member of one or more of the diverse groups in the society, should have a political education which will enable him to relate, via the group (or groups), to the government and to acquire the virtue of tolerance of other

[17] I do not here want to enter into what would necessarily be a lengthy account of democratic government and its justification. Let me simply say, therefore, that I am assuming that the democratic state is characterized primarily by its attempt to govern according to the moral principles of justice, freedom, and consideration of interests. It might be objected that this is not what 'democracy' means. In that case I would say that, whatever term is applied to it, I am interested here in the state-trying-to-govern-according-to-moral principles. Its justification, therefore, would be that of conducting public life according to moral principles and this ultimately, to compress considerable argument, would rest on the justification of the moral principles themselves. Here I would closely follow the kind of justification put forward by R. S. Peters in *Ethics and Education* (London: Allen & Unwin, 1966), chapters iv, vi, vii, and xi.

[18] Conceivably, as I suggested earlier, a similar conclusion might be reached using Barry's definition of interest: an appropriate political education is in the public interest because it is a means to the democratic government the public wants. Therefore, even if the second sense of interest cannot be sustained (or if democracy cannot be justified in the way I suggested in note 17), in those cases where the public do want democratic government, the implications for the curriculum which are developed below would still follow.

groups with different values, interests, and so on. I have in mind a political education resting on the pressure-group theory of democracy. This can be stated rather baldly as that theory which sees government in a democracy as primarily related and responsible to *groups* within the society rather than directly to *individuals* and, conversely, individuals related to the government not primarily as individual citizens but through their membership of certain groups, as, e.g. householders, tenants, members of a white collar union, members of a minority religion, etc. The groups relate to the government in two main ways. On the one hand in so far as they can by themselves pursue their own goals (e.g. their religious worship or union activities) the government's only function is to keep the ring between the various groups engaged in their individual pursuits. The government acts as a kind of referee, making sure everyone observes the rules demanded by tolerance. On the other hand in so far as there are goals which can most conveniently be pursued by the government, e.g. the establishment of internal law and order, defence against external enemies, the government will react like a kind of barometer to the pressure put on it by different groups to adopt this policy rather than that or adjust this policy and amend that one. In such a society the appropriate political education—to develop a little what I have already indicated—will have two main aspects. Children will have to learn when and how to put pressure on the government; and they will have to learn to value tolerance and to operate the various procedures devised to institutionalize it. This sketchy picture could be more convincingly elaborated, but no more than these bare bones are needed to indicate its inadequacy, because this stems, not from the educational policy *per se*, but from the limited view of democracy on which it rests.

The liberty to pursue one's own good with like-minded people and tolerance of others behaving similarly are only two values. A democratic state must embody others, like justice and consideration of interests, in its institutions.[19] Indeed on these grounds three objections can be made to the state outlined. First, governing justly demands more of a government than simply keeping the ring between groups pursuing their own goods. To do only this would be to accept the *status quo* as just. Justice may well demand that the government alter the relationship between groups, as, e.g., in the redistribution of wealth in a society. Secondly, the government's obligation to consider the interests of the people may well not allow it to operate a policy of pure tolerance. It may have

[19] See note 17.

to suppress some groups (e.g. groups whose aim is to victimize minorities within the society); it may have to pay more attention to other groups than the pressure they could exert in a completely competitive situation would warrant (old age pensioners in our society). Thirdly, a government's commitment to the principles of justice and consideration of interests means that its responsibility for its citizens must extend beyond groups to individuals. It must be prepared, if necessary, to safeguard the rights of minorities of one.

These criticisms of pure pressure-group democracy, to which, of contemporary democratic systems, the American system most closely approximates in practice, are not unfamiliar. R. P. Wolff makes some similar points in his essay 'Beyond Tolerance' and ends with a possible solution to the problem which can be shown to yield a *second* view of political education. He argues that

> We must give up the image of society as a battleground of competing groups and formulate an ideal of society more exalted than the mere acceptance of opposed interests and diverse customs. There is a need for a new philosophy of community, beyond pluralism and beyond tolerance.[20]

How far this is an acceptable solution depends on what is meant by 'a new philosophy of community'. Earlier in the essay Wolff mentions with approval the views of Burke and Durkheim, interpreting them as claiming that:

> The involvement of each with all which to Mill was a threat and an imposition, is to such critics of liberalism as Burke and Durkheim a strength and an opportunity. It is indeed the greatest virtue of society, which supports and enfolds the individual in a warm, affective community stretching backwards and forwards in time and bearing within itself the accumulated wisdom and values of generations of human experience.[21]

and 'The only hope is for men to huddle together and collectively create the warm world of meaning and coherence which impersonal nature cannot offer.'[22] It is not clear to me that Burke and Durkheim are making such 'cosy' proposals as this, rather than, in the former case, points about the logic and application of political principles and, in the latter, logical points about which it is for something to be a society, but

---

[20] See R. P. Wolff, 'Beyond Tolerance', in R. P. Wolff, B. Moore, Jr., and H. Marcuse, *A Critique of Pure Tolerance* (Boston: Beacon Press, 1965), p. 52.

[21] Ibid., p. 29.

[22] Ibid., p. 31.

this is not the place to go into exegesis of Burke and Durkheim. In any case it would be irrelevant because, whatever they are in fact saying, some contemporary American educational practice is based on a 'philosophy of community' very similar to that indicated by Wolff. This is reflected in recent studies of children's political education in schools in the United States.[23]

The education system reflects, on the one hand, the pluralistic nature of the society by providing many optional courses, from which pupils may put together their own education in a do-it-yourself kind of way. As new interests arise in the society so relevant curriculum subjects find their way into schools and colleges (cf. the notorious new degree courses, in, e.g., driver education, often commented on). This diversity is underpinned, however, with what is felt to be an appropriately cohesive political education. Here, if one accepts the accounts and criticisms of some American commentators, the emphasis is on solidarity, fraternity, the community-spirit, and the nation as one big happy family with the President as a benevolent father figure. This state of affairs is produced, as far as the school is concerned, by an 'indoctrination in a kind of goody-goody civics',[24] in which the aim is to instil obedience to rules and laws and develop respect for authority, backed up by 'the inculcation of a kind of ethos of sociability, with a faint *Animal Farm* aroma'.[25] This is to put the state of affairs very extremely, of course. In practice, as the literature and these comments indicate, the emphasis is not entirely on the community spirit. There is usually some minimal attempt to acquaint children with the political forms of the society, although the accuracy and appropriateness of the teaching cannot always be guaranteed.[26]

However, whether in its extreme or less extreme forms, as an education for democracy, it must be counted a failure. This must be so, if what is understood by the promotion of feelings of fraternity is simply getting people to feel kinship to others who are perceived as sharing some valued characteristic, in this case getting children to value fellow

[23] See, e.g., F. I. Greenstein, *Children and Politics* (New Haven & London: Yale University Press, 1965); R. D. Hess and J. V. Torney, *The Development of Political Attitudes in Children* (Chicago: Aldine, 1967); also *Harvard Educational Review*, Vol. 38, No. 3 (1968).

[24] R. Kirk, 'Political Socialization in the Schools', *Harvard Educational Review*, Vol. 38, No. 3 (1968), p. 548.

[25] Ibid., p. 546.

[26] See R. D. Hess, 'Political Socialization in the Schools', in *Harvard Educational Review*, Vol. 38, No. 3 (1968).

Americans, simply because they are fellow Americans. Clearly there is more to education for democracy than the inducing of this sort of feeling in children—and this quite apart from more stringent criticisms which might be made of too rigid an application of this limited form of regard for others. If one tries to base the complex machinery of a modern democratic state on an education like this, the system is likely, at best, to function inadequately and perhaps in time to break down. What will determine which it is to be is the proportion of 'other political education' (i.e. the promotion of other values, like freedom, information about particular political institutions of the society, etc., which could, of course, come from outside the formal education system) to the promotion of the community spirit. This follows from a quite general logical point. The political education in any given society must appropriately match the political system, if the system is to be maintained. Indeed there are actual examples of systems which have broken down for just this lack of fit.[27, 28]

It is possible to take a somewhat different view of the 'community spirit' which is promoted in this second conception of the democratic state. As just described, it is very much the huddling together in the warm world which Wolff sees Burke and Durkheim emphasizing, but one could think rather of getting people to be concerned about the common good, the public interest. Indeed towards the end of his article it seems that Wolff must, at least, also have something like this in mind. He talks about the need for a concern with the common good to deal with problems like the preservation of natural beauty, public order, and the cultivation of the arts which are not the special interest of any identifiable social group.[29] But, paradoxically, even encouraging future citizens to concern themselves with what is in the public interest would not of itself be sufficient for a political education in the public interest in

---

[27] See R. P. Bolgar, 'The Training of Elites in Greek Education', in R. Wilkinson (ed.), op. cit., for a discussion of this general point with regard to political education in ancient Greece.

[28] This point about the 'lack of fit' between the education and the political system and its dangers suggests a possible explanation of the political attitudes of some young Americans. Confronted by the, to them, totally bewildering complexities of a modern political system, their school-induced feelings of fraternity and perception of the state as a happy family fail to persist. Frustrated by their almost total incapacity to understand and operate the system, they conclude that it is 'fixed' against them and become alienated and hostile to it.

[29] See R. P. Wolff, op. cit., pp. 49–50.

a democracy. There are other values, besides the common good (e.g. the good of particular individuals and groups of individuals), which must be taken into consideration; also, being able to care about the common good presupposes an enormous amount of non-moral knowledge. A political education would have to take account of these considerations.

V

Putting together the emphases and defects of the previous examples provides the main lines of such an education.

(i) Its primary objective must be to get pupils to acquire the values which underlie the democratic system. These will include, of course, the values of tolerance and fraternity emphasized in the previous examples, although the fraternity cannot be the vague, amorphous feeling sketched before but a feeling of kinship to other democratic citizens as democratic citizens. Unless citizens can feel akin to others as people sincerely committed to the same values as themselves, the operation of any democratic machinery will be hampered by suspicions and crises of confidence. In addition these values must be supplemented by those of justice and consideration of interests, understood as individual and sectional interests as well as the public interest.

(ii) These values will, of course, be embodied in particular institutions in any democratic state and children will need to be brought to understand and know how to work these—something very much lacking in the fraternity example. There is a great deal of philosophical and other work to be done here on what the precise content of the teaching should be in this area.[30] One wants to avoid at all costs children coming to believe, e.g. that what it means to decide something democratically, is to take a vote on it. One wants rather to get across the view that any particular democratic institutions are potentially improvable attempts to institutionalize certain values, which might well be better institutionalized in some other way.

(iii) However, the knowledge which the democratic citizen requires is not limited to the knowledge of democratic values and the operation of institutions mentioned under (i) and (ii). For if a child is correctly to apply the democratic values in particular cases, their acquisition will

---

[30] See B. Crick, 'The Introducing of Politics', in *The Teaching of Politics*, ed. D. B. Heater (London: Methuen, 1966), esp. pp. 6, 15.

have to go along with the kind of liberal education described by Hirst as an initiation into all the forms of knowledge.[31] This is a crucial element lacking in both the American examples, for actually to act intelligently on the values mentioned in (i) the child will have to *know* a great deal. Care and concern for others' interests, for instance, may be enough to earn one the label of a 'good-hearted soul who means well' but they are not sufficient, without a background of knowledge, to enable one to act wisely.

To make this kind of claim, i.e. that citizens in a democracy need a broad general education, is to enter on the very complex question of exactly how much citizens in a democracy need to know to be able to function as citizens and this is a question—a crucially important one for education—which as far as I know has never been tackled in any systematic and rigorous way. Therefore I can only indicate what seems to me a possible argument for it here. It is clear of course that all citizens in a democracy do not need to have—and of course could not have—*all* the relevant knowledge necessary for taking *all* the political decisions in the society. The government must draw on experts in deciding whether or not to reinflate the economy, retain a certain military base, and so on. But this is quite compatible with the government's decisions on these matters being democratic, as long as citizens can check that all relevant interests are being considered, i.e. as long as the government is accountable to the people. But it is precisely what comes out of an examination of what is involved in a government's being accountable that constitutes the argument for a liberal education. For if the government is to be accountable, the citizen must be able to judge that it has taken all the relevant factors into account (i.e. called in all the relevant experts) in making its decision. This will be impossible unless he has some awareness of the considerations which *could* bear on practical political decisions. In addition, of course, the citizen will have to consider the relative weighting given to different considerations, e.g. the aesthetic as against the economic in the siting of power stations, but this only underscores the main point—this further step presupposes that he is already acquainted with what might count as different relevant considerations.

There still might remain some doubt, however, as to whether *all* the forms of knowledge are really necessary to a political education what-

[31] See P. H. Hirst, 'Liberal Education and the Nature of Knowledge', in *Philosophical Analysis and Education*, ed. R. D. Archambault (London: Routledge & Kegan Paul, 1965).

ever their value as a liberal education might be. Hirst lists mathematics, the physical sciences, social sciences and history, moral knowledge, philosophy, religious knowledge, and aesthetics as identifiable forms of knowledge.[32] Reviewing this list, mathematics, and possibly philosophy too, might be regarded somewhat sceptically by someone reflecting on the political decisions ordinary citizens are called upon to assess. For instance, one might question whether a knowledge of mathematics, beyond basic arithmetic, was likely to be of any use in assessing a government's strike policy, its housing programme, its defence policy ... and the list could be extended to include a number of familiar contemporary government policies without its becoming apparent that a knowledge of mathematics was crucial to the assessment of any one of them. Such an extension would not show, though, that mathematics could be omitted. The reason for this is that the liberal education outlined by Hirst is not one characterized by a certain kind of *content*. The liberally educated man is not characterized by the items of knowledge he possesses—knowledge of the second law of thermodynamics, acquaintance with the Elgin marbles, *Middlemarch*, the book of Job, and so on—but by the fact that he can think in these various ways, knowing, for instance, what a truth of mathematics is as distinct from a truth of science. Of course, he, logically, has to think about *something* and he may well contingently know the things mentioned, but the point remains that he is generally educated in virtue of the fact that he is able to think in these various forms of thought and not because of any particular stack of items of knowledge he may possess. The importance of this point to political education is that in so far as the citizen is acquainted in this way with the structure of knowledge he is acquainted with *all* the *kinds* of considerations which could bear on, and indeed define, political problems. It may well be that some of these considerations, e.g. mathematical ones, bear on political problems more rarely than others, but with political problems, as with moral ones, one cannot say in advance what knowledge will bear on them and what not. For this reason the education cannot be limited in such a way as to exclude mathematics or indeed any other form of knowledge.

The fact that the liberal education is part of a political education has no effect, therefore, on the *number* of forms of knowledge to which the child is introduced. He must be acquainted with them all if the

[32] See P. H. Hirst, op. cit. See also P. H. Hirst and R. S. Peters, *The Logic of Education* (London: Routledge & Kegan Paul, 1970), chapter iv.

education is to be adequate. It can, however, have some effect on the particular *content* of the education. Hirst, in discussing the notion of a liberal education, suggests that if the aim is simply to give children a liberal education, the criterion for choosing a particular content within the various forms is simply the extent to which any given content exemplifies the form.[33] Using this as the sole criterion one would choose to teach, for instance, those parts of science or history which best exemplify the scientific or historical forms of thought. However, in so far as one had political education in mind one would have another criterion for choosing content. One would choose those items which would give most help to the child in understanding democracy and the democratic society in which he lives. One might choose to teach statistics within mathematics, for instance, political philosophy within philosophy, and within the social science category selected parts of economics, sociology, and history. These examples necessarily only give the most general indication of the way in which content might be selected using this criterion because the details will be influenced very much by local conditions. The science taught in the context of a political education might be very different in the U.S.A. from, say, in Africa. The science lying behind the atmosphere and water pollution in the U.S.A. would be of little value as part of a political education in Nigeria (whatever its merits in demonstrating the scientific mode of thought).

How much weight the political education criterion should have in determining the content of the curriculum in, for instance, state primary and secondary schools is a question which can only be raised here. Its solution depends on a number of factors. For instance, it depends partly on the answer to the question raised above as to how much citizens in a democracy need to know and partly on what other criteria are relevant to curriculum planning and what the priorities are amongst the various criteria. The final form of any given curriculum therefore would depend on a number of detailed considerations and local factors which it would be foolish to attempt to anticipate here. The only general conclusions I want to maintain are (*a*) that a liberal education, i.e. an acquaintance with all the forms of knowledge, is essential to a political education and (*b*) that *a* criterion (it will not be the sole one for the reasons I have just suggested) governing the content of such a liberal education should be the understanding it gives of democracy and the democratic system in which the child lives.

[33] See P. H. Hirst, op. cit., pp. 133–4.

Conclusion

From this examination of education and the public interest I would like to draw out the following conclusions:

1. There is at least *one* policy which *must* be in the public interest in a democracy. This is an appropriate education for a democracy.

2. This policy passes the tests, outlined above, which any such policy must pass.

(i) The claim that it is in the public interest, i.e. good for people as members of the public, can be justified by reference to the democratic system. That is, in so far as it is good for people to be governed democratically, such a policy is in the interest of the public of a democracy.

(ii) It is in *everyone's* interest as a member of the public and not only in the interest of some section of the public. That is, it is clearly in the interest of all, and not, for instance, just those being educated, that all citizens should be initiated into the system.

(iii) There is no indefensible limit on the public.

3. An examination of what is involved in an education for democracy actually establishes a large part of what *must* be the common content of the curriculum in any pluralistic democracy.

A case is made out for

(i) the values of tolerance, fraternity, justice, and consideration of interests;

(ii) the knowledge of particular political and social institutions, embodying the values outlined, and how to operate them;

(iii) and a liberal education covering all the forms of knowledge.

All of these are often, rightly, argued for on grounds of the individual's good but these are not the only grounds. And if the already powerful arguments for, e.g. (iii)[34] are now reinforced by 'public interest' arguments, it is hard to see how, on rational grounds, curriculum reform along these lines can be much longer resisted.

4. An attempt has been made to suggest more concretely what the *content* of a liberal education might be. With this end in mind a criterion has been suggested for choosing what is to be the particular content

[34] See P. H. Hirst, op. cit.; R. F. Dearden, *The Philosophy of the Primary School* (London: Routledge & Kegan Paul, 1968), esp. chapter iv.

of the curriculum in the various forms of knowledge—namely the understanding promoted by the content of democracy and the democratic system in which the child lives. This criterion, it is suggested, might be seen as one step towards establishing a set of non-arbitrary principles for determining the precise content of the curriculum.

XII

THE JUSTIFICATION OF EDUCATION

R. S. PETERS

Introduction

To be educated is thought by many to be a desirable condition of mind, but it obviously does not encompass all that is desirable. Uneducated people can be compassionate and courageous and there is surely some value in such mental dispositions. On the other hand educated people often lack perseverance and integrity, which are also generally thought to be valuable. So even though there may be value in being educated it must be associated with some specific types of value. What then are the values which are specific to being educated and what sort of justification can be given for them? It is to these limited questions that I propose to address myself in this article rather than to wider questions of value with which I was concerned in *Ethics and Education*, and with which, in places, I confused these limited questions—owing perhaps to certain inadequacies in the analysis of the concept of 'education' with which I was then working.

1. *The Values Specific to Education*

What, then, are the values which are specific to being educated? This depends on whether 'education' is being used in a general or in a specific sense.[1] There is a general concept of 'education' which covers almost any process of learning, rearing, or bringing up. Nowadays, when we speak of education in this general way, we usually mean going to school, to an institution devoted to learning. In this sense of 'education' almost any quality of mind can be deemed a product of it—compassion and perseverance included. To say that such qualities of mind are the product of education is to say that they are learned. Education,

My thanks are due to colleagues and friends who helped me by their criticism of early versions of this paper, especially Paul Hirst and A. Phillips Griffiths.

[1] R. S. Peters, 'Education and the Educated Man', *Proceedings of the Philosophy of Education Society of Great Britain*, Vol. 4 (Jan. 1970).

in this sense, can be accorded any kind of instrumental value and so is not of any significance for its valuative suggestions.

Of more relevance is the specific concept of 'education' which emerged in the nineteenth century as a contrast to training. Various processes of learning came to be termed 'educative' because they contribute to the development of an educated man or woman. This was an ideal which emerged in opposition both to narrow specialization and to the increasingly instrumental view of knowledge associated with the development of technology. It was, of course, as old as the Greeks, though it was not previously picked out by the concept of an 'educated man'. Thus (a) the educated man is not one who merely possesses specialized skills. He may possess such specific know-how but he certainly also possesses a considerable body of knowledge together with understanding. He has a developed capacity to reason, to justify his beliefs and conduct. He knows the reason why of things as well as that certain things are the case. This is not a matter of just being knowledgeable; for the understanding of an educated person transforms how he sees things. It makes a difference to the level of life which he enjoys; for he has a backing for his beliefs and conduct and organizes his experience in terms of systematic conceptual schemes. (b) There is the suggestion, too, that his understanding is not narrowly specialized. He not only has breadth of understanding but is also capable of connecting up these different ways of interpreting his experience so that he achieves some kind of cognitive perspective. This can be exhibited in two sorts of ways. Firstly he is not just embedded in one way of reacting to what he encounters. He can, for instance, combine a knowledge of how a car works with sensitivity to its aesthetic proportions, to its history, and to its potentiality for human good and ill. He can see it as a problem for town-planners as well as a fascinating machine. Secondly he is ready to pursue the links between the different sorts of understanding that he has developed. Any moral judgement, for instance, presupposes beliefs about people's behaviour and many moral judgements involve assessments of the consequences of behaviour. An educated person, therefore, will not rely on crude, unsophisticated interpretations of the behaviour of others when making moral judgements; he will not neglect generalizations from the social sciences, in so far as they exist, about the probable consequences of types of behaviour. If these are at all sophisticated he will have to bring to bear some rudimentary understanding of statistics. Similarly, as a scientist he will not be oblivious of the moral presuppositions of scientific activity nor of the aesthetic features of theories; neither will he be insensitive to the relevance of his findings to wider issues of belief and action.

(c) In contrast, too, to the instrumentality so often associated with specialized knowledge, the educated person is one who is capable, to a certain extent, of doing and knowing things for their own sake. He can delight in what he is doing without always asking the question 'And where is this going to get me?' This applies as much to cooking as it does to chemistry. He can enjoy the company of a friend as well as a concert. And his work is not just a chore to be carried out for cash. He has a sense of standards as well as a sense of the setting of what he is doing between the past and the future. There are continuities in his life which reflect what he cares about. He takes care because he cares.

(d) *Processes of education.* Processes of education are processes by means of which people become this way, by means of which they are gradually initiated into this form of life. They are not to be regarded strictly as means to being educated, if 'means' is taken as indicating a process which is both valuatively neutral and related to the end purely causally as taking a drug might be related to a tranquil state of mind. For these processes are processes of learning, and this always involves some kind of content to be mastered, understood, remembered. This content, whether it is a skill, an attitude, an item of knowledge, or a principle to be understood must be intimated, perhaps in embryonic form, in the learning situation. There must, therefore, be some link of a logical rather than a causal sort between the 'means' and the 'end' if it is to be a process of learning. If anyone, for instance, is to learn to think mathematically or morally, the learning situations must include some kind of experiences of a mathematical or a moral sort. Learning may be aided by the temperature of the room, by constant repetition, by smiling at the learner or rewarding him. Some of these conditions of learning may be of a causal type. But there must be some kind of logical link between the content to which the learner is introduced in the learning situation and that which is constitutive of his performance when he has learnt.

Because of this logical type of relationship between means and ends in education it is not appropriate to think of the values of an educational process as contained purely in the various attainments which are constitutive of being an educated person. For in most cases the logical relationship of means to ends is such that the values of the product are embryonically present in the learning process. Suppose, for instance, that children learn to think scientifically by being set simple problems to solve in chemistry and physics. Some of the values of scientific thinking—for instance being clear and precise, looking for evidence, checking results and not cooking them—are instantiated in the learning situation.[2] This would suggest that, from the point of view of value, there is little difference between the learning situation and that of the exercise of what has been learnt. This has led thinkers such as Dewey to claim that the values of living are no different from those of education. For both the learner and the liver exhibit the virtues of critical, open-ended, disciplined inquiry.

On the other hand there is the type of difference to which Aristotle drew attention in his paradox of moral education which is really the paradox of all education. This is that in order to develop the dispositions of a just man the individual has to perform acts that are just, but the acts which contribute to the formation of the dispositions of the just man are not conceived of in the same way as the acts which finally flow from his character, once he has become just. Similarly doing science or reading poetry at school contribute to a person being educated. But later on, as an educated person, he may conceive of them very differently. He may do them because he is drawn to their underlying point or because he sees their relevance to some issue of belief or conduct. This makes the justification of values immanent in such activities very complicated. However, nothing yet has been said about the justification of any of the values of being educated.

2. Instrumental Justifications of Education

The most all-pervading type of justification for anything in our type of society is to look for its use either to the community or to the individual; for basically our society is geared to consumption. Even the work of the artist, for instance, is not always valued for the excellences which are intrinsic to it. Rather it is valued because it attracts more people to a public place, because it provides a soothing or restful atmosphere for people who are exposed to it, or because of the prestige of the artist which rubs off on to the body which commissions him. Music is piped into railway stations and air terminals to make people

[2] In other cases, however, the logical relationship of the learning process to the product is that of being a necessary preliminary rather than a full-blooded instantiation. Reading, for instance, is often taught as a kind of discrimination skill. Practising such discriminations may be thought of as instantiating little that is valuable. It is valuable only as a necessary preliminary to reading poetry with sensitivity and expression, or to reading George Eliot's novels.

feel cheerful just as heat is piped through radiators to make them warm. Art and music can be thought of in this way irrespective of how the artists or musicians conceive of what they are doing. The same sort of thing can happen to education, though there are difficulties in thinking of education in this way if all its criteria are taken into account. To make this point I will consider its aspects separately.

(a) *Knowledge and understanding.* It can be argued cogently that the development of knowledge, skill, and understanding is in both the community's and the individual's interest because of other types of satisfaction which it promotes, and because of distinctive evils which it mitigates. Skills are an obvious case in point. Whatever their intrinsic value as forms of excellence the learning of them is obviously necessary for the survival of a community. Many of them also provide an individual with a living and hence with food, shelter, and a range of consumer satisfactions.

A strong instrumental case can also be made for the passing on of knowledge and understanding. Knowledge, in general, is essential to the survival of a civilized community in which processes of communication are very important. For 'knowledge' implies at least (i) that what is said or thought is true and (ii) that the individual has grounds for what he says or thinks. It is no accident that all civilized societies have such a concept. As far as (i) is concerned, most forms of communication would be impossible if people did not, in general, say what they thought was true. It is socially important, therefore, to have a special word to mark out communications drawing attention to what is true. (ii) The evidence condition is also socially very important because of the value of reliability and predictability in social life. Most of human behaviour depends on beliefs which are expressed and transmitted by means of language. If such beliefs were entirely based on guesses, on feelings which people had in their stomachs, or on various forms of divination, a predictable form of social life would be difficult to imagine. It is no accident, therefore, that civilized societies have the special word 'knowledge' which signals that the person who uses it has good grounds for what he says or thinks.

'Understanding' is equally important; for it suggests that a particular event can be explained in terms of a general principle or shown to fit into some kind of pattern or framework. This permits a higher degree of predictability because of the recourse to generality or to analogy. The context of predictability is thus widened. And, needless to say, the development of knowledge and understanding has an additional social benefit because it permits better control over and ultilization of the natural world for human purposes as was emphasized by thinkers such as Bacon, Hobbes, and Marx. Hence the social value of highly specialized knowledge with the development of industrialism.

The development of understanding is particularly important in a modern industrialized society in which the skills required change rapidly. Industrialists do not demand that the schools should provide a lot of specialized technical training. They prefer to do this themselves or to arrange courses in technical colleges for their employees. If people just serve an apprenticeship in a specialized skill and if they are provided only with a body of knowledge which is necessary to the exercise of that skill under specific conditions, then they will tend to be resistant to change and will become redundant when there is no longer need for this particular skill. If, on the other hand, they have also some understanding in depth of what they are about, they will, at least, be more flexible in their approach and more ready to acquire new techniques. This applies also to social understanding, some degree of which is necessary for working with others; for, as Marx showed, changes in techniques bring with them changes in social organization. If a builder or a teacher is both limited in his understanding and rigid in his attitudes, he is not likely to be good at adapting to changes in organization brought about by changes in techniques.

(b) *Breadth of understanding.* The importance of social understanding suggests an instrumental type of argument for the other aspect of being educated which is incompatible with narrow specialization, namely that of 'breadth'. But what kind of case, in terms of providing services, can be made for typists, dentists, and shop stewards being aesthetically sensitive, and alive to their historical situation and religious predicament? A case can be made for such breadth of understanding as being an important aspect of political education in a democracy along the lines argued by Mrs. White in her article in this collection. It is, however, often said that such people make more efficient employees than those with a narrow training. But if this is true, which is questionable, it may not be due to the breadth of their understanding and sensitivity but to the fact that, in studying various subjects, they become practised in the generalizable techniques of filing papers and ideas, mastering and marshalling other people's arguments, of presenting alternatives clearly and weighing them up, of writing clearly and speaking articulately, and so on. Their academic training in the administration of ideas may prepare them for being administrators.

Of course it may be argued that educated people are of benefit to the professions and to industry because the breadth of their sensitivities helps to make their institutions more humane and civilized. But this is to abandon the instrumental form of argument in which qualities of mind are regarded purely as contributing to the efficiency of the service provided judged by some obvious criterion such as profit, number of patients cured, amount of food produced, and so on. As soon as industry or the professions come to be looked at not simply as providing profit, goods for consumption, or services to the public, but as being themselves constitutive of a desirable way of life, then the values associated with consumption begin to recede. And this introduces the third aspect of being educated.

(c) *Non-instrumental attitude.* It is difficult to make explicit quite what is involved in this non-instrumental attitude. The key to it is that regard, respect, or love should be shown for the intrinsic features of activities. This can be exemplified in at least the following ways. Firstly it involves doing things for reasons that are reasons for doing this sort of thing rather than for reasons that can be artificially tacked on to almost anything that can be done. By that I mean that most things can be done for profit, for approval, for reward, to avoid punishment, for fame, for admiration. Such reasons are essentially extrinsic, as distinct from intrinsic reasons which are internal to the conception of the activity. If, for instance, a teacher changes his methods because his pupils seem too bored to learn, that is a reason intrinsic to the activity; for 'teaching' implies the intention to bring about learning.

Secondly, if things are done for some end which is not extrinsic in this sense, the features of the means matter. If, for instances, someone wants to get to another town or country and is absolutely indifferent to the merits of different ways of travelling, save in so far as he arrives quickly at his destination, then he has an instrumental attitude to travelling.

Thirdly, well established activities such as gardening, teaching, and cooking have standards which are constitutive of performing them well. These are usually related to the point of the activity. If the individual cares about the point of the activity he will therefore care about the standards which are related to its point. If, for instance, he is committed to an inquiry because he genuinely wants to find something out, he will value clarity, will examine evidence carefully, and will attempt to eliminate inconsistencies.

The ingenious could, no doubt, give arguments from the outside in terms of benefits to consumers for the capacity for doing and making things out of love for the job rather than for some extrinsic reason. It could be claimed, for instance, that bricklayers or doctors in fact render better service to the public if they approach their tasks with this attitude rather than with their minds on their pay packet or someone else's satisfaction. But this is like the utilitarian argument in favour of encouraging religious belief if it comforts the believer and ensures his social conformity. In both cases the practice is looked at without any regard to its intrinsic nature. It is assessed from the outside purely in terms of its actual results, not at all in terms of how it is conceived by its participants. This, of course, is not an entirely irrelevant or immoral way of looking at a practice. But if it predominates a widespread and insidious type of corruption ensues. For the point of view of participants in a practice becomes of decreasing importance. They are regarded basically as vehicles for the promotion of public benefit, whose queer attitudes may sometimes promote this, though no thought of it ever enters their heads. This is the manipulator's attitude to other human beings, the 'hidden hand' in operation from the outside.

3. *The Incompleteness of Instrumental Justifications*

All these arguments for education deriving from social benefit could also be put in terms of individual benefit with equal plausibility or lack of it. For it merely has to be pointed out that if certain types of knowledge and skill are socially beneficial, then it will be in the individual's interest to acquire some of them; for he has to earn a living and he will be likely to get prestige and reward for his possession of skills and knowledge that are socially demanded. He is afloat in the pool of relevantly trained manpower. There is also a lot of knowledge which will help him spend and consume more wisely—e.g. about types of food, house purchase, income tax, and so on. So the same kind of limited instrumental case can be made for education when it is looked at externally from the individual's point of view as when it is looked at from the point of view of social benefit. But there is an obvious incompleteness about these sorts of social justification, even if they are quite convincing—e.g. the justification for specialized knowledge. For what, in the end, constitutes social benefit? On what is the individual going to spend his wages? If approval is the lure, why should some things rather than others be approved of? What account is to be given of the states of affairs in relation to which other things are to be thought of as instrumental?

The answer of those whose thoughts veer towards consumption is that social benefit is constituted by various forms of pleasure and satisfaction. This, however, is an unilluminating answer; for pleasure and satisfaction are not states of mind supervenient on doing things. Still less is happiness. They are inseparable from things that are done, whether this be swimming, eating a beef-steak, or listening to a symphony. And if it is said that such things are pleasures or done for the pleasure or satisfaction that they give, this is at least to suggest that they are done in a non-instrumental way. The reasons for doing them arise from the intrinsic features of the things done. So this is to repeat that they need no instrumental justification; they are indeed the sorts of things for the sake of which other things are done. It can then be asked why some pleasures rather than others are to be pursued. For many the pursuit of knowledge ranks as a pleasure. So this is no more in need of justification than any other form of pleasure—and no less.

The question, therefore, is whether knowledge and understanding have strong claims to be included as one of the goods which are *constitutive* of a worth-while level of life and on what considerations their claims are based. This is a particularly pertinent question in the context of the value of education. For it was argued that the instrumental arguments for the breadth of knowledge of the educated man are not very obvious. Also it has been claimed that the educated person is one who is capable, to a certain extent, of a non-instrumental outlook. This would suggest that he does not think of his knowledge purely in terms of the uses to which he can put it. How then can it be justified?

4. *Non-instrumental Justifications of Education*

Questions about the intrinsic value of states of mind and of activities are often put by asking whether they are 'worth while'. This term is often used, of course, to raise questions of extrinsic value. If a man is asked whether gardening is worth while he may take it to be a question about its cash value. The term, too, is often used to draw attention to an individual's benefit, or lack of it, from something—e.g. 'It simply is not worth while for him to change his job just before he retires.' But even in its intrinsic uses it has ambiguities. (*a*) It can be used to indicate that an activity is likely to prove absorbing, to be an enjoyable way of passing the time. (*b*) Alternatively it can point to 'worth' that has little to do with absorption or enjoyment. Socrates obviously regarded questioning young men as being worth while; for it was an activity in which they came to grasp what was true, which, for him was a state of mind of ultimate value. But at times he may have found it a bit boring. Let us therefore explore the 'worthwhileness' of education in these two senses.

(a) *Absence of boredom.* An educated person is one who is possessed of a range of dispositions connected with knowledge and understanding. These will be revealed in what he says, in his emotional expressions, and in what he does. Of particular importance are the activities on which he spends time and the manner in which he engages in them. Activities can be more or less interesting, absorbing, or fascinating, depending on the dispositions and competences of the agent and the characteristics of the activity in question. Fishing, for instance, is more absorbing in one respect for a man who depends on fish for his meals or livelihood than for one who does it for sport; but in another respect the interest depends not so much on the urgency of the objective as on the skill there is in it. The more occasions there are for exercising skill in dealing with the unexpected, the more fascinating it becomes as an activity.

Some activities are absorbing because of their palpable and pleasurable point, such as eating, sexual activity, and fighting. But erected on this solid foundation of want is often an elaborate superstructure of rules and conventions which make it possible to indulge in these activities with more or less skill, sensitivity, and understanding. Such activities become 'civilized' when rules develop which protect those engaged in them from brutal efficiency in relation to the obvious end of the exercise. Eating could consist in getting as much food into the stomach in the quickest and most efficient way—like pigs at a trough. Civilization begins when conventions develop which protect others from the starkness of such 'natural' behaviour. The development of rules and conventions governing the manner in which these activities are pursued, because of the joys involved in mastery, generates an additional source of interest and pleasure.

To take part in activities of this civilized type requires considerable knowledge and understanding. The possession of it at least makes life less boring, as well as making possible levels of boredom beyond the ken of the uneducated. A case may be made, therefore, for the possession of knowledge in so far as it transforms activities by making them more complex and by altering the way in which they are conceived. This can take place in the pursuit of pleasures like those of the palate; it can also take place in spheres of duty which are sometimes regarded as boring. And in spheres like those of politics, or administration, which can be looked at both as pleasures and as duties, the degree of knowledge with which the activities are conducted makes a marked difference. For what there is in politics, administration, or business depends to a large extent on what a person conceives of himself as doing when he engages in them.

Another way in which knowledge can exert a transforming influence on conduct is in the sphere of planning—not just in the planning of means to ends within activities but in the avoidance of conflict between activities. This is where talk of happiness, integration, and the harmony of the soul has application. The question is not whether something should be indulged in *for the sake* of something else but whether indulging in some activity to a considerable extent is compatible with indulging in another which may be equally worth while. A man who wants to give equal expression to his passions for golf, gardening, and girls is going to have problems, unless he works out his priorities and imposes some sort of schedule on the use of his time. The case for the use of reason in this sphere of planning is not simply that by imposing coherence on activities conflict, and hence dissatisfaction, are avoided; it is also that the search for order and its implementation in life is itself an endless source of satisfaction. The development of knowledge is inseparable from classification and systematizing. In planning there is the added satisfaction of mastery, of imposing order and system on resistant material. Children begin to delight in this at the stage of concrete operations, and, when more abstract thought develops, it is a potent source of delight. The love of order permeates Plato's account of reason and Freud regarded it as one of the main effective sources of civilization.

The mention of the pursuit of knowledge introduces another type of justification for knowledge and hence for education. For so far the case for knowledge in relation to the avoidance of boredom has been confined to its transforming influence on other activities. A strong case can be made for it, however, as providing a range of activities which are concerned with its development as an end in itself and which provide an endless source of interest and satisfaction in addition to that concerned with the love of order.

Philosophers from Plato onwards have made strong claims for the pursuit of knowledge as providing the most permanent source of satisfaction and absorption. They have claimed, not altogether convincingly, that the ends of most activities have certain obvious disadvantages when compared with the pursuit of truth. The ends of eating and sex, for instance, depend to a large extent on bodily conditions which are cyclic in character and which limit the time which can be spent on them; there are no such obvious limitations imposed on theoretical activities. Questions of scarcity of the object cannot arise either; for no one is prevented from pursuing truth if many others get absorbed in the same quest. There is no question either, as Spinoza argued so strongly, of the object perishing or passing away.

Theoretical activities could also be defended in respect of the un-ending opportunities for skill and discrimination which they provide. Most activities consist in bringing about the same state of affairs in a variety of ways under differing conditions. One dinner differs from another just as one game of bridge differs from another. But there is a static quality about them in that they both have either a natural or a conventional objective which can be attained in a limited number of ways. In science or history there is no such attainable objective. For truth is not an object that can be attained; it is an aegis under which there must always be progressive development. To discover something, to falsify the views of one's predecessors, necessarily opens up fresh things to be discovered, fresh hypotheses to be falsified. There must therefore necessarily be unending opportunities for fresh discrimina-tion and judgement and for the development of further skills. An educated person, therefore, who keeps learning in a variety of forms of knowledge, will have a variety of absorbing pursuits to occupy him. The breadth of his interests will minimize the likelihood of boredom.

These arguments carry weight, but they are not entirely convincing. Even an educated person might claim that they are one-sided. In rela-tion to the nature of the ends of activities he might argue that evanes-cence is essential to the attraction of some pursuits. What would wine-tasting or sexual activity be like if the culminating point was too per-manent and prolonged? And is there not something to be said for excursions into the simple and brutish? Does not intensity of pleasure count as well as duration? In relation, too, to the arguments in terms of the open-endedness and progressive features of the pursuit of knowledge, it might well be said that the vision of life presented is alto-gether too exhausting. It smacks too much of John Dewey and the frontier mentality. It takes too little account of the conservative side of human nature, the enjoyment of routines, and the security to be found in the well-worn and the familiar.

(b) *The values of reason*. The major objection to these types of argument for the pursuit of knowledge, or for the transformation of other activities by the development of knowledge, is not to be found, however, within these dimensions or argument. It is rather to exclusive reliance on this form of argument. It is to the presupposition that, leaving aside straightforward moral arguments in terms of justice or the common good, science or wisdom in politics have to be defended purely hedonistically. This is not to say that arguments for education in terms of absorption and satisfaction are not important. Of course they are—especially with the increase in leisure time in modern society and the boring character of so many jobs. It is only to say that this is only one way of justifying education. To gain a fuller perspective we must turn to the other sense of 'worth while'.

In section 2(a) the connection between 'knowledge' and 'truth' was spelled out. To 'know' implies that what is said or thought is true and that the individual has grounds for what he says or thinks. The utilitarian case both for having a concept of knowledge and for the importance of knowledge in the life of the society and of the individual was briefly indicated. But being concerned about truth has another type of worth. It can be regarded as having a worth which is independent of its benefit. Indeed the state of mind of one who is determined to find out what is true and who is not obviously deluded or mistaken about how things are can be regarded as an ultimate value which provides one of the criteria of benefit. This was the central point of Socrates's answer to Callicles in Plato's *Gorgias*. Someone who values truth in this way may find the constant effort to free his mind from prejudice and error painful; he may sometimes find it wearisome and boring; but it matters to him supremely, even if he falls short of the ideal which he accepts.

Three points must be briefly made to explain further this ideal. Firstly no finality is assumed or sought for. It is appreciated that error is always possible. Value attaches as much to the attempt to eradicate error as it does to the state of not being in error. Secondly no positivistic view of truth is being assumed, which claims that true statements can only be made in the realms of empirical science, logic, and mathematics. Rather the term is being used widely to cover fields such as morals and understanding other people in which some kind of objectivity is possible, in which reasons can be given which count for or against a judgement. Thirdly there is a group of virtues which are inseparable from any attempt to decide questions in this way. They are those of truth-telling and sincerity, freedom of thought, clarity, non-arbitrariness, impartiality, a sense of relevance, consistency, respect for evidence, and for people as the source of it—to mention the main ones. These must be accepted as virtues by anyone who is seriously concerned with answering questions by the use of reason.

How, then, is this concern for truth relevant to the attempt to justify knowledge and understanding? Surely because the activity of justification itself would be unintelligible without it. If a justification is sought for doing X rather than Y, then firstly X and Y have to be distinguished in some way. To distinguish them we have to rely on the forms of discrimination which are available, to locate them within some kind of conceptual scheme. For instance, if the choice is between going into medicine or going into business some understanding of these activities is a prerequisite. Understanding such activities is an open-ended business depending upon how they are conceived and how many aspects of them are explored. So an open-ended employment of various forms of understanding is necessary. And such probing must be conducted at least on the presupposition that obvious misconceptions of what is involved in these activities are to be removed. There is a presumption, in other words, that it is undesirable to believe what is false and desirable to believe what is true.

Secondly, if a reason is to be given for choosing X rather than Y, X has to be shown to have some feature which Y lacks which is relevant to its worth or desirability. If smoking in fact is a threat to health and chewing gum is not, these are relevant considerations, given the assumption that health is desirable. And this, in its turn, presupposes two types of knowledge, one about the effects of smoking as distinct from chewing gum, and the other about the desirability of health. Further questions can, of course, be raised about the desirability of health, which may lead to questions in moral philosophy about the existence and epistemological status of ultimate ends. But whatever the outcome of such explorations they too are part of the quest for further clarity and understanding. Maybe the inquirer will be chary of saying that what he ends up with is 'knowledge', but at least he may claim to have eliminated some errors and to have obtained more clarity and understanding of the issues involved. Arbitrary assertions will have been rejected, irrelevant considerations avoided, and generalizations queried for their evidential basis. These procedures, which are constitutive of the search for truth, are not those for which some individual might have a private preference; they are those which he must observe in rational discussion. This would be unintelligible as a public practice without value being ascribed at least to the elimination of muddle and error.

It might be admitted that there are links of this sort between justification and forms of knowledge in that to ask for reasons for believing or doing anything is to ask for what is only to be found in knowledge and understanding. But three sorts of difficulties might be raised about ascribing value to this concern for what is true. Firstly, the value of justification itself might be queried. Secondly, it might be suggested that this does not establish the value of *breadth* of knowledge. Thirdly, it might be argued that this only establishes the instrumental value of attempts to discover what is true. These three types of difficulty must be dealt with in turn.

(i) *The value of justification.* The difficulty about querying the value of justification is that any such query, if it is not frivolous, presupposes its value. For to discuss its value is immediately to embark upon reasons for or against it, which is itself a further example of justification. This is not, as might be thought, a purely *ad hominem* argument which might be produced to confound a reflective sceptic. For to give reasons why unreflective people should concern themselves more with what they do, think, and feel is to accept the very values that are at issue. No reason, therefore, can be given for justification without presupposing the values which are immanent in it as an activity.

It might be thought that this smacks of arbitrariness. But this is not so; for 'arbitrariness' is a complaint that only has application within a context where reasons can be given. To pick out the values presupposed by the search for reasons is to make explicit what gives point to the charge of arbitrariness. There is an important sense, too, in which anyone who denies the value of justification, not by making a case against it, which is to presuppose it, but by unreflectively relying on feelings in his stomach or on what other people say, is himself guilty of arbitrariness; for human life is a context in which the demands of reason are inescapable. Ultimately they cannot be satisfied by recourse to such methods. So anyone who relies on them is criticizable in the sense that he adopts procedures which are inappropriate to demands that are admitted, and must be admitted by anyone who takes part in human life.

To explain this point properly would require a treatise on man as a rational animal. All that can be here provided is a short sketch of the broad contours of the demand for justification that is immanent in human life. Human beings, like animals, have from the very start of their lives expectations of their environment, some of which are falsified. With the development of language these expectations come to be formulated and special words are used for the assessment of the content of these expectations and for how they are to be regarded in respect of their epistemological status. Words like 'true' and 'false' are used, for instance, to appraise the contents, and the term 'belief' for the attitude of mind that is appropriate to what is true. Perceiving and remembering are distinguished by their built-in truth claims from merely imagining. Knowledge is similarly distinguished from opinion. In learning we come up to standards of correctness as a result of past experience. Our language, which is riddled with such appraisals, bears witness to the claims of reason on our sensibility. It reflects our position as fallible creatures, beset by fears and wishes, in a world whose regularities have laboriously to be discovered.

The same sort of point can be made about human conduct. For human beings do not just veer towards goals like moths towards a light; they are not just programmed by an instinctive equipment. They conceive of ends, deliberate about them and about the means to them. They follows rules and revise and assess them. Assessment indeed has a toehold in every feature of this form of behaviour which, in this respect, is to be contrasted with that of a man who falls off a cliff or whose knee jerks when hit with a hammer. Words like 'right', 'good', and 'ought' reflect this constant scrutiny and monitoring of human actions.

Man is thus a creature who lives under the demands of reason. He can, of course, be unreasonable or irrational; but these terms are only intelligible as fallings short in respect of reason. An unreasonable man has reasons, but bad ones; an irrational man acts or holds beliefs in the face of reasons. But how does it help the argument to show that human life is only intelligible on the assumption that the demands of reason are admitted, and woven into the fabric of human life? It helps because it makes plain that the demands of reason are not just an option available to the reflective. Any man who emerges from infancy tries to perceive, to remember, to infer, to learn, and to regulate his wants. If he is to do this he must have recourse to some procedure of assessment. For how else could he determine what to believe or do? In their early years all human being are initiated into human life by their elders and rely for a long time on procedures connected with authority and custom. They believe what they are told and do what others do and expect of them. Many manage most of their lives by reliance on such procedures. This fact, however, is a reflection of human psychology rather than of the logic of the situation; for ultimately such procedures are inappropriate to the demand that they are meant to serve. For belief is the attitude which is appropriate to what is true, and no statement is true just because an individual or a group proclaims it. For the person whose word is believed has himself to have some procedure for determining what is true. In the end there must be procedures which depend not just on going on what somebody else says but on looking at the reasons which are relevant to the truth of the statement. The truth of a lot of statements depends upon the evidence of the senses; and all men have sense-organs. Similarly reasons for action are connected with human wants; and all men have wants. There may be good reasons, in certain spheres of life, for reliance on authorities; but such authorities, logically speaking, can only be regarded as provisional. They cannot be regarded as the ultimate source of what is true, right, and good. This goes against the logic of the situation.

Thus those who rely permanently and perpetually on custom or authority are criticizable because they are relying on procedures of assessment which are not ultimately appropriate to the nature of belief and conduct. To say, therefore, that men ought to rely more on their reason, that they ought to be more concerned with first-hand justification, is to claim that they are systematically falling down on a job on which they are already engaged. It is not to commit some version of the naturalistic fallacy by basing a demand for a type of life on features of human life which make it distinctively human. For this would be to repeat the errors of the old Greek doctrine of function. Rather it is to say that human life already bears witness to the demands of reason. Without some acceptance by men of such demands their life would be unintelligible. But given the acceptance of such demands they are proceeding in a way which is inappropriate to satisfying them. Concern for truth is written into human life. There are procedures which are ultimately inappropriate for giving expression to this concern.

This is not to say, of course, that there are not *other* features of life which are valuable—love for others, for instance. It is not even to say that other such concerns may not be more valuable. It is only to say that at least some attempt must be made to satisfy the admitted demands that reason makes upon human life. If, for instance, someone is loved under descriptions which are manifestly false, this is a fault. If, too, a person is deluded in thinking that he loves someone—if, for instance, he mistakes love of being loved for loving someone, this too is a criticism.

This argument, which bases the case for the development of knowledge and understanding on its connection with justification, does not make a case for the pursuit of any kind of knowledge. It only points to the importance of knowledge that is relevant to the assessment of belief, conduct, and feeling. It does not show, for instance, that there is value in amassing a vast store of information, in learning by heart every tenth name in a telephone directory. And this accords well with the account of the sort of knowledge that was ascribed to an educated person. For to be educated is to have one's view of the world transformed by the development and systematization of conceptual schemes. It is to be disposed to ask the reason why of things. It is not to have a store of what Whitehead called 'inert ideas'.

(ii) *The case for breadth.* It might still be claimed, however, that this type of argument only shows the value of some sort of knowledge; it does not establish the value of the breadth of understanding characteristic of the educated man. A man might just look for grounds of a certain sort of beliefs—e.g. empirical grounds. He might only value philosophy.

The case for breadth derives from the original link that was claimed between justification and forms of knowledge. For if a choice has to be made between alternatives these have both to be sampled in some way and discriminated in some way. It is not always possible to do the former but the latter must be done for this to rank as a choice. The description of possible activities open to anyone and hence the discussion of their value is not a matter of mere observation. For they depend, in part, on how they are conceived, and this is very varied. If the choice is, for instance, between an activity like cooking or one like art or science, what is going to be emphasized as characterizing these activities? Many such activities—chess, for instance, or mathematics —are difficult to understand without a period of initiation. But they cannot simply be engaged in; they have to be viewed in a certain way. And this will depend upon the forms of understanding that are available and the extent to which the individual has been initiated into them. It would be unreasonable, therefore, to deprive anyone of access in an arbitrary way to forms of understanding which might throw light on alternatives open to him. This is the basic argument for breadth in education.

In the educational situation we have positively to put others in the way of such forms of understanding which may aid their assessment of options open to them. It is of great importance in a society such as ours in which there are many life-styles open to individuals and in which they are encouraged to choose between them, and to make something of themselves. But this value accorded to autonomy, which demands criticism of what is handed on and some first-hand assessment of it, would be unintelligible without the values immanent in justification. Indeed it is largely an implementation of them. For it demands not only critical reflection on rules and activities, with the search for grounds that this involves, but also a genuineness which is connected with the rejection of second-hand considerations. By that I mean that a conventionally minded person goes on what others say. If he has reasons for doing things these are connected with the approval which he will get if he does them and the disapproval if he does not. These are reasons of a sort but are artificially related to what is done. They are reasons for doing a whole variety of things, not this thing in particular. If, for instance, people refrain from smoking because they are disapproved of if they do, this is not connected with smoking in the way in which the probability of lung cancer is connected. As Hume put this point in the context of morality: 'no action can be virtuous or morally good unless there be in human nature some motive to produce it distinct from the sense of its morality'. The same sort of point can be made about other forms of judgement—e.g. aesthetic, scientific, religious. So if the individual is to be helped to discriminate between possibilities open to him in an authentic, as distinct from a second-hand way, he has to be initiated into the different forms of reasoning which employ different criteria for the relevance of reasons.

A corollary of this type of argument for breadth of understanding would be that some forms of knowledge are of more value from the point of view of a 'liberal education' than others, namely those which have a more far-reaching influence on conceptual schemes and forms of understanding. There are forms of understanding such as science, philosophy, literature, and history which have a far-ranging cognitive content. This is one feature which distinguishes them from 'knowing how' and the sort of knowledge that people have who are adepts at games and at practical skills. There is a limited amount to know about riding bicycles, swimming, or golf. Furthermore, what is known sheds little light on much else.

Science, history, literary appreciation, and philosophy, on the other hand, have a far-ranging cognitive content which gives them a value denied to other more circumscribed activities. They consist largely in the explanation, assessment, and illumination of the different facets of life. They can thus insensibly change a man's view of the world. The point, then, about activities such as science, philosophy, and history is that they need not, like games, be isolated and confined to set times and places. A person who has pursued them systematically can develop conceptual schemes and forms of appraisal which transform everything else that he does.

(iii) *An instrumental type of argument?* But, it might be said, this shows only the *instrumental* value of breadth of understanding and imagination. It does not show that a variety of forms of knowledge should be pursued for any other reason, particularly if they are rather boring. This argument also shows the great importance of physical education. For without a fit body a man's attempts to answer the question 'Why do this rather than that?' might be sluggish or slovenly. So it provides, it seems, a transcendental deduction of the principle of physical fitness! The seeming correctness of such a deduction, if the empirical connection were to be shown, does not establish that physical exercise has any value except of an instrumental sort.

There is, however, a confusion in this comparison between physical exercise and the pursuit of knowledge in their relations to justification; for the former is suggested as an empirically necessary condition and hence is properly regarded as instrumental, whereas the latter is connected by logical relationships such as those of 'relevance', 'providing evidence', 'illuminating', and 'explaining'. Indeed the latter is in an educational type of relationship to justification in that it suggests avenues of learning which are relevant to choice, and this is not properly conceived of as an instrumental relationship, as was argued in section 1(d). In engaging in the activity of justification the individual is envisaged as exploring the possibilities open to him by developing the ways of discriminating between them that are available to him— i.e. through the different form of understanding such as science, history, literature which the human race has laboriously developed. This process of learning is logically, not causally related, to the questioning situation. He will be articulating, with increasing understanding and imagination, aspects of the situation in which he is placed, and in pursuing various differentiated forms of inquiry he will be instantiating, on a wider scale, the very values which are present in his original situation—e.g. respect for facts and evidence, precision, clarity, rejection of arbitrariness, consistency, and the general determination to get to the bottom of things. If, for instance, he considers one of the possibilities open to him as desirable he must, as has already been argued, view this under a certain description. The question then arises whether this description is really applicable and whether there is any other way of looking at this possibility which might be relevant. The ethical question immediately articulates itself into other sorts of questions. The values of reason, such as those of consistency, relevance, and clarity, inherent in such educational explorations are the values of the starting-point 'writ large'.

It is important to stress the values of reason which are immanent in such attempts to discriminate alternatives with more clarity and precision rather than the 'means–end' type of link between questioning and forms of knowledge that can often be both logical, and of the means–end type, as in the case of the relationship between learning to read and reading George Eliot, previously explained (above p. 242, n. 2). Socrates, it seems, gave up his pursuit of knowledge in the physical sciences in favour of devotion to ethics and psychology. It could be argued that, leaving aside *other* questions to do with what he found absorbing, he could well have thought that he ought to study psychological questions deeply only because of their logical links with ethical questions. He had reason to engage in such a disinterested inquiry but did not value this form of knowledge 'for its own sake'. But this is to misconceive the way in which the value of concern for truth enters into both answering justificatory questions *and* into asking them. The point is that value is located in the procedures necessary to explicate what is meant by *justification*. In other words the value is not in the acquisition of knowledge *per se* but in the demands of reason inherent both in answering questions of this sort and in asking them. Evidence should be produced, questions should be clearly put, alternatives should be set out in a clear and informed way, inconsistencies and contradictions in argument should be avoided, relevant considerations should be explored, and arbitrariness avoided. These monitoring and warranting types of relationships, which are characteristic of the use of reason, are not instrumental types of relationship. They are articulations of the ideal implicit in thought and action. We are drawn towards this ideal by what I have elsewhere called the 'rational passions'.[3] And this ideal may draw us towards

[3] See R. S. Peters, 'Reason and Passion', in G. Vezey (ed.), *The Proper Study*, Royal Institute of Philosophy (London: Macmillan, 1971).

types of inquiry which we do not find particularly absorbing in their own right.

To put this point in another way: much has been said in this section about the 'concern for truth' and 'the demands of reason'. The value picked out by these expressions is not to be thought of as a kind of consumer value which bestows importance on the accumulation of countless true propositions. Devotion to the pursuit of knowledge, in this sense, may also be fascinating, and a case can be made for it in terms of the first sense of 'worth while'. But that type of argument is not now being used either. Value rather is being ascribed to the quality of knowledge rather than to its amount or to its capacity to mitigate boredom. It is being claimed that what is valuable is inherent in the demand that what is done, thought, or felt should be rationally scrutinized.

It will not do to suggest that this concern for truth is instrumentally valuable just because people need to know in order to satisfy their wants, including their desire for knowledge itself, unless 'want' is used in a very general sense which makes it a conceptual truth that anything which people can value must be, in some sense, what they want. For, firstly, to want is always to want under some description that involves belief; hence wants can be more or less examined. Secondly, one of the most perplexing questions of conduct is whether, in any ordinary sense of 'want', people ought to do what they want to do. Thirdly, the very notion of 'instrumentality' presupposes the demand of reason. For, as Kant put it, taking a means to an end presupposes the axiom of reason that to will the end is to will the means. Thus the demands of reason are presupposed in the form of thought which might lead us to think of its value as being instrumental.

On the other hand the demand for truth is not an absolute demand in the sense that it can never be over-ridden. It sometimes can be, if, in some situation, some other value is more pressing. In general, for instance, it is undesirable that people should ignore facts about themselves or about others which are relevant to what they should do. But on a particular occasion, when someone's suffering is manifestly at stake for instance, it might be argued that it is just as well for a person not to be too persistent in his demand for truth, if satisfying this demand would occasion great suffering. The values of reason are only one type of value. As has been argued from the start, there are other values, e.g. love for others, the avoidance of suffering. But situations like this, in which there is a conflict of values, do not affect the general status of the concern for truth. As E. M. Forster put it: 'Yes, for we fight for more than Love or Pleasure: there is Truth. Truth counts. Truth does Count.'[4]

This type of argument for the value of knowledge helps to explain the value inherent in being educated not only of breadth of knowledge, as previously explained, but also of what was called 'cognitive perspective'. What was suggested is that an educated person is not one who has his mind composed of *disconnected* items of knowledge. What he knows and understands should be seen to be interrelated in terms of consistency, relevance, evidence, implication, and other such rational connections. If his knowledge is linked together in this way it is 'integrated' in one sense of the term. It may well be, too, that certain studies such as philosophy, which explicitly examines grounds for different types of knowledge and their interrelationship, and literature, which imaginatively depicts people in situations in which they have to make complex judgements and respond emotionally to perplexing situations, contribute to the development of this cognitive perspective.

Those who favour certain educational methods might argue that the exploration of literature, of history, and of philosophy should not begin until children begin to be troubled or curious about various aspects of the human condition. And certainly, if inquiries and explorations move outwards from a centre of puzzlement and concern, they are more likely to be genuine and to instantiate the values immanent in justification in a first-hand way. Others, however, might argue that one way of generating such concern and puzzlement in people is to initiate them into our human heritage. This kind of imaginative situation may be necessary to make people more alive to their position in the world as believers and choosers. But there is the danger of the second-hand in this approach. There is also the possibility that individuals may fail to connect, to transfer values learnt in a specialized context to wider contexts. A person, for instance, may be ruthless in demanding evidence for assumptions when learning history or social science. But he may not show the same ruthlessness when having to make up his mind about policies presented to him by politicians. This raises questions which are, in part, empirical about transfer of learning. But it does not, I think, affect the basic point about the non-instrumental features of the relationship between justification, and the forms of understanding which contribute to it.

[4] E. M. Forster, *A Room with a View* (Harmondsworth: Penguin Books, 1955), p. 218.

In a purely philosophical context it might be said, then, that the demand for justification presupposes the acceptance of the values implicit in it. In an educational context, however, children must be initiated somehow into those forms of understanding which are of particular relevance to justification. It is, of course, no accident that there should be these two ways of explicating this relationship. For processes of education are processes by means of which people come to know and to understand. These are implementations, through time, by means of learning, of the values and procedures implicit in justification. Education, properly understood, is the attempt to actualize the ideal implicit in Socrates' saying that the unexamined life is not worth living.

5. *The Non-instrumental Attitude*

An educated person, it was argued, is characterized not just by his abiding concern for knowledge and understanding but also by the capacity to adopt, to a certain extent, a non-instrumental attitude to activities. How can this attitude be justified? This is not difficult; for the justification of it is implicit in what has already been said. It is presupposed by the determination to search for justification. Anyone who asks the question about his life 'Why do this rather than that?' has already reached the stage at which he sees that instrumental justifications must reach a stopping place in activities that must be regarded as providing end-points for such justifications. To ask of his pattern of life 'What is the point of it all?' is to ask for features internal to it which constitutes reasons for pursuing it. A stage has been reached at which the ordinary use of 'point' has no application—unless, that is, the same types of question are transferred to an afterlife or to the life of future generations. So a person who asks this type of question seriously demonstrates that he is not a stranger to this attitude. To what extent it will in fact transform his way of going about particular activities within his life cannot be inferred from this capacity for reflection. It is, to a certain extent, an empirical question—but not entirely empirical, because of the logical connection between the general capacity to reflect and particular instantiations of it.

In so far, however, as he values knowledge and understanding he values one very important ingredient in the non-instrumental attitude; for this attitude requires attention to the actual features of that with which he is confronted, as distinct from tunnel vision determined by his own wants. He is concerned about what is 'out there'. Even at the crudest level a person who *just* regards a piece of fish as a way of satisfying his hunger, or a glass of wine as a way of satisfying his thirst, ignores a range of features. He fails to discriminate the variety of tastes. Conversely he will think nothing of using a beautiful glass to house his tooth-brush—unless, of course, he thinks that it is worth a lot of money and that he might break it. In sexual activity, too, he will regard a woman as a necessary object for satisfying his lust; he will be indifferent to her idiosyncrasies and point of view as a person. He will only listen to people in so far as they share his purposes or provide, by their remarks, springboards for his own self-display. His interest in people and things is limited to the use he can make of them. He lacks interest in and concern for what is 'out there'.

A person, on the other hand, who presses the question 'Why do this rather than that?' already accepts the limitations of his egocentric vision. He is not satisfied with a life geared to unexamined wants. He wonders whether some of the things that he wants are really worth wanting or whether he really wants them. He wonders about the relevance of his wants. In attempting to find out what is the case he may reveal features of situations that in no way serve his wants and which indeed may run counter to them. An unreflective businessman, for instance, might visit an undeveloped country with a view to setting up a factory. But, on going into all the details of what this would involve, he might become more and more aware of the disruption of a way of life that is entailed. He might 'not want to know' or he might begin to question the whole enterprise. And if he began to question this particular feature of business life he might begin to query the way of life more generally.

Another aspect of the instrumental attitude is the view of time that goes with it. For the instrumentally minded good lies always in future consumption. The present has to be hurried through for the sake of what lies ahead. It is not to be dwelt in and its aspects explored. To a person who uses his reason this attitude is just as unreasonable as the opposed cult of instancy. For, as Sidgwick put it, to a rational person, 'Hereafter as such is to be regarded neither more no less than now.'[5] Reasons have to be given for instant or delayed gratification other than temporal position—e.g. 'If you wait you won't be able to have it at all' or 'If you wait there will be more of it.' The important thing for a

[5] H. Sidgwick, *The Methods of Ethics* (Papermac ed., London: Macmillan, 1962), p. 381.

man is to connect, to grasp the features of objects and situations and the relationships which structure his life. It is not, therefore, the fact that the pleasure of smoking is to be had now or in five minutes that matters; it is rather how it is to be conceived and its relation to other things in life. Can smoking, like sexual activity, be conceived of not simply as a physical pleasure, but also as an expression of love? Can it be done with skill and grace like dancing? And are its relationships to other human activities anything other than detrimental?

To ascribe a non-instrumental attitude to a person is not, of course, to lay down that he will indulge in some activities rather than others. It is only to indicate the way in which he will go about activities and conceive them. He will not always do things for the sake of some extrinsic end. He will, first of all, enjoy performing well according to the standards required. He will have an attitude of care in other words. But this care will be related to the point of the activity. He will feel humility towards the givenness of the features of the activity, towards the impersonal demands of its standards. And he will have a sense of its connection with other things in life, a wary consciousness of the past and the future and of the place of what is being done in the passage through the present. Indeed, as Spinoza put it, he should be capable of viewing what he does 'under a certain aspect of eternity'.

6. Concluding Problem

There is a major outstanding problem to which this approach to justification gives rise. Two types of value have been distinguished, which underpin the life of an educated person, leaving aside moral values such as justice, and the minimization of suffering, which structure the interpersonal realm of conduct. These are (i) values relevant to the avoidance of boredom, in relation to which the pursuit of knowledge was accorded a high place, and (ii) values implicit in the demands of reason which give rise to virtues such as humility, hatred of arbitrariness, consistency, clarity, and so on. If a reasonable person examines his beliefs or conduct these virtues govern his conduct of the inquiry; but he does not necessarily find this kind of examination enjoyable or absorbing.

Now, for reasons that were explained in Section 1(d), when dealing with processes of education, a person can only *become* educated if he pursues theoretical activities such as science and literature and/or practical activities which require a fair degree of understanding; but why, having become educated, should he devote himself much to activities of this sort? Why should he choose to spend much of his time in reading, taking part in discussions, or in demanding practical activities such as engineering? On occasions, of course, in acknowledgement of the demands of reason, he may feel obliged to enlighten himself on some issue, to seek information which is relevant to his beliefs and action. And while so doing he submits to the standards of such a disinterested pursuit. But why should he seek out *any* such pursuits? To take a parallel in the moral sphere: why should a person who accepts the principle of justice, and who acknowledges its demands on his life by relevant actions and inquiries when occasions arise, pursue the promotion of justice as an *activity*—e.g. by working as a judge or as a social reformer? Similarly in this sphere of worth-while pursuits why should not an educated man settle for an undemanding job which allows him plenty of time for playing golf which is the one activity which he really enjoys apart from eating, sun-bathing, and occasionally making love to his wife? He is, of course, capable of seeing point in a more Dewey type of life of expanding experience and understanding. He is not a philistine; neither is he particularly instrumental in his outlook. He just loves his game of golf more than any of the more intellectually taxing types of pursuits. Golf is to him what he presumes science is to the other fellow.

Could the answer be connected with the fact, already pointed out, that the use of reason itself exemplifies the two types of value? On the one hand is the absorption springing from curiosity and from the love of order, etc. Human beings, it might be said, 'naturally' find discrepancies between what they expect and what they experience intolerable. This is what leads them to learn according to cognitive theories of motivation stemming from Piaget. On the other hand there are the normative demands connected with the use of reason. Inconsistencies and confusions in thought ought to be removed; evidence ought to be sought for and arbitrariness avoided. Is it conceivable that the latter type of value could be accepted by a person who was unmoved by curiosity and by the desire to sort things out? Is this not like saying, in the moral sphere, that respect for persons, as a moral attitude, could exist without some natural sympathy for them?

There may well be some relationships, which are not purely contingent, between the 'natural' and the normative aspects of the use of reason, which may parallel those between sympathy and respect, but it would require another paper to elucidate them. The doubt, as far as this paper goes, is whether such connections need be strong enough to carry the required weight. It might be shown that acceptance of the demands of reason presupposes certain 'natural' passions such as curiosity and the love of order, but would it show enough to make it necessarily the case that an educated person must not only proceed in a rational way with regard to his beliefs and conduct but must also adopt some pursuits for their own sake which provide ample scope for curiosity or which are taxing in relation to the level of understanding that they require? Does not Dewey's educational method, which requires that learning should always be harnessed to spontaneous interest and curiosity, seem appropriate because so many people emerge from school and university with some degree of sophistication and capacity for rational reflection, but with a singular lack of enthusiasm either for further theoretical pursuits or for practical activities that make frequent and open-ended demands on their understanding? Could not his methods be seen as an attempt to close the gap between the two types of value? And does not this suggest that, as closing this gap depends upon empirical conditions underlying methods of learning, the connection in question is an empirical connection? Indeed is not one of the main tasks of the educator the devising of procedures which are likely to minimize this type of gap?

This sounds plausible but a nagging doubt remains. The problem can be summarized as follows:

(i) There are activities such as science, engineering, the study of literature, etc., by engaging in which a person becomes an educated person— one who has breadth and depth of understanding and who is prepared to examine his beliefs and conduct.

(ii) As an educated person he may, later on, see reason to pursue such activities on occasions, if he sees their relevance to some issue of belief and conduct, though he may not find them particularly absorbing. Such exercises will be manifestations of his acceptance of the demands of reason.

(iii) But, as an educated person, he will do *some* things for their own sake. Whatever he does will be, to a certain extent, transformed by his level of understanding, but will he necessarily pursue, for their own sake, some activities of the sort that he pursues or has pursued in contexts (i) and (ii), which make demands on his understanding? Is it intelligible that he should both be educated and find *all* such activities too frustrating or boring to pursue for their own sake? Would such a man be any more intelligible than Kant's moral being who is virtuous only out of respect for the law? Socrates may have sometimes regarded his pursuit of truth with others as a boring duty, though we know that he did not always find it so. But does it not seem inconceivable that he could *always* have found it boring? And is this *simply* because of the empirical fact that he spent a lot of time that way?

NOTES ON THE CONTRIBUTORS

R. S. PETERS, the editor of this volume, is Professor of the Philosophy of Education at the Institute of Education of the University of London.

JOHN WOODS is a member of the Department of Philosophy at the University of Victoria, British Columbia.

W. H. DRAY is in the Philosophy Department at Trent University, Ontario.

I. SCHEFFLER is a Professor of the Harvard Graduate School of Education.

P. H. HIRST is Professor of Education in the University of Cambridge.

P. HERBST is in the Philosophy Department at the Australian National University at Canberra.

MARY WARNOCK, now a Research Fellow of Lady Margaret Hall, Oxford, was formerly Headmistress of Oxford High School for Girls.

R. PRING, now in the Department of Curriculum Studies at the Institute of Education in London, was formerly a Research Fellow at the Cambridge Institute of Education.

D. W. HAMLYN is Professor of Philosophy at Birkbeck College, University of London, and is the editor of *Mind*.

MRS. P. A. WHITE is on the Philosophy of Education staff at the Institute of Education in the University of London.

H. SOCKETT is Tutor in the Philosphy of Education at the Cambridge Institute of Education.

BIBLIOGRAPHY

THERE are several introductory books on philosophy of education but, as yet, no satisfactory introduction has emerged which is both philosophically competent and suitable for students with no previous experience of philosophy. D. J. O'Connor's *An Introduction to the Philosophy of Education* (London: Routledge & Kegan Paul, 1957) is still the nearest approach to this. But it is more an introduction to philosophy in general than to the philosophy of education in particular, and its stance in philosophy rather reflects the positivistic period of A. J. Ayer's *Language, Truth and Logic*. A completely different approach is represented by L. A. Reid's *Philosophy and Education* (London: Heinemann, 1962). Reid was the first occupant of the chair in the philosophy of education at the University of London, and this book is the fruit of his reflection on fundamental issues underlying education. He raises most of these issues in a very perceptive way. But he tends to paint with his pen rather than to lay out systematic arguments.

G. Langford's *Philosophy and Education* (London: Macmillan, 1968) is a more straightforward introduction from the point of view of modern analytical philosophy, but is rather colourless because the analysis is not always closely related to central educational issues. A briefer introduction from an analytic point of view, which is more restricted in its scope, is J. F. Soltis's *An Introduction to the Analysis of Educational Concepts* (Addison-Wesley, 1968). *The Logic of Education* by P. H. Hirst and R. S. Peters (London: Routledge & Kegan Paul, 1970) is an introduction within the analytic tradition aimed at more advanced students. But it is written with the additional purpose of providing a reconciliation between subject-centred and child-centred approaches to education. It is, therefore, not just a neutral introduction; for it adopts a distinctive point of view about the nature of education and explores the implications of this for the curriculum, for teaching, and for the authority structure of schools and colleges. R. D. Archambault's *Philosophical Analysis and Education* (London: Routledge & Kegan Paul, 1965) is the first British collection of articles in philosophy of education from the analytic point of view and represents a lively introduction to a wide range of issues. There is, finally, R. F. Dearden's *The Philosophy of Primary Education* (London: Routledge & Kegan Paul, 1968) which explores in a very clear and competent manner the main philosophical issues which are of relevance to primary education.

Another introductory approach to the philosophy of education, which might appeal to many students, is via some of the great educators whose educational theory is closely connected with a systematic philosophical position. If the students were to read Plato's *Republic*, Rousseau's *Émile*, and

Dewey's *Democracy and Education* or *Experience and Education*, with appropriate commentaries, a good grounding would be provided in the ways in which views about education presuppose different positions in ethics, epistemology, philosophy of mind, and social philosophy. Kingsley Price's *Education and Philosophical Thought* (Rockleigh, N.J.: Allyn and Bacon, 1962) is a useful book to read in conjunction with these historical texts; for it tries to separate out the distinctively philosophical components in these classical theories of education. C. D. Hardie's *Truth and Fallacy in Educational Theory* (New York: Teacher's College, Columbia University, 1962) provides a critique of some of these theories from the point of view of analytic philosophy, and W. Frankena expounds and comments on the views of Aristotle, Kant, and Dewey in his *Three Historical Philosophies of Education* (Glenview, Ill., Scott Foresman, 1965).

There are many ways in which issues raised in the first section of the collection on 'The Concept of Education' could be further explored. Some of the classics on the subject could be read—e.g. Herbert Spencer's *Essays on Education* (Everyman Edition, London: Dent & Sons, 1911), A. N. Whitehead's *Aims of Education* (London: Macmillan, 1929), and John Dewey's *Democracy and Education* (London: Macmillan, 1916) in which much is said about 'aims'. There are some controversial thoughts about 'aims of education' in R. S. Peters's *Authority, Responsibility and Education* (London: Allen and Unwin, 1959). Various aims of education are discussed in a collection of articles by R. F. Dearden, P. H. Hirst, and R. S. Peters entitled *Education and the Development of Reason* (London: Routledge & Kegan Paul, 1972). There is also a collection of articles edited by T. H. B. Hollins, entitled *Aims in Education: the Philosophical Approach* (Manchester: Manchester University Press, 1964) which contains papers on educational aims. Another collection by J. Doyle entitled *Educational Judgments* (London: Routledge & Kegan Paul, 1972) contains articles by W. Frankena and A. Edel on the concept of 'education'. W. Frankena has also put together a collection of different positions about the aims of education in his *Philosophy of Education* (London: Macmillan, 1965). In one of the earliest and most influential books in modern philosophy of education called *The Language of Education* (Springfield, Ill.: Charles Thomas, 1960) Israel Scheffler illustrated the influence of metaphors and slogans on concepts of education.

A general discussion, from a philosophical point of view, of the central issues of the curriculum can be found in H. S. Broudy, B. O. Smith, and J. R. Burnett, *Democracy and Excellence in the American Secondary School* (New York: Rand McNally, 1964), and H. Taba's *Curriculum Development* (New York: Harcourt Brace, 1962) sets out the general problems of curriculum planning. There are also several papers by P. H. Hirst on epistemological issues underlying the curriculum which should soon appear in a collection entitled *Knowledge and the Curriculum* to be published by Routledge & Kegan Paul. Israel Scheffler's *Conditions of Knowledge* (Glenview, Ill.: Scott Foresman, 1965) also discusses fundamental issues in epistemology and indicates their relevance to education. Jane Martin's collection *Readings in the Philosophy of Education: A Study of Curriculum* (Rockleigh, N.J.: Allyn and Bacon, 1970) contains many of the best recent papers on this topic and Martin Levit's collection called *Curriculum* (Urbana: University of Illinois Press, 1971) ranges more widely over the classical and modern period. Both R. Whitfield, in his collection *Disciplines of the Curriculum* (New York: McGraw-Hill, 1971), and K. Dixon, in his *Philosophy of Education and the Curriculum* (Oxford: Pergamon Press, 1972), put together articles which attempt to show the contributions of various school subjects to the curriculum. The more aesthetic aspects of the curriculum are treated in D. Arnstine, *Theory of Knowledge and Problems of Education* (Urbana: University of Illinois Press, 1969).

There are chapters on teaching in the introductions by Langford, and Hirst and Peters, and in I. Scheffler, *The Language of Education* (Springfield, Ill.: Charles Thomas, 1960), and most of the growing literature on teaching, learning, and allied concepts is now availble in collections. Articles on the different ways of bringing about learning can be found in R. S. Peters (ed.), *The Concept of Education* (London: Routledge & Kegan Paul, 1967). A group of influential papers on teaching is available in C. J. B. MacMillan, and T. W. Nelson (eds.), *Concepts of Teaching* (New York: Rand McNally, 1968). B. P. Komisar and C. B. J. MacMillan (eds.), *Psychological Concepts in Education* (New York: Rand McNally, 1967) and B. O. Smith and R. H. Ennis (eds.), *Language and Concepts in Education* (New York: Rand McNally, 1961) contain many useful papers on a variety of topics in this area. I. Snook has also put together a collection on *Concepts of Indoctrination* (London: Routledge & Kegan Paul, 1972) and has himself written a monograph on this topic as a companion to his collection entitled *The Concept of Indoctrination* (London: Routledge & Kegan Paul, 1972). There are also two influential articles on indoctrination by R. Hare and J. Wilson in T. H. B. Hollins (ed.), *Aims in Education: the Philosophical Approach* (Manchester: Manchester University Press, 1964).

The justification of education is one of the least explored areas of the philosophy of education. There has been little of a systematic sort before or after R. S. Peters's *Ethics and Education* (London: Allen and Unwin, 1965) which was an over-hasty attempt to 'provide a few signposts for others and to map the contours of the field for others to explore in a more leisurely and detailed manner'. In this book the ethical basis of education and of its social principles, such as freedom, authority, equality, respect for persons, punishment, and democracy is examined, and a particular point of view within moral theory is developed and defended. A classic, with a similar type of coverage but with a less analytical approach, is W. H. Kilpatrick *Philosophy of Education* (London: MacMillan, 1951). To pursue such topics further the student will have either to turn to the standard philosophical texts on ethics and social philosophy or to return to the classical works of Dewey, Spencer, Mill, Rousseau, Kant, Aristotle, and Plato.

A larger collection of articles with a somewhat similar structure to this collection is I. Scheffler *Philosophy and Education* (Rockleigh, N.J.: Allyn and Bacon, 2nd edition, 1966). This also includes articles on moral and political education, together with a section on the nature of educational theory.

INDEX

INDEX OF NAMES

(not including authors mentioned only in the Bibliography)

Anscombe, G. E. M., 47, 188 n.
Arendt, H., 5, 58
Aristotle, 112, 142, 147
Austin, J. L., 75
Ausubel, D., 22

Bacon, Francis, 244
Barry, B., 217 n., 218–20, 228 n.
Benn, S. I., 218, 220
Bernstein, B., 136
Biran, M. de, 188
Bolgar, R. P., 232 n.
Borger, R., 179 n.
Bradley, F. H., 131
Broad, C. D., 1
Burke, Edmund, 230–2

Carnap, R., 132
Chomsky, N., 6, 7, 181–6, 191, 192
Cohen, J. M., 180 n.
Coleridge, S. T., 112, 118
Comenius, J. A., 1
Comte, A., 132
Crick, B., 233 n.

Dewey, J., 1, 12, 20, 23, 27, 83, 89, 130, 131, 142, 143, 250, 266
Dray, W. H., 4, 39–43, 46
Dressel, P. L., 124, 125
Durkheim, E., 230–2

Freud, S., 249
Froebel, F. W. A., 1, 2, 130 n.

Gagné, R. M., 155
Gibson, J. J., 188

Hamlyn, D. W., 6, 156, 179 n.
Hardie, C. D., 1, 2

Hare, R. M., 41
Hart, H. L. A., 218, 223 n.
Hebb, D. O., 191
Hegel, G. F. W., 131
Herbart, J., 1, 2
Herbst, P., 5
Hirst, P. H., 5, 7, 146, 153, 158, 159, 234–6
Hobbes, T., 244
Hume, D., 257

James, C., 141

Kant, I., 181, 190, 197, 266
Keller, Helen, 193
Komisar, B. P., 165 n., 169 n.

Lawrence, D. H., 26
Lawton, D., 132

MacMillan, C. B. J., 7
Maritain, J., 89
Marx, K., 244
Mill, J. S., 157, 230
Moore, G. E., 1

Nelson, T. W., 7
Nowell-Smith, P. H., 95 n.
Nunn, Sir Percy, 1

Oakeshott, M., 111, 150, 151

Peirce, C. S., 80, 143
Peters, R. S., 4, 7, 29–39, 158, 218, 228 n.
Peterson, A. D. C., 96, 97
Piaget, J., 6, 7, 181–6, 193, 198, 203, 205, 208–12, 265
Plato, 1, 69, 187, 249, 251

Popper, Sir Karl, 150, 151
Pring, R., 6

Rousseau, J.-J., 1
Russell, B., 130
Ryle, G., 16

Scheffler, I., 5
Seabourne, A. E., 179 n.
Sidgwick, H., 263
Sockett, H., 6
Spinoza, B., 264

Taylor, C., 178
Tinbergen, N., 189

Warnock, H. M., 5
White, P. A., 17, 244
Whitehead, A. N., 1, 256
Wittgenstein, L., 43, 149, 173, 189
Wolff, R. P., 230–2
Wollheim, R., 227
Woods, J., 4, 34, 39, 43, 44, 46–9
Wordsworth, W., 112, 113